PRESIDENTIAL

GOVERNMENT

The Crucible
of Leadership

Books by
James MacGregor Burns

PRESIDENTIAL

GOVERNMENT

★ ★ ★ ★ ★ ★ ★ ★ ★ ★

The Crucible

of Leadership

James MacGregor Burns

Sentry Edition
with a new Preface
by the author

Houghton Mifflin Company Boston

Second Printing Sentry Edition c

Copyright © 1965, 1973 by James MacGregor Burns

ISBN: 0-395-14095-1 SENTRY
Printed in the United States of America

★ ★ ★

For Carl

1921–1965

I must study politics and war, that my sons may have liberty to study mathematics and philosophy. My sons ought to study mathematics and philosophy, geography, natural history and naval architecture, in order to give their children a right to study painting, poetry, music, architecture, statuary, tapestry and porcelain.

JOHN ADAMS

PREFACE TO THE

SENTRY EDITION

We KNOW almost everything about Presidents, I suggest in these pages, but far too little about the Presidency. That paradox has not changed markedly during the eight years since this book was written — four years of Lyndon Johnson and almost four of Richard Nixon. We have had a super-abundance of information about the man in the oval office, his wife, daughters, sons-in-law, his daily routine, moods, entertainments, travels. But we know all too little about the vast gray executive establishment that expands, proliferates, and partially devours the decision-making apparatus of the rest of the government, behind the pleasantly deceptive "low profile" of the White House.

Perhaps it was not surprising that the executive office should become bigger and more institutionalized during Johnson's full term in the White House. Liberal Democratic Presidents are expected to be "strong" chief executives; Johnson had a huge agenda of domestic and foreign policy goals; and in any event the momentum of the Roosevelt, Truman, and Kennedy Administrations could be expected to put pressure on and dilate the executive bureaucracy. The test would come when a Republican entered the White House with the aim not only of curbing big government in general but of curtailing the "unbridled executive power" that good Republicans are taught from the cradle to abhor.

President Nixon faced and — from a conservative Repub-

lican point of view — flunked that test. The presidential
establishment — that is, the White House and the functional
agencies of the Executive Office of the President, such as the
Council of Economic Advisers and the Office of Science and
Technology — have continued to dominate the whole executive branch. Mr. Nixon promised to restore the Cabinet as
a key instrument of presidential decision-making; he took
pains to introduce his Cabinet choices before the television
public and to vest them with a sense of importance and independence. But soon the old tendencies, as described in this
book, manifested themselves. Cabinet members complained
that they had inadequate access to the President, that the
White House staff was making the main decisions in their
fields of responsibility, that the Cabinet was failing to serve
as a collective decision-making institution.

In some respects, indeed, Nixon outdid his Democratic
predecessors as he smoothly changed direction and supported
a big, institutionalized Presidency. For years Democratic Administrations had struggled with the question of whether
they should institutionalize the advisory and policy-making
activities of the presidential staff even more than had been
done under Roosevelt, Truman, and Eisenhower. A specific
aspect of this problem was whether the Budget Bureau should
take a larger and more formal responsibility for policy development, the President's legislative program, and administrative management; presidential Democrats had never quite
got on top of this problem. In 1970 Nixon acted decisively
on this score. He transformed the Budget Bureau into a new
Office of Management and Budget, and he established formally a Cabinet-level Domestic Council, soon to be led by
his closest advisers.

Presidential government has continued and expanded

under President Nixon in other ways. In sheer scope and bulk the executive office is at least as vast as when he took office. In the executive office, as in all classic bureaucracies, work has become more specialized, systematized, and routinized. The old "kitchen cabinet" seems to have become even further institutionalized; the distinction between the high-powered White House inner circle of staff generalists and the more specialized Executive Office agencies has continued to sharpen.

The most dramatic example of Nixon's inability to reverse the thrust of presidential government has been in foreign policy making. He had promised in particular to restore the State Department to its one-time preeminence in foreign relations, and he appointed one of his closest and most trusted friends as Secretary of State. But he also had inherited the formidable machinery of national security policy making and crisis management, and he proceeded to appoint the equally formidable Henry Kissinger as his national security adviser. Knowing the personalities involved and, even more, knowing the absolute indispensability of a powerful, talented, and ever-present staff carefully tailored to the President's needs, one could have little doubt which would win out, the "little State (and Defense) Department" in the White House, or the old-line agency in Foggy Bottom. But one could hardly have expected that the competition would be so brief, so uneven, so public — and so frustrating for the State Department.

Thus the basic tendencies toward presidential government set forth in this book have continued under a Republican administration. Discontinuities have, of course, been evident. In the wake of various actions and statements by President Nixon, Vice President Agnew, and Attorney General Mitchell, I would not speak so confidently today of the forces in presidential government protecting individual liberty; on the other hand, I would want to know the extent to which institutional factors in presidential government operated to protect civil liberty in the face of the bias of individual Nixonites in favor of "law and order." I might also speak less confidently of the "presidential press"; but here again one would need to differentiate sharply between attacks by the "Eastern liberal establishment press" on Johnson and Nixon as Presidents and the general encouragement by the media of — and indirect participation in — the institutionalized Presidency, as described in these pages.

If the pressures toward a bigger, more powerful, more institutionalized Presidency leave their mark on Republican as well as Democratic administrations, the problems of presidential government heighten too. The desperate ordeal of Vietnam has exemplified, far more than I could have predicted, the problem of consensus versus creativity presented in the last chapter of this book. In my view, the early years of our intervention in Indochina — an intervention supported by a wide consensus of men making up the presidential establishment and the Democratic and Republican presidential parties — provide only the cruelest example of the dangers of the presidential delusion that if the President honestly acts and speaks for "all the nation" and for the "national interest," he must automatically be right.

The candidacies of Robert Kennedy and Eugene McCarthy in 1968, and the nomination of George McGovern in 1972, were protests against the strong consensus Presidency as well as against Vietnam. In this respect the key question for the 1970s is not whether presidential government will continue; it can be trimmed here and there but it will continue, if only because of the huge domestic commitments facing it. The question is whether the "out" party can fashion an opposition that could challenge the consensus Presidency and present the voters with a compelling and credible alternative. It is still my thesis that a new type of checks and balances operates to put some curb on presidential government from within, and that trying to restore the old checks and balances outside the Presidency would be both ineffective and undesirable. The trauma of the last few years has fortified my view that the great job of institution-building lies in fashioning a "Shadow Presidency" — critical, competitive, creative — that can restrain presidential government in an effective, appropriate way. Such an opposition Presidency came under discussion during the 1972 presidential campaign, and it is well that the issue is now out in the open. The Shadow Presidency could offer relentless criticism in the free press, hold hard-fought elections at regular intervals, and thereby present an arresting and responsible alternative to the incumbent administration.

J.M.B.

THE THIRD MODEL:
A PERSONAL PREFACE

SHORTLY after John Kennedy's election to the Presidency in November 1960 I had an appointment with him at his home in Georgetown. My recollection is still vivid. As I arrived the narrow old street was full of excitement. From the front stoop the President-elect was announcing a cabinet appointment; a knot of reporters, their fingers numb with cold, were trying to capture his staccato sentences; television and movie cameras whirred; and from a gaping crowd across the street a woman cried out in a voice of anguish, "Jack, what about Adlai Stevenson for Secretary of State?" Except for the cameras it was a scene out of the Jacksonian era. Kennedy waved stiffly to the crowd and withdrew; shortly I was admitted.

Inside Kennedy sat sprawled in a chair; occasionally he hunched forward to scan a newspaper spread before him on the floor. All at the same time he was chatting with an aide and one or two visitors, trying to get a Senator on the phone to inform him of an appointment, and hunting for something in the paper. Apart from the phone it was the setting of a much earlier time: the ivory-walled room with its prints and stuffed chairs and French decor; the tall windows with the little garden beyond; antique tables uncluttered by paper. Unable to complete the phone call, Kennedy rose, greeted me with that briskly friendly way of his, and led me up a narrow stairs to a tiny room on the second floor.

I had come on a strange mission, or so it must have seemed to him. A year and a half before, I had accompanied him on a hedge-hopping tour of the Midwest. He had said to me one day — suddenly, when I would have supposed him preoccupied with the endless minor crises of the campaign — that he had been interested by some articles I was doing for the *Atlantic*. In these articles I contended that American government was caught in deadlock and delay, that no matter whether Nixon or Kennedy won in 1960 the new President would face legislative stalemate and slowdown, and that only radical political planning and action could equip a President with the party and electoral support necessary to put through a big legislative program. I seized on his remark to ask if he would be interested in my developing these ideas further. He would.

Now he was President-elect and I was there to press my point. It was clear to us both that his razor-edge popular margin and his dubious majorities in Congress would make it difficult for him to live up to his key campaign promise of "getting the nation moving." I urged him to devote some time in his first term to reorganizing and strengthening the Democratic party, planning for the congressional elections of 1962, and trying to win in 1964 not only a mandate for his program but a political base for broadening his program after 1964. I said: "I am a professional worrier about presidential second terms."

He was thinking about his first term, not his second. Outside the reporters were waiting; across the nation men were hoping for a phone call; around the world politicians were weighing the new President by the Cabinet he was so carefully measuring and fitting. Even so he listened, understood, responded — the supreme compliment he would pay his visitors, including academics. After further talk about other, more mundane matters, I rose to go, and while following him down the narrow stairs I got in one more thrust: "You must be the Jefferson of the twentieth century."

From time to time I saw the President in action during his thousand days in the White House. I had no part in Administration councils but Kennedy did permit me some glimpses of his Presidency — of the pre-Inaugural planning at Palm Beach, of a discussion with his aides of a forthcoming trip to Latin America, of legislative and executive staffwork, of talks with the press, of White House ceremonial and display. Several times he talked with me about the Presidency. I think of him leaning back in his rocker, squinting down the length of a cane, talking simply, directly, skeptically about both the Presidency and its critics. And each time I saw him I raised the old issue or left a memorandum.

In January 1963, halfway through Kennedy's term, I published *The Deadlock of Democracy,* a study of what I called four-party politics in America. Whatever his feelings about the main title, the President seemed interested in the thesis. I contended that Presidents faced a choice between two basic presidential strategies or "models." They could try to operate on the basis of the old Madisonian model — the model of checks and balances, bargaining among minority coalitions, limited presidential power, and the inability of government to make major departures in policy except on the basis of a popular consensus. Or they could act on the basis of another model that had far less legitimacy in the minds of most Americans — the Jeffersonian. This was the model of executive teamwork and leadership, majority rule, party responsibility. (These two models, and a third, are developed historically and conceptually in Chapter I of the present book and spelled out in the last section of Chapter IV.) Only a strategy drawn from the Jeffersonian model, I proposed to the President, could give him the ample and dependable political support necessary to enact his program.

At that time Kennedy's major proposals were still bogged down in Congress. It seemed to me imperative that he now mount a great effort in the latter part of his term to revitalize the torpid state and local parties, recruit able young candidates for Congress, help them win elections by a generous sharing of his coattails, attract liberal and moderate Republicans into the Democratic party as well as into his personal following, and plan to reform and strengthen both houses of Congress. Some in Washington believe that Kennedy was planning to conduct this kind of political strategy — that he was quietly interesting men in the idea of running for Congress, for example. I am not so sure that he would have made the tremendous political commitment to the Democratic party that such a strategy would have demanded.

But the President was doing something else that was at least as important. He was showing what could be done with the federal government without reforming it. As Chief Executive and Chief of State he was leading the executive branch with such vigor and style and imagination that in a sense he was "tuning high" the whole national government, just as Alexander Hamilton had once done. This was nothing new. Historians and political scientists have long apotheosized the "strong" Presidents who, despite the Madisonian checks and balances, exercised leadership by expertly mobilizing influence through a combination of frontal attacks on the opposition, by dramatic executive action, and by the exertion of constant pressure across a long battlefront — and also through deft and even Machiavellian maneuvers in the interstices of the political system. But in Kennedy's case it seemed to me a more directed and determined effort than it had been with most earlier Presidents, for as a student of American history and politics he well knew the alternatives.

Even more, Kennedy was supporting this kind of strategy with a political resource that had not been available to some of the earlier Presidents who had tried to exercise leadership. This was a huge, heavily institutionalized presidential office. He had inherited an elaborate staff mechanism from Eisenhower, and however critical Kennedy may have been of the General's numerous staff committees, he was soon using a big staff of his own, though in a different way than Eisenhower had. Lyndon Johnson in turn inherited this super-office, and in the fall of 1964, on spending some time in the White House, I was struck most of all by the continuities of the White House staff. It was clear that Johnson was neither following the Madisonian model, nor was he rebuilding the Democratic party. Like Kennedy he was nurturing his own personal party, exerting heavy pressure on Congress, and marshaling influence in every way he could. He was following a third strategy and (perhaps less consciously than Kennedy) was working according to a third model.

It is this third model that poses the great practical problem of the Presidency and the theoretical problem of this book. By model I do not mean something that is necessarily good, something that should be imitated or desired, like a mannequin's mink coat. Nor do I mean the rigorously analytical model used in mathematics or the physical sciences. I use the term as a shorthand way of communicating with the reader about recurring patterns of presidential behavior. I also use the term as an aid to analyzing complex political variables and relationships. More hopefully, a model enables us to select political data — about institutions or events or processes — to clarify their interrelationships and begin to develop theory. As a mathematician has said, models in the nonexact sciences can have such uses,[1] but we must not put too heavy a burden on them.

I stress the use of models because my aim in this book is to help fashion a theory of the American Presidency. Thanks to reporters and historians we have had a superabundance of facts about American Presidents. No agency in the Western world, save perhaps the Kremlin and the Vatican, is under such close and intense surveillance — and the Kremlin and Vatican know how to keep out reporters. No institution of American government suffers so much from what David Easton calls hyperfactualism. In a sense we know everything about the Presidents and nothing about the Presidency.

On April 30, 1964, President Johnson invited a group of historians and political scientists to the White House for a celebration. It was the 175th anniversary of George Washington's taking of the oath of office. In his proclamation President Johnson noted that the Presidency had long since come to transcend its occupants, that the Presidency "has made every man who occupied it, no matter how small, bigger than he was; and no matter how big, not big enough for its demands." Presidents might be partisan, he said, but the office was "national and not partisan." And he urged scholars and other Americans during the ensuing year to devote new study to the origins, history, and functions of the Presidency.

As one who always obeys the government — especially Presidents — I was happy to comply. I had, indeed, already planned to spend that period in restudying the office. I do

[1] Anatol Rapoport, "Various Meanings of 'Theory,'" *The American Political Science Review,* Vol. 52, No. 4, December 1958, p. 982.

not consider this book a final or definitive attempt to develop a theory of the Presidency; another twenty years could well be devoted to that. But as Justice Holmes said, sometimes problems must be presented obscurely before they can be presented clearly. I can only hope that I have developed some of the presidential problems, potentials, and paradoxes that wiser men than I will continue to explore.

J.M.B.

CONTENTS

Contents

★ PART ONE ★

THE PRESIDENCY
IN HISTORY

I

The Hamiltonian Model

THE AMERICAN CONSTITUTION is the most audacious example of political planning in the Western world. In this day, when it is comforting to dream small dreams and fashionable to dismiss the story of man as a tragicomedy of blind gropings, sheer accidents, and feeble improvisations, it is good to look back upon that Philadelphia summer in 1787 when a body of men deliberately and self-consciously set about planning a government in the grand manner and for all time. They succeeded magnificently. Today we conduct our affairs within the framework of this charter of government; we expand or limit public power by the devices — federalism, balanced powers, the Bill of Rights — that were part of the Constitution of 1787 or implicit in it; and our continuing debates over great constitutional issues have hardly improved on the quiet, probing discussions in Philadelphia.

The Framers could plan boldly and brilliantly because they combined a grasp of theory with direct experience, often during crisis, in the management of public affairs. Thus with cold realism they could measure their visions of the ideal commonwealth against the harsh conditions that would face thirteen struggling states federated under a new instrument of government. They were uninhibited political theorists. From Hume and Machiavelli and Locke and Blackstone and Montesquieu and others they had learned something of the iron ambitions of power seekers, the need for constitutional

restraints on rulers, the mechanics of the rule of law, the ways
that different powers and interests in society and government
can be nicely balanced against one another. Grappling with
knotty colonial affairs, disunity, revolution, and war taught
them much about practical statecraft.

Each one of us, in his own way, is a political theorist; each
one of us is a practical man; our difficulties arise in relating
the one to the other. The intellectual talent of the Framers
lay in their uniting theory and practice, ends and means, the
is and the *ought*. Their political genius lay in their realistic
view of human nature and their capacity to design a democratic government that would survive despite the frailties of
the leaders who would run it and of the great number of men
who would have to sustain it. The architects of the Constitution had neither a utopian nor a pessimistic view of the nature of man; they saw him as a mixture of selfishness and generosity, of stupidity and rationality, with the less becoming
elements predominating, perhaps, but not so much that they
could not be cushioned by prudent governmental arrangements. Political leaders they saw as a baffling mixture of good
and evil, but as men who could be subject to constitutional
restraints. The Framers also had a grasp of immediate possibilities and of practical politics; otherwise they never could
have brought off the feat of gaining ratification of a new Constitution that, in shifting power from states to the central government, and from legislators to executives, touched the most
sensitive political nerves in America.

In this sunburst of political wisdom, however, there was
one great region of doubt and murk. The Framers had a
clear understanding of the power that the new national government would need (though they were not sure how much
power the anti-Federalists would yield). They had no doubt

that the new federal legislature would be the engine of law and policy. They assumed that the new federal judiciary would hold at least enough power over the political branches to protect its own independence. But the shape of the new national executive confounded them. How should the President be selected? How long should his tenure be? How much power should he have?

The Framers floundered in dealing with these questions because neither theory nor practice was of much help. Machiavelli and a host of others had written much about the ways and wiles of princes, but not in a manner that had much relevance to the executive in a representative republic. Locke had preached the rights of popular assemblies against kings, but he had been vague about the place of the executive in a republican system; he had written about an executive "prerogative" that, the more one studied it, seemed to give the executive an almost bottomless reservoir of power. The lessons of experience were also ambivalent. Colonial leaders had had a bellyful of executive interference and bullying from royal governors and other minions of the Crown (and the stories of interference tended to be inflated with the retelling); but at the same time many Revolutionary and post-Revolutionary leaders yearned for stronger governors who could control unruly state assemblies, and for a stronger national executive under the Articles of Confederation.

There was one member of the Constitutional Convention, however, who had a most definite conception of the executive power: Alexander Hamilton. The New Yorker's reading of history, especially classical history; his experience as aide-de-camp to General George Washington; his observation of the conduct of public affairs in the colonies and states and under the Articles; and — perhaps most important — his own pushing, dominating nature, all convinced him, as he wrote in his column in the *New York Packet* in March 1788, that "energy in the Executive is a leading character in the definition of good government." "It is essential to the protection of the community against foreign attacks; it is not less essential to the steady administration of the laws; to the protection of property against those irregular and high-handed combinations which sometimes interrupt the ordinary course of justice; to the security of liberty against the enterprises and assaults of ambition, of faction, and of anarchy." A feeble executive, he went on, implied a feeble execution of the government; and a government ill executed, whatever it may be in theory, must be, in practice, a bad government.[1]

On June 18, 1787, Hamilton had risen in the constitutional convention in Philadelphia to "give my sentiments of the best form of government — not as a thing attainable by us, but as a model which we ought to approach as near as possible." For five hours he lectured his colleagues, while James Madison and several others scribbled the notes that have given us such an intimate view of the proceedings. His "model" was a bold one; Hamilton dreamed of a mighty continental nation and had thought unthinkable thoughts about the concentration of power in the new national government. He would strip the states of most of their powers and make them little more than administrative departments of the new national government. And he would create a new national Executive who would hold his position for life and who would have the power of "negativing all laws — to make war or peace, with the advice of the senate — to make treaties with their advice, but to have the sole direction of all military operations, and to send ambassadors and appoint all military

1 *The Federalist,* no. 70.

officers, and to pardon all offenders, treason excepted, unless by advice of the senate." [2] His object, said Hamilton, was to unite public strength and individual security.

Hamilton recognized the sweep and audacity of his proposals. He was not sure that a really effective executive could ever be established on republican principles. But, he said, "Our situation is peculiar — *it leaves us Room to dream* as we think proper." [3] Yet his was a dream about the strength and mechanics of government, not its ultimate purpose.

The delegates quickly dismissed Hamilton's daring proposal to abolish the states; this was theoretically undesirable and politically impossible. But the presidential provisions that emerged in September from the convention's labors showed the influence of Hamilton and of the other proponents of executive power. The new President would serve only a four-year term, but he would be indefinitely re-eligible; he would be chosen by electors and not by the legislature; he would have only a limited veto over congressional measures but still an important one; he would hold extensive power over foreign policy and the making of war. Perhaps the greatest concession the convention made to Hamilton in the final document was to leave executive power and organization rather undefined, as compared to the long list of fairly specific powers, and the bicameral organization, of Congress.

Clearly the executive office would take its shape largely from the men who first manned it.

2 Harold C. Syrett (ed.), *The Papers of Alexander Hamilton*, vol. 4 (New York: Columbia University Press, 1962), p. 201.

3 Quoted in John C. Miller, *Alexander Hamilton: Portrait in Paradox* (New York: Harper & Brothers, 1959), p. 160.

The Vital Precedents

"It squints toward monarchy," Patrick Henry had cried out in Philadelphia against the proposed presidency, ". . . your President may easily become King." He would rather have a King, Lords, and Commons, Henry said, than an executive who would have the army in his hands. But the Framers did not heed him, partly because they fenced the office in with countervailing powers, partly because they had vast confidence in the man who would obviously be the first President. It was easy to grant general and undefined authority to an office that would be filled by the august and steadfast George Washington. In this the Framers were realistic; Washington turned out to be almost exactly the kind of President they had envisaged.

The first President clearly understood the vital precedents he would be setting. "Many things, which appear of little importance in themselves and at the beginning," he said two weeks after his first inauguration, "may have great and durable consequences from their having been established at the commencement of a new general government." [4] Although he presided over a cabinet of such strong and clashing spirits as Hamilton and Thomas Jefferson, Washington took broad command of his administration and hence of the precedents that were set. While for the most part he played the role of mediator, harmonizer, and balancer of competing policies and factions, and was not a creative innovator in his own right, his subordinates cleared major decisions with him and

[4] W. C. Ford (ed.), *The Writings of George Washington* (New York: G. P Putnam's Sons, 1891), vol. 30, p. 393.

secured his approval. By staying somewhat above the battle Washington consolidated the people's support for him, lent his name and prestige to the new republic, and ultimately helped convert his charismatic appeal and authority into the popular and constitutional legitimacy so badly needed by the new Republic.[5]

The activist, the operator, the dynamo of the first administration was the Secretary of the Treasury, Alexander Hamilton. He combined a belief in positive leadership with a clear idea of the potential role of the Treasury Department and its head. During the Revolution he had written in his Artillery Company Account Book a quotation from Demosthenes' orations that revealed his concept of the leader: "As a general marches at the head of his troops, so ought wise politicians, if I dare use the expression, to march at the head of affairs. . . . They ought not to wait the event, to know what measures to take; but the measures which they have taken, ought to produce the *event*." [6] Now he had his chance to exercise this kind of leadership.

Few were surprised that Hamilton sought to dominate the executive life of the Administration, that he intruded into other departments' administrative affairs, or that he ceaselessly pursued his ideal of a "high-toned" government. The main question was the extent to which he would burst outside the executive establishment and try to influence the making of domestic and foreign policy and hence establish vital precedents for the relation of President and Congress. Hamilton's critics did not have long to wait. Appointed Secretary of the Treasury in September 1789, he made clear almost from

5 Seymour Martin Lipset, *The First New Nation* (New York: Basic Books, Inc., 1963), pp. 16–23.
6 Cited in Miller, *op. cit.*, p. 228.

the start that he would not feel unduly confined by the nice
balancing and compartmentalizing of governmental power of
which the Framers had been so proud. His legislative strategy
was quite simple: to intervene in the framing of bills at the
start and at the finish and all the way in between.

Although the Constitution had given the President the
power "from time to time" to "give to the Congress Information of the State of the Union, and recommend to their Consideration such Measures as he shall judge necessary and expedient," it was generally assumed that Congress would be
the main source of policy. Hamilton saw the immense advantage of gaining the initiative in the field of legislation. Not
content with the familiar argument that Congress held broad
powers implied by the general grants of authority given it, he
acted on the far bolder proposition that the *President* could
exercise implied powers.[7]

Drawing up the details of legislation was not enough; what
Hamilton wanted was the power to frame the great programs
that would dominate legislative strategy in Congress. Like
Demosthenes' general, he would march at the head of the
troops. Spurred by the Secretary's Federalist friends in Congress, the House of Representatives formally asked Hamilton
for advice on the fiscal problems facing the new nation.
These requests paved the way for the great reports on public
credit, a national bank, and manufactures that laid the foundations not only of Federalist measures but of national economic policy for decades to come. Hamilton's reports also set
the precedent for the presidential commissions that in later
decades would challenge Congress for supremacy in dramatizing alternatives of national policy.

[7] Clinton Rossiter, *Alexander Hamilton and the Constitution* (New York:
Harcourt, Brace and World, Inc., 1964), p. 211.

Once his measures were before Congress, Hamilton threw himself into the legislative battle. Since Washington did not have a congressional floor leader to represent the Administration, Hamilton unofficially filled this role. The disorderly factions and coteries in Congress aroused in him the same instinct for coordination and control as guerrilla troops arouse in a military commander. An anti-Federalist Senator wrote in his diary that "It is totally vain to oppose this [Bank] Bill," that Congress might as well go home, for "Mr. Hamilton is all-powerful, and fails in nothing he attempts," that Hamilton was even influencing the selection of committees and attending committee meetings to give advice.[8] He reported that Hamilton "was here early to wait on the Speaker, and I believe spent most of his time in running from place to place among the members."

Whatever the exaggerations, it was clear that a fundamental reversal had taken place in the balance of legislative power between President and Congress. The President, through Hamilton and other cabinet members, was dominating the legislative process. Leadership of Congress was being supplied from outside and not just from within. Not that Hamilton won all his battles. On one occasion he evidently wanted to bring in person his financial program before the House of Representatives, but after a brief debate the House decided that the report must be brought before it in writing, so the personal appearance of a cabinet member before Congress was a precedent that Hamilton did *not* establish. But there were more important precedents that he did set, for use by later Presidents if they so wished.

---

[8] *Journal of William Maclay* as cited in Ralph V. Harlow, *The History of Legislative Methods in the Period Before 1825* (New Haven: Yale University Press, 1917), p. 141.

It was paradoxical that Hamilton established these precedents in the area of policy that Congress was supposed to guard most jealously. Historically republicanism had stood for popular control of fiscal measures against the executive. Some of the Framers had spoken strongly for subordinating the Treasury directly to Congress and thus moving its chief out of the orbit of executive control. Some had favored continuing the old Treasury Commission, of three members, that existed under the Articles of Confederation, doubtless with the hope that a commission of three would be more deliberate and less zealous than a single Secretary. There had even been serious discussion of a proposal for the election of the Secretary of the Treasury by Congress. Here again experience with excessive legislative control of finance cautioned the Framers against such schemes, but they still planned and assumed that Congress — especially the House of Representatives — would be dominant in the fiscal field. To them it seemed as though the ink was hardly dry on the new charter when Hamilton was reversing their intention — to the point where one Representative complained that "according to the ideas of some gentlemen, the House had no right to add to the appropriations proposed by the Secretary." [9]

It was in foreign policy making, however, that Hamilton staked out his widest claim for executive power. Here he was moving much more with the thrust of the Constitution than against it; still, the Framers had left to Congress the basic constitutional power over the broad direction of foreign policy, the backing up of treaties with funds (such as payments to Indian tribes), and the actual declaration of war. To be sure, the President had the power to make treaties, but many Framers expected that the Chief Executive would consult closely with the Senate during negotiations and allow Sena-

[9] *Annals,* 1st Cong., II, p. 1449.

tors to make known their views on the coverage of the treaty, on the conditions, limitations, concessions, and compromises.

With Hamilton's full backing Washington took a series of steps asserting presidential control of foreign policy making. He exercised sole discretion in the reception of envoys and hence in the recognition of nations — a crucial precedent, considering the turbulent European situation. He refused to accede to a call from the House of Representatives for papers relating to the negotiation of the Jay Treaty. He issued a Proclamation of Neutrality in 1794 on his own discretion; because of American feelings about France and Britain this was a most controversial step, but the precedent stood. In a famous incident he tried to consult the Senate on a treaty, was rebuffed, and withdrew in chagrin; the Senate may have won that skirmish, but it lost the war, for the President never again collaborated directly with the Senate in the treaty-forming process and thus the Senate lost an opportunity to affect the shape of treaties at the critical stages.

Thus in foreign policy making, even more than domestic, Congress was left with neither the crucial power of original formulation of policy nor, save in the case of treaties, with the final power of consent or veto; the President in effect exercised both. He dominated the start and the finish of the legislative process and many of the stages in between. While Congress during these early years retained essentially a kind of advisory, delaying, modifying, and sometimes vetoing power, things had moved a long way from the bold, categorical words of Article I of the Constitution: "All legislative Powers herein granted shall be vested in a Congress of the United States . . ."

As for the power to make war, there had never been much question of the clear primacy of the executive. The nation became involved in no major war during Washington's presi-

dency, but the Whiskey Rebellion gave Hamilton the chance
to laud the force and vigor that could be forthcoming only
from the President. "In emergencies, great and difficult, not
to act with an energy proportioned to their magnitude and
pressure, is as dangerous as any other conceivable course. In
the present case, not to exert the means which the laws pre-
scribe for effectuating their own execution would be to
sacrifice [those] laws, and with them the Constitution, the
Government, the principles of social order, and the bulwarks
of private right and security." [10] Hamilton had lived most of
his life in crisis times; he knew that, whatever the dangers to
ordinary constitutional processes, emergency conditions required concentration of power in the hands of the most vigorous and single-minded branch of government.

Although Hamilton did not have the sweeping influence
that the Republicans imputed to him as Washington's "evil
genius," he held a pivotal role in most of the decisions. It was
an awkward but not insuperable problem for him that he was
only Secretary of the Treasury and not also Secretary of State.
He blithely issued instructions to American envoys abroad,
conferred with the British Minister, and even undermined
Washington's neutrality policies. In much of this Hamilton
was simply being realistic. No Secretary of the Treasury
could divorce himself from foreign policy. Hamilton's early
decision to pay off foreign debts in itself had a major influence on foreign relations, and almost all foreign policy making would affect taxing or spending and hence ultimately
come back to the Treasury Department.

Still, the net effect of Hamilton's activities was an audacious extension of executive power over foreign policy. He
had also shifted in his public pronouncements on the matter.

[10] Henry Cabot Lodge (ed.), *The Works of Alexander Hamilton* (New York:
G. P. Putnam's Sons, n.d.), vol. 6, p. 397.

"The history of human conduct," he had written for the *Federalist,* doubtless with an eye to suspicious Republicans, "does not warrant that exalted opinion of human virtue which would make it wise in a nation to commit interests of so delicate and momentous a kind, as those which concern its intercourse with the rest of the world, to the sole disposal of a magistrate created and circumstanced as would be a President of the United States." Five years later he was asserting that the direction of foreign policy was essentially and inherently an executive function — that the executive had the right "in certain cases, to determine the condition of the nation, though it may, in its consequences, affect the exercise of the power of the legislature to declare war." Professor Corwin has summed up his position neatly: "In short, the President has all powers that the facts of international intercourse may at any time make conveniently applicable if the Constitution does not vest them elsewhere in clear terms. Ordinarily this means that the *initiative* in the foreign field lies with him. He is consequently able to confront the other departments, and Congress in particular, with *faits accomplis* at will, although, on the other hand, Congress is under no *constitutional* obligation to back up such *faits accomplis* or to support the policies giving rise to them." [11] Congress and the President shared concurrent powers, but the latter held the lion's share.

"For god's sake, my dear Sir," Jefferson wrote to Madison on reading Hamilton's defense of executive power, "take up your pen, select the most striking heresies and cut him to pieces in the face of the public." [12] All these constitutional controversies, then as now, took their form and heat from the

[11] Edward S. Corwin, *The President: Office and Powers, 1787–1957,* 4th ed. (New York: New York University Press, 1957), pp. 179–80.
[12] Quoted in Nathan Schachner, *Thomas Jefferson* (New York: Thomas Yoseloff, 1951), p. 499.

political battles between Federalists and Republicans and factions thereof. As the party excluded from influence in the White House, the Republicans naturally tried to thwart Federalist policy by hobbling the instrument of that policy, the Presidency. The great test of the Republicans' constitutional consistency would come if and when they won the Presidency.

Men differed then as now over Hamilton's motives and nature. To many a Republican he was simply a monarchist who was trying to introduce into America the trappings and the authority of the British Crown. To Madison and Jefferson he was a man on the make who, though born a bastard, or perhaps because of it, was trying to take over the government. To John Adams he was a man whose fierce ambitions sprang from a "superabundance of secretions" that he "could not find whores enough to draw off." [13] Historians and political scientists have found more of a pattern in Hamilton. In view of his interference in the affairs of the Secretary of War and of the Attorney General as well as of the other cabinet departments, it has been suggested that he was consciously trying to ape the British cabinet system, with himself as first minister under a ceremonial and magisterial President. His sympathetic biographer of many years later, Henry Cabot Lodge, wrote that Hamilton "could not rid himself of the idea that he was really the prime minister, a notion encouraged by the way in which Congress had thrown all sorts of questions into his hands for decision." [14]

Perhaps so; but the more one studies Hamilton's role, the more he appears the utter opportunist seeking any tolerable means of gaining the policies he favored. "The contingencies

[13] Quoted in Miller, *op. cit.,* p. 523.
[14] Henry Cabot Lodge, *Alexander Hamilton* (Boston: Houghton, Mifflin and Company, 1899), p. 156.

of society are not reducible to calculations," he said.[15] They could not be fixed or bounded, even in imagination. He wanted sweeping presidential power so that the national government could deal quickly and flexibly with rapidly moving events, especially events abroad. His own hopes and ambitions were caught up in the exercise of that executive power, of course, but he wished no fixed pattern. For example, despite his preaching about cabinet unity — essential to the British-type cabinet system — he had little compunction about opposing and even maneuvering against the President's neutrality policy. The modern theory of presidential power, Edward Corwin concluded after a long study of the Presidency under the Constitution, is the contribution primarily of Alexander Hamilton.[16] If he had a limited influence on the Constitution of 1787, he had a substantial influence on the Constitutions of 1789 and 1792 and 1795 and hence all the later ones.

"Other men," Professor Rossiter has said, "responding to the challenge of mighty events, have made the Presidency the splendid instrument of constitutional democracy it is today; other men, attempting to find a pattern of constitutional logic in these responses, have piled construction upon construction to give the theory of the Presidency a content far more detailed than he was able to work out. Yet all these responses and all these constructions have been, in one sense, merely an elaboration of the principle he first announced as Pacificus: 'that the *executive power* of the nation is vested in the President; subject only to the *exceptions* and *qualifications* which are expressed in the instrument.' " [17]

15 Miller, *op. cit.,* p. 265.
16 Edward S. Corwin, *Constitution Annotated,* p. 381.
17 Rossiter, *op. cit.,* p. 348.

Rebuffed by his colleagues in Philadelphia in 1787, Hamilton by 1795 had presented the world with the Hamiltonian model in action — a model not in the technical or scientific sense, but as he himself used the word[18] — as a general plan of government that would best unite "public strength" and "individual security," and a model too that would both shape crucial precedents at the start and help legitimate a particular type of government. It was the model, in short, of *presidential government* — of a government in which the President would act vigorously and creatively, dominating the legislative process as well as the executive, upsetting the carefully contrived balance of powers between nation and states and between President and the other branches, and being curbed less by formal constitutional restrictions than by the pressures and exigencies of the political arena — by what the people, or their leaders, would bear at the moment.

It was a model, too, in that it brilliantly related means to immediate ends — it related governmental mechanics, such as presidential power, to a coherent set of limited or instrumental ends, such as national economic strength. But it failed to relate its means and its instrumental ends to broader, more ultimate goals — and this leads us straight to the great failing of the Hamiltonian model.

The Fox and the Hedgehog

Isaiah Berlin has recalled to us the line from Archilochus: "The fox knows many things, but the hedgehog knows one big thing." Taken figuratively, Berlin goes on, "the words

18 Syrett (ed.), *Papers*, vol. IV, *op. cit.*, p. 200.

can be made to yield a sense in which they mark one of the deepest differences which divide writers and thinkers, and, it may be, human beings in general. For there exists a great chasm between those, on one side, who relate everything to a single central vision, one system less or more coherent or articulate, in terms of which they understand, think and feel — a single, universal, organizing principle in terms of which alone all that they are and say has significance — and, on the other side, those who pursue many ends, often unrelated and even contradictory, connected, if at all, only in some *de facto* way, for some psychological or physiological cause, related by no moral or aesthetic principle; these last lead lives, perform acts, and entertain ideas that are centrifugal rather then centripetal, their thought is scattered or diffused, moving on many levels, seizing upon the essence of a vast variety of experiences and objects for what they are in themselves, without, consciously or unconsciously, seeking to fit them into, or exclude them from, any one unchanging, all-embracing, sometimes self-contradictory and incomplete, at times fanatical, unitary inner vision. . . ." [19]

Without overly burdening this insight — and Berlin does not — we can include Hamilton among the foxes who spurn ideological systems, monistic and all-inclusive creeds, and systematic interpretations of the nature of man and society, among the foxes who work toward fairly specific and tangible ends, who act experimentally and empirically, who unite the appropriate and concrete means with manageable and immediately realizable instrumental ends. Such men are highly *operational* — and if they limit their ends to the fulfillment of narrow and even selfish ambitions of their own, we call them "operators."

[19] Isaiah Berlin, *The Hedgehog and the Fox* (New York: New American Library, 1957), pp. 1–2.

Hamilton was operational without being simply an operator. He knew exactly what he wanted the new national government to do and how it must be organized and operated to
do it. He wanted a government that would be able to attract
the support of moneyed and prestigeful Americans (and foreigners) who would be willing to invest in the banks and fac-
tories and canals and ships that would start the new nation
toward industrial strength and greatness. He wanted a national government powerful enough to prevent the states —
and popular majorities within the states — from actions that
would undermine confidence in the American economy. He
wanted an executive branch that would exert vigorous leadership in stabilizing and expanding the economy and would
prevent popular and democratic forces in Congress from raising hob with what Hamilton considered the preconditions of
economic development and national greatness.

All this might seem to make Hamilton a hedgehog in Berlin's sense. But something was lacking — an understanding of
the relation of these means and these instrumental ends to
ultimate goals or values. One reason that Hamilton was so
effective operationally was the immediacy and manageability
of his objectives. He could lecture brilliantly to the constitutional convention, write a masterful series of essays defending
the new Constitution, set up a new Treasury Department,
push his measures through Congress, dominate Washington's
Cabinet, organize a Society of Useful Manufactures, pay off
the foreign and domestic debt, establish a national bank, out-
wit and outmaneuver his opponents, not only because of his
extraordinary intelligence and vigor but because his instrumental ends — mainly national economic development —
very clearly shaped his means.

But he did not have a central vision of ultimate goals; he

did not have a single, universal, organizing principle in terms of which elitist politics and his developmental economics took on continuing meaning for the American people. He did not ask the ultimate question: For whom was the new economy being developed? For whom was the new policy being shaped? The new economy would bring prosperity to the nation — but how widely would that prosperity be shared? To what extent would the great number of people share in the decisions as to who got what, when, and how out of the new order of things? And if the people were to share, by what political and economic mechanism would the sharing take place?

It was all the more imperative that Hamilton address himself to such questions because so many of his constitutional positions and economic policies fortified the impression that he was a monarchist, an oligarchist, or at least an inegalitarian. Doubtless he was — but then he still must, if he were to be anything more than a superior kind of fox, show how his means and instrumental ends related to the ultimate goals of virtue, welfare, excellence, happiness, or such other ends as he valued.

But Hamilton had no wish to be a hedgehog, in this sense, and opposed the "speculative philosophers" who made so much of lofty problems. The most speculative of these philosophers was Thomas Jefferson. And here we have an interesting contrast. Jefferson was as confused and self-contradictory as to his intermediate ends as Hamilton was clear and consistent. He held biases against the city, in favor of the farmer, in favor of states' rights, against a strong Presidency, in favor of a minimum of government, against urbanization and industrialization, against a strong national government, that made many of his political and economic policies irrelevant to, or even a handicap to, the strength of the new republic.

But Jefferson had one supreme value, a monistic vision if you will, that gave him the posture and strength of Archilochus' hedgehog. This was a simple faith in the people — in all the people, in the living people, in the present generation, in the right of one generation to change the arrangements of a previous one, in the superior right of a majority over a minority simply because a majority embraced more people than a minority. Above all, he believed in liberty and equality. Through all his twistings and windings (and contradictions — see Chapter 8) Jefferson was able in the end to stick to the central values of democracy — of government by and for and of the people — that can be captured now only in hackneyed words simply because they *have* become the central political values of the American people.

Hamilton's limitations in this area had immensely important implications for American politics, for the Presidency, and for the careers and historical reputations of himself and Jefferson — implications that were far more practical than he ever would have dreamed when he denounced the impractical speculators and philosophers:

Hamilton's first miscalculation lay in the method of electing the President. With the image of Washington fixed in his mind, he must have shared his colleagues' assumption that presidential electors in the states would consider disinterestedly the possible candidates and finally agree on some wise and good man — like George Washington. As long as Washington was around, the idea worked. But after Washington? Many of the Framers had expected that the electors might not be able to agree and hence that the presidential election would be thrown into the House of Representatives. What they did not fully understand was that the Presidency would be the grand prize of American politics, that anyone connected with filling it, whether elector or congressman, would be drawn into the orbit of political ambitions, loves and hatreds, coteries and coalitions — in short, into politics — and that the dream of impartial wise men calling some Cincinnatus from his plow to the Presidency was just a dream.

This miscalculation led to a more serious one, which would have special poignancy for Hamilton's career.

Jefferson might indeed have gone down in history as just a speculative and ineffectual man, and Hamilton as a wholly practical and successful one, if Jefferson had been content to leave his idea of democracy and popular rule in the realm of wishful thinking. But he was not. After some backing and filling, Jefferson worked out means that were brilliantly suited to his ultimate ends, and those ends — liberty and equality, under government by the people—were loftier than Hamilton's and more suited to the political aspirations of the American people. If Jefferson's theoretical answer to Hamilton was the viability of rule by the people instead of rule by an elite, his practical answer was the political party.

Hamilton himself had founded the nation's first party, but it was not a party in the modern sense. It was an Administration party embracing most of the Cabinet and officialdom, those Senators and Representatives who supported Hamilton and the Federalist cause, and clusters of Federalist families, cliques, factions, and leaders in the states. Hamilton was not consciously a party builder in the modern sense. The only party model he had to go by, as Chambers has pointed out, was the English type, which then was "still a helter-skelter of personal maneuverings and personal 'connexions' — in the old spelling and the old style — of ties based on family, narrow bonds of special interest, or friendship." [20] In the last analysis politicians might have to appeal to voters, but the electorate was very limited; probably only one or two out of ten white males voted in the elections of 1788 and 1789. Hamilton simply looked around for whatever help he could find for his fiscal and other measures; he had little need for — and less interest in — grass-roots support.

The first Republican party was also a highly limited enterprise. Founded as a counterorganization to the Hamiltonian clique or faction, it was centered in the Republican members of Congress and their friends, allies, and supporters in the states and districts. Madison was the leader of this faction and deserves a place in history as the founder of the "Congressional Republican" party. But the man who had once written and spoken so brilliantly against the dangers and violence of faction still had doubts about a widely inclusive politics that would bring the ambitious politicians more directly into the councils of state. Hamilton too opposed party; his writings are filled with denunciations of the "petulance" and "rage" and "delirium" of party — which he continued to define as a small faction of ambitious, selfish, and pugnacious power seekers.

Given this prejudice against big popular parties, the critical question was whether either of the party leaderships would overcome their prejudice and would broaden their party appeal for the very practical purpose of winning votes and political office. This is where Jefferson's hedgehog vision made all the difference.

Jefferson too had been against parties. But this was one of his means that he could easily reshape — to the perplexity of

20 William Nisbet Chambers, *Political Parties in a New Nation* (New York: Oxford University Press, 1963) , p. 3.

his friends and the annoyance of his enemies — as he clung to his central ends. Since Jefferson retained his abiding faith in the common sense of the people, it was easier for him than for Hamilton to accept — and ultimately to direct — the formation of a party that depended both on popular votes and a belief in popular rule to attain success.

So during the 1790's the Republicans brought off a brilliant job of party building. They had one advantage that the Federalists lacked — the rise in a number of states of Democratic Societies that provided something of a popular basis for the Republicans. But most of the work was done by the tireless politicians of Philadelphia. In the House, Madison united Republicans and Independents against Hamilton; set up a Ways and Means committee to counter his fiscal measures; and inveighed against his "monarchical" and "English" ways.

Slowly the party lines formed. Washington, despite his distaste for party and faction, was drawn increasingly into the Federal orbit. His Secretary of State Jefferson resigned from the Cabinet at the end of 1793 and moved gradually into the opposition. Madison and Jefferson worked closely together in one of the most fruitful partnerships in American politics; but it was Jefferson — signer of the Declaration of Independence, successor to Benjamin Franklin in Paris, and the great philosopher of the rights of man — who headed steadily toward the role of national spokesman and leader of the Republicans. Elected Vice-President in 1796, he had the ideal office — visibility and prestige, without much to do — from which he could lead the opposition to Adams.

The election of 1800 acted as a catalyst of party. Under Jefferson's leadership, Republican party activists simply outorganized and outmobilized the Federalists. The Adams Administration had good leaders, good issues, and a good record; it simply lacked a base in the electorate. Chambers has well summarized the situation: "The Federalists achieved party structure earlier and found a substantial popular power base; and yet they never quite transcended their ministerial, English-oriented, elitist origins. They represented interests, shaped opinion, and offered choices to the electorate; but they were not given to encouraging intra-party popular participation. They always depended on a comparatively close nucleus of leaders in government, and their attitude toward the public and electorate was always an uncertain mixture of condescension and fear. The Republicans on the other hand, although slower to form, finally established a close rapport between leaders and followers." [21] The best test of the intensified party politics was the extent of voting, which rose to almost 40 percent of adult white males in 1800.

So in the end it was that most practical of men, Alexander Hamilton, whose theoretical predilections hindered him from meeting the Federalist party crisis of 1800, and it was that speculative philosopher Thomas Jefferson who led his party in getting out the vote and in achieving that most practical goal for politicians, winning a national election. And if there was still any doubt as to Jefferson's understanding of the possibilities of party action and party leadership, it was removed during his Presidency. As many studies have shown, he perfected his party in Congress so that he could easily marshal support for his policies. He exerted party discipline even to the extent of easing a Republican dissident out of the chairmanship of the Ways and Means Committee. And he won a tremendous victory in the election of 1804.

The final denouement for Hamilton was grievous. At a

21 *Ibid.,* p. 106.

time when Jefferson's sun was brightest, Hamilton was reduced to hardly more than a local politician and back-stairs intriguer. His ideas were turned upside down. He had fought for a strong President without sensing the danger that some day the Presidency might become a popular instrument, the Tribune of the People, and that "demagogues" and "democrats" and "jacobins" might occupy it; he lived to see Jefferson occupy it. The firm constitutionalist of 1787 was so fearful of Republican victory in 1800 that during the election he proposed to John Jay a change in the rules of the game; Jay, a more principled man, spurned the idea. Much of the despair that Hamilton suffered after 1800 stemmed from his fear that Jefferson would occupy the Presidency for life; hence Hamilton regretted his proposals of 1787 for a President during good behavior. Both the original proposal and the later fear were demolished by Jefferson's demeanor in office and his willingness to relinquish it.

In 1805 Aaron Burr, Jefferson's man in New York City whom Hamilton once had criticized for having no "theory" or "general principles," blew out the brains of the Federalist party in the duel on the heights of Weehawken. That brain had been an eminently operational one; quick, sensitive, versatile, and productive, it had helped plan a new system and fashion a powerful executive but it had not come to grips with either the popular forces or the popular ideas that were reshaping the foundations of American democracy.

The Three Models

It is a measure of both the genius and the flexibility of the Constitution that the first three Presidencies provided three different models of government under the great charter. The first was the Hamiltonian model of a vigorous executive working within the system of checks and balances. After his earlier doubts that executive power and good republicanism were compatible, Hamilton succeeded in "tuning Government high" — so high that Washington's administration stands as one of the truly creative Presidencies in American history.

The second great experiment I have labeled the Madisonian model after the "father of the Constitution," who mainly established it in theory and in law, but it was first tried out in practice by John Adams.[22] While not himself a member of the Constitutional convention, Adams had long preached the need of governments with countervailing powers and had fashioned for Massachusetts a marvelously contrived instrument that balanced powers within the executive and legislative branches as well as between them. A believer in prudent, orderly, and stable government and in an ordered set of individual liberties and responsibilities, President Adams dissolved many of the Hamiltonian arrangements and tried to carry out a model of government quite close to the hopes and expectations of most of the Framers.

The third model was the Jeffersonian. Within fifteen years of the framing of the Constitution the first Republican Presi-

[22] James MacGregor Burns, *The Deadlock of Democracy* (Englewood Cliffs, N.J.: Prentice-Hall, Inc., 1963), ch. 1.

dent was presiding over a strong national party, dominating the legislature, and even trying to subdue a Federalist-controlled judiciary. If the Hamiltonian model implied a federal government revolving around the Presidency, and depending on energy, resourcefulness, inventiveness, and a ruthless pragmatism in the executive office, and if the Madisonian model implied a prudent, less daring and active government, one that was balanced between the legislative and executive forces and powers, the Jeffersonian model was almost revolutionary, implying government by majority rule, under strong presidential leadership, with a highly competitive two-party system and with a more popular, democratic, and egalitarian impetus than the Madisonian. The Hamiltonian model was perhaps a more resourceful and flexible kind of government, the Madisonian more stable and prudent, and the Jeffersonian more democratic and potentially more powerful.

During the next fifty years American Presidents governed in the light of these models or variations of them. They did not, of course, consciously try to adhere to a set general design, but they were influenced by memories of the early great Administrations, by precedents, by institutional arrangements, by popular expectations, and by speeches and dicta that ran back to the first three Presidencies.

Madison himself tried to shape and administer his government in the true spirit of the checks and balances. Since he lacked Washington's prestige, Hamilton's ability to manipulate people, and Jefferson's strength as national party leader, he soon discovered that centrifugal forces in the government were frustrating his plans; that if he did not exert force through the political circuits, his opponents would exert pressure through the same circuits against him; that political structure could never be neutral; that even carefully designed checks and balances favored some interests and policies against others. The Cabinet, supposedly an instrument of executive power, was turned against President Madison by congressional forces that blocked him from appointing the Secretary of the Treasury he wanted. The Vice-President acted virtually as he wished against the President. The Speakership, the caucus, the committee system were also turned against him.

We need not here review the tortuous history of the Presidency between Madison's time and Abraham Lincoln's. Nor is it necessary to squeeze the various administrations into any one of our three models in order to find pattern or continuity. Some administrations — most notably Andrew Jackson's — had a sharply Jeffersonian cast; buttressed by a strong Democratic party, by a rising tide of votes and local party politicians, and by his own demagogic appeal, Jackson even more than Jefferson made the Presidency the Tribune of the People. Here was a President that would really have horrified Hamilton and vindicated his worst fears. Other Presidencies had more of a Hamiltonian cast, as the Chief Executives opportunistically sought to keep or expand their power as political conditions made it possible. Most of the Presidencies were closer to the Madisonian model. It was not, in general, a time of executive leadership or creativity.

The vital question is not how well various administrations fit various models, but the implications for us today of the Hamiltonian, Jeffersonian, and Madisonian approaches to government. Each of these models was a way of granting and withholding power to the President, which meant granting and withholding power to the party and group interests represented by the President. Each model was subject to distortion and caricature. The Democratic party use of patronage under Jackson and other Presidents was party government carried to extremes. Calhoun's theory of concurrent majority rule was virtually a caricature of the Madisonian model and its checks and balances; Calhoun would give a veto not simply to an institution representing (in some form) the whole nation, but to any substantial region or interest even if in the minority.

What about the Hamiltonian model — the model that lent itself most easily to opportunism, experimenting, manipulation, pressuring, and perhaps endless expansion? Since the essence of Hamilton's political tactics, especially in enacting his fiscal measures, had been the exertion of influence regardless of constitutional theory and principle, what were the natural limitations on the exercise of this power? Or were there none? Was there no limit to expediency? Hamilton in office had been limited less by constitutional niceties or principle than by counterpressure and counterorganization. What if the Hamiltonian impulse should be projected in a time when the natural counterforces to political pressure were enfeebled? Partial answers to these questions would not come until the latter years of the first century of the American Republic.

II

The Rise of
Presidential Government

T HE CENTURY after 1787 witnessed severe oscillations in the power relations of President and Congress. Within a few years of the adoption of a Constitution designed to secure the affirmative policy-making power in Congressional hands, as we have seen, Hamilton was framing momentous fiscal measures and pushing them through the House and Senate. John Adams restored the essential balance anticipated by the Framers, only to be followed by a Jefferson who blithely ignored his own constitutional principles of earlier days and established a powerful regime of party government. The pendulum of presidential-congressional relations swung back toward presidential weakness with Madison and continued to oscillate sporadically and unpredictably in presidential successions such as those of John Quincy Adams and Jackson, James Polk and Franklin Pierce, James Buchanan and Lincoln.

Walter Lippmann has suggested that the relation of executive and legislature, as well as government and people, somewhat resembles that of the two sexes. "The executive is the active power in the state, the asking and the proposing power. The representative assembly is the consenting power, the petitioning, the approving and the criticizing, the accepting and the refusing power. . . . In the act of reproduction each sex has an unalterable physiological function. If this function is devitalized or is confused with the function of the other sex, the result is sterility and disorder." [1] This analogy is useful only if we assume considerable volatility and even turbulence in the relation of the sexes. Time and again in the first century, Congress did become the active, proposing power, and the President the petitioning, accepting and refusing power; whether this overturn of the "normal" relationship produced sterility and disorder is an open question.

There was always a limit, however, to the oscillation of power between President and Congress. The balance never swung so far to one side or the other as to destroy either branch as an institution, to reduce it to utter impotence, or to prevent its later resurrection as political forces shifted direction. However unbalanced the relation might be at any one time, the underlying system of checks and balances retained its potency. This was a result of the constitutional planning of the Framers. They could not prevent gusts of public opinion, the coming of new leaders, and the rush of events from temporarily upsetting the nice balance they preferred over the long run. What they could do and did do was to build under each branch institutional and political foundations that would shore it up and sustain it in the face of fluctuating political pressures. Their method of accomplishing this equipoise was spelled out by Madison in the Tenth and Fifty-first Federalist Papers: first "by enlarging the sphere of government and hence breaking society into a greater variety of interests and passions," and secondly by making President, Senate, and House elected by, and responsive to, different elements and combinations in that wider sphere. As long as the larger society retained its diversity, and as long as men retained their ambitions and fought for office in a variety of

1 Walter Lippmann, *The Public Philosophy* (Boston: Little, Brown and Company, 1955), p. 30.

different, overlapping, and mutually hostile or competitive constituencies, the institutional apparatus for sustaining the checks and balances would be intact, even though the actual balance of power might teeter at various times.

Still, there was never any predictability as to when the balance might be restored. The pendulum oscillated erratically especially in the mid-nineteenth century. In the crucible of civil war Abraham Lincoln overrode his Whig heritage and provided a pragmatic, opportunistic Presidency in the fullest Hamiltonian tradition. The Civil War was followed by a crisis in the Presidency, and this was followed by a remarkable period of Congressional government. That period in turn was the prelude to the rise of presidential government.

Lincoln:
The Paradox of the Presidency

Abraham Lincoln more than any other important American politician illustrated the jumbling and deranging of means and instrumental goals and ultimate ends that characterized the relations between American ideology and American political practice. As a congressman and a Whig he had denounced the Democratic party's vigorous use of presidential power. "Were I President," he had said, "I should desire the legislation of the country to rest with Congress, uninfluenced by the executive in its origin or progress, and undisturbed by the veto unless in very special and clear cases." [2] It was the fate of this man, coming to the Presidency with a

---

[2] John G. Nicolay and John Hay, *Abraham Lincoln: Complete Works* (New York: Century Company, 1894), vol. 1, p. 134.

modicum of executive experience, to turn the Whig conception of the Presidency upside down.

The extent of the overturn has long entranced historians — even those historians who implicitly favor some variation of the Madisonian model. "No one can ever know just what Lincoln conceived to be limits of his powers," Binkley has concluded. "Even a partial review of them presents an imposing list of daring ventures. Under the war power he proclaimed the slaves of those in rebellion emancipated. He devised and put into execution his peculiar plan of reconstruction. In disregard of law he increased the army and navy beyond the limits set by statute. The privilege of the writ of habeas corpus was suspended wholesale and martial law declared. Public money in the sum of millions was deliberately spent without congressional appropriation. Nor was any of this done innocently. Lincoln understood his Constitution. He knew, in many cases, just how he was transgressing and his infractions were consequently deliberate." [3]

It is a striking fact, according to the leading authority on Lincoln's constitutional role, that Lincoln, "who stands forth in popular conception as the great democrat, the exponent of liberty and of government by the people, was driven by circumstances to the use of more arbitrary power than perhaps any other President has seized." [4] "Unquestionably the high-water mark of the exercise of executive power in the United States is found in the administration of Abraham Lincoln," Binkley wrote in 1947. "No President before or since has pushed the boundaries of executive power so far over into the legislative sphere." [5]

[3] Wilfred E. Binkley, *President and Congress* (New York: Alfred A. Knopf, 1947), p. 129.
[4] James G. Randall, *Constitutional Problems under Lincoln* (New York: D. Appleton and Company, 1926), p. 513.
[5] *Op. cit.*, p. 126.

Particularly daring was Lincoln's challenge to the fiscal supremacy of Congress. The Whigs had railed against Jackson's "usurpations" in this area; Lincoln went much further than Old Hickory. Early in the war, when Congress was not in session — Lincoln had preferred not to call it into session — the President instructed his Secretary of the Treasury to give two million dollars to three New Yorkers for the payment of certain military expenses. He later defended his action to Congress not on constitutional grounds but on the grounds — with tongue in cheek? — that not a dollar of the funds had been lost or wasted.

Lincoln's candid defense of his constitutional usurpations has also impressed historians. "Was it possible to lose the nation and yet preserve the Constitution?" Lincoln demanded. "By general law, life and limb must be protected, yet often a limb must be amputated to save a life, but a life is never wisely given to save a limb. I felt that measures otherwise unconstitutional might become lawful by becoming indispensable to the preservation of the Constitution through the preservation of the nation. . . ." [6]

Lincoln could act with such certainty and defend his acts with such assuredness because he had a clear and set aim — victory and restoration of the Union. If men and treasure could be sacrificed to that aim, certainly the Constitution could. And here, although he would never have considered himself a Hamiltonian, Lincoln was acting in the tradition of Hamiltonian operationalism. And he was involved in the same confusion of ends and means as Washington's first secretary.

Lincoln recognized that Union or Reunion was not an end

[6] John G. Nicolay and John Hay (eds.), *Complete Works of Abraham Lincoln* (Lincoln Memorial University, 1894), vol. 10, p. 66.

in itself, or an ultimate end; it was an instrumental goal to something more central and vital to the people. "This is essentially a people's contest," he told Congress. "On the side of the Union it is a struggle for maintaining in the world that form and substance of a government whose leading object is to elevate the condition of men — to lift artificial weights from all shoulders; to clear the paths of laudable pursuit for all; to afford all an unfettered start, and a fair chance in the race of life. . . ."

"To elevate the condition of man" — here was a noble aim, one that issued from Lincoln's mind and heart, as well as from the liberal and popular tradition in America. Here apparently was Lincoln's ultimate end — one sufficient unto itself. The question we must raise — especially from the vantage point of the racial struggles and tension of the seventh decade of the twentieth century — is how well did Lincoln make his magnificent operationalism a servant to his ultimate ends, and his ends a guide to his operationalism?

It would be easy to answer this question by observing that Lincoln was mainly concerned with the future of free white labor, not of the Negroes, despite the sweep of his pronouncements about mankind — despite, for example, his use of the word "all" three times even in the short statement quoted above. Certainly to Lincoln, with his border background and his reservations about racial integration, the Negro was secondary to the white laborer, as Hofstadter has noted.[7] But this was not the whole story. As the war became increasingly a struggle not just for the Union but for the Negro, as a result of ideological and social forces precipitated by the war, Lincoln became increasingly implicated in the popular commit-

---

[7] Richard Hofstadter, *The American Political Tradition* (New York: Vintage Books, 1954), p. 131.

ment to emancipation and to equality for the Negro. It was in the relation of Lincoln's instrumental aim — restoring the Union — and his ultimate aim — elevating all men — that Lincoln's operationalism served him ill.

The problem is that any major political action or operation releases and reinforces certain tendencies, and blocks or diverts other tendencies in a manner that creates consequences for broader goals and values than the immediate objective in hand. The more that a political leader concentrates on his immediate objective, the more he may be limiting himself in his capacity to plan or influence more remote ends that may be equally important for him — ends, indeed, that can supply the only final vindication for the instrumental ends on which he is concentrating. It is the ultimate end, not the instrumental end, that can vindicate opportunistic and "illegal" or "unconstitutional" means. In Lincoln's case, his overturn of constitutional practice can be justified only in terms of the fundamental objective of Lincoln himself, of his party, of the bulk of the Northerners behind him, of the Constitution itself — the elevation of all men.

Most historians believe that Lincoln's governmental means were well suited to his military aims. Some members of Congress, of course, believed devoutly at the time that congressional leaders could do a better job of military direction than Lincoln was doing, indeed, that no one could do worse than the inexperienced, indecisive, small-town politician from Illinois, but history has dealt harshly with such critics and their views. For the North did win, Lincoln did handle a multitude of complex political and military problems with shrewdness and foresight, and even many professional politicians in the end paid tribute to his tactics. So we do not need to reconsider here Lincoln's operationalism. It is his ability to act in terms of broader goals and more remote — but equally compelling — objectives that concerns us here, because this question sheds light on the possibilities and limitations of the Hamiltonian approach to politics.

Lincoln was as candid about his priority of instrumental ends as he was about his flouting of the Constitution. It was Union first, Emancipation second. In answer to an eloquent editorial by Horace Greeley — "The Prayer of Twenty Millions" — in favor of early Emancipation, Lincoln wrote: "I would save the Union. I would save it the shortest way under the Constitution. . . . My paramount object in this struggle *is* to save the Union, and is *not* either to save or to destroy slavery. If I could save the Union without freeing *any* slave I would do it, and if I could save it by freeing *all* the slaves I would do it; and if I could save it by freeing some and leaving others alone I would also do that. What I do about slavery, and the colored race, I do because I believe it helps to save the Union; and what I forbear, I forbear because I do *not* believe it would help to save the Union. . . ." [8] This single-minded concentration on the highest priority of national survival has been widely applauded. But what consequences did this exclusive attention on military victory have for the Negroes — for whom many Northerners felt the war was being fought?

Lincoln never wavered in his subordination of the race issue. Although he patiently heard out the Radicals who were pressing for emancipation, he could privately refer to "the petulent and vicious fretfulness of many radicals." [9]

In the early months of the war he made clear that it was not being waged to interfere with slavery in the seceded states;

[8] Roy P. Basler (ed.), *The Collected Works of Abraham Lincoln* (New Brunswick: Rutgers University Press, 1953), vol. 5, p. 388.

[9] Quoted in J. G. Randall and Richard N. Current, *Lincoln the President: Last Full Measure* (New York: Dodd, Mead & Company, 1955), p. 185.

these states could return to the Union with slavery intact. As the months passed, Lincoln did abandon some of his earlier positions — for example, his support on the eve of hostilities of a constitutional amendment designed to prevent the federal government from ever interfering with slavery — but it is significant that Lincoln's shifts were mainly in response to military, congressional, and narrowly political pressures. Taking a stronger line against slavery was an operational necessity. He issued the Emancipation Proclamation — itself an unimpassioned document except for the words "act of justice" inserted on the urging of Secretary Salmon P. Chase — partly as a military measure and partly to make concessions to the ever more militant radicals. Lincoln knew that he had to hold the support of elements cool to emancipation, such as sections of the border states, Northern conservatives, and some army officers and troops. He performed a prodigious balancing act between radicals and conservatives and averted crisis.

Perhaps most revealing of Lincoln's operationalism were his repeated proposals for the colonization of American Negroes in other parts of the world. He advocated this policy in 1854 and favored it as late as August 1862, when he had already decided to issue the Emancipation Proclamation.[10] Lincoln also saw practical problems in racial integration. In words often quoted since by segregationists, he told a group of Negroes in August 1862: "You and we are different races. We have between us a broader difference than exists between almost any other two races. Whether it is right or wrong I need not discuss, but this physical difference is a great disadvantage to us both, as I think your race suffer very greatly,

[10] John Hope Franklin, *The Emancipation Proclamation* (Garden City, N. Y.: Doubleday & Company, Inc., 1963), pp. 33–34.

many of them by living among us, while ours suffer from your presence. In a word we suffer on each side. If this be admitted, it affords a reason at least why we should be separated." [11] While this utterance was more a defense of colonization than domestic segregation, it had a practical implication for race relations at home.

Still, one has a sense that Lincoln's operationalism lived uneasily with his inmost thoughts and values. Perhaps the most important words in the last quotation are the words: "whether it is right or wrong I need not discuss." At the core of his being, behind all the compromises and expediencies, historians have found a humanity, charity, egalitarianism, and sheer humanness that have lifted Lincoln far above the ruck of American politicians. He made a major distinction between his public responsibilities (compromise on the issue of slavery) and his private views (opposition to slavery). In the last month of his life he wrote a friend: "I am naturally anti-slavery. If slavery is not wrong, nothing is wrong. . . . And yet I have never understood that the Presidency conferred upon me an unrestricted right to act officially upon this judgment and feeling. . . . And I aver that, to this day, I have done no official act in mere deference to my abstract judgment and feeling on slavery." [12]

This is a remarkably revealing observation. It suggests a gap between private feeling and public action that could characterize an operationalist only of Lincoln's genius. Yet it simply poses the question again: what price may be paid by this intensive concentration on the job at hand, regardless of moral convictions or broader political pressures relating to ultimate ends?

11 Roy P. Basler (ed.), *The Collected Works*, vol. 5, p. 371.
12 *Ibid.*, vol. 7, p. 281.

The moral issue of the Civil War became the very practical problem of the postwar period — so practical a problem, indeed, that the same issue confronts us one hundred years later: what arrangements for the freedmen? And it is here that Lincoln's operationalism broke down. So cautious had he been not to interfere with military necessities, and so orthodox about the powers of the states, that the North ended the war without clear guidance from the fallen leader — with his prestige now immensely heightened — as to postwar policies that might carry out the great moral commitment of the North to the freedmen. To the extent that Lincoln's wartime position affected postwar reconstruction strategy, it was, on balance, to hinder the enactment of the humane and creative policies that might have been possible, given the state of Northern feeling and Northern resources.

We now know that the vital issue facing the nation in 1865 was whether the power of the nation that had been employed in subduing the South could now be used to prepare the ground for the protection and elevation of the southern Negro. We now know that the only way to prepare the ground was to provide the freedmen with schooling, jobs, civil rights, including the right to vote, that in the long run would enable him to exercise democratic citizenship. We now know that the Southern states, whether controlled by white Southerners, Negroes, or carpetbaggers, had neither the economic resources nor the governmental procedures and skills to carry out this tremendous effort.

We now know all this — but it is not merely hindsight, nor merely the benefit of later experience with the reconstruction of conquered nations, such as Japan and Germany. Many politicians and publicists, especially among the Radicals, perceived at the time the problems and potentialities of postwar

Reconstruction policies. They wanted to reorganize Southern society; to distribute land to the freedmen; to outlaw discrimination at the polls, in education, in public places. They also foresaw the perils of allowing the old slaveowning class to retain power in the Southern states, and the Southern states to retain power over the Southern social structure. They realized that the perpetuation of the old oligarchies plus states' rights would mean the perpetuation in Congress of Southern delegations representing the oligarchies and actually enjoying increased numbers in Congress as a result of the ending of the old provision for three-fifths representation for slaves. The Southerners would combine with Northern Democrats and border state conservatives to control Congress and thwart the Republican party and its reconstruction policies.

Everything depended on the treatment of "states' rights" — on the willingness of the North at least for a time to override the political and social structure of the old South and to establish the foundations for Negro opportunity and eventual equality. And this is where Lincoln's operationalism proved critical. As the price of immediate political and military necessity he had never faltered in his public position in favor of states' rights — including Southern states' rights. Even as late as December 1863, when Lincoln presented his general proposals for postwar policy, military considerations dominated his thinking. Critics were disturbed at the time, W. R. Brock has noted, "by the President's deliberate sanction to the continuance of prewar State constitutions and legal codes which had included discriminatory treatment of free negroes." [13]

It can be argued, of course, that military necessity — win-

---

[13] *An American Crisis* (London: St. Martin's Press, 1963), p. 23.

ning the war as efficiently as possible, with the least possible
bloodshed and destruction — was all that Lincoln could or
should have been concerned about. But such an argument
overemphasizes immediate military ends and underempha-
sizes the great objectives — reunion and, increasingly, protection for the freedmen — for which the war was being
fought, and which gave it ultimate meaning. And in this respect Lincoln's operationalism had special poignancy. His example of compassion, tolerance, and forgiveness was badly
needed in Southern reconstruction policy; nothing could
have reflected those qualities more practically than the generous use of national authority in behalf of equal rights and
racial opportunity. When national authority was finally
brought to bear on the South, Lincoln's compassion seemed
to have little weight; hopes for a bold and sweeping social and
political reorganization of the South perished in a welter of
arguments over less crucial matters, such as punitive measures
for the old elite and the deeds and misdeeds of white and
black politicians. What the South needed was the only kind
of policy that would have made a difference in the long run —
not rule by carpetbaggers or by the old oligarchs or by inexperienced Negroes, but long-run development programs
sponsored by the federal government, like those that have become familiar to us in recent years and that were not un-
known to men of vision in the 1860's. Granted that such a
development program for the South would have been extremely difficult without a trained cadre to replace the old
elite and without the expertise we have since accumulated in
aiding the developing nations abroad. The important fact is
that such a policy was never tried. It was not tried because
the intellectual commitment had not been made. If it had
been, the nation, even though failing initially, might have

come back to such a program before a whole century had passed.

This was the paradox of Lincoln: a failure in the end to relate his instrumental goals — a strong Presidency, victory, reunion — to the benign and compassionate values that we know he cherished.

Doubtless he was aware of the problem, for he considered himself a captive of immediate popular pressures and public opinion. "I claim not to have controlled events but confess plainly that events have controlled me," he said.[14] To Lincoln events were the immediate political pressures, the palpable needs and demands, the military crises — all the specific forces that beat on him relentlessly day after day. He improvised skillfully and untiringly in the face of these felt events. But looking back we see other "events" and it is precisely in the perception of events that the tests of great presidential leadership lie.

The paradox of Lincoln is the paradox of the Presidency. The more the President becomes a captive to the immediate pressures on him, the more he may become drawn away from the more significant but more remote and long-run problems of his time. The more practical, pragmatic, and operational he becomes, the more he is a victim of events rather than a shaper of events. And the more he enhances presidential power in coping with immediate crisis, the more open and unresolved he leaves the relation between the powerful instrumentality of the Presidency and the ultimate values and goals of the American people.

[14] Quoted in Hofstadter, *op. cit.*, p. 130.

The Era of
Congressional Government

The historic era of congressional government, stretching through the last thirty years of the last century, was ushered in by an abnormal period of Congressional power, especially Senate power. The story of Senate hegemony during Reconstruction has often been told, sometimes in lurid terms, but the sweep of congressional control was indeed startling. To the consternation of the Radicals, the new President, Andrew Johnson, continued Lincoln's policy of restoring civil government to the recently seceded states. He also emulated Lincoln in proceeding with reconstruction without calling a special session of Congress. There followed a battle between presidential veto and congressional counter-veto. When Johnson, acting out of his (and Lincoln's) states' rights principles, vetoed the Civil Rights bill, he challenged the Radicals' conviction that the civil rights of the freedmen could be protected only through the use of national authority. Congress not only overrode the veto, in the most sweeping exercise of that power until that time, but protected this reconstruction policy from presidential interference by taking the first steps to write the policy into the Constitution in the form of an amendment (the Fourteenth). More vetoes and overridings of vetoes followed.

"Two thirds of each house united and stimulated to one end can practically neutralize the executive power of the government and lay down its policy in defiance of the efforts and opposition of the President," James G. Blaine observed.[15]

15 Quoted in Wilfred E. Binkley, *President and Congress* (New York: Alfred A. Knopf, 1947), p. 135.

The power of Congress over the President became even more assured when Johnson's opponents carried the congressional elections of 1866 almost three to one. Staying in almost continuous session, Congress took command of basic Reconstruction policy, established control over executive personnel policy through the Tenure of Office Act (1867), which required Senate approval of removal of a presidential appointee, and finally impeached and almost convicted the beleaguered Johnson.

Would the normal balance of presidential-congressional power be re-established after the unusual conditions of the 1860's? Ulysses S. Grant, the man who succeeded Johnson, was a popular President who had little interest in converting his popularity into political influence. During his two terms Congress strengthened the powers and procedures that were to underlie its dominance during the rest of the century. Legislative control of men, money, and measures constituted the three foundations of congressional government during this period.

Congressional influence over the recruitment and tenure of officials provoked the most open and dramatic conflicts during these years. The impeachment of Johnson, precipitated by the President's dismissal of Secretary of War Stanton, was less a judicial trial than an effort to seize control of the executive power and hence of the thousands of officials who would be running the government, and especially directing Reconstruction. Unable to employ the European parliamentary device of a vote of no confidence, the Radicals were hoping to use the weapon of impeachment as a means of establishing an equivalent parliamentary supremacy. It was an awkward device, but one that came within one vote in the Senate of being operational.

The struggles over control of personnel during the next

thirty years were less dramatic but no less important for the
everyday making and administering of policy. The Tenure
of Office Act remained on the statute books for some time
and, in the words of Congressman James A. Garfield, "has virtually resulted in the usurpation, by the senate, of a large
share of the appointing power . . . has resulted in seriously
crippling the just powers of the executive, and has placed in
the hands of senators and representatives a power most cor-
rupting and dangerous." [16]   President Rutherford B. Hayes
challenged the Senate oligarchy and after a struggle established his right — and in effect the right of future Presidents
— to choose their own cabinets, but the day-to-day control of
personnel remained subject to a seesaw battle. In the absence
of a professional merit system, Congress insisted on the advice
and consent of the Senate not only in the appointment of
high officials but of many subordinate ones as well. For example, deputy controllers and deputy auditors in the Treasury Department and even melters and coiners in the local
mints were subject to Senate confirmation.[17] Congressmen
were especially interested in the thousands of routine patronage appointments. Presidents often complained about the
pressure of the job seekers, but the department and agency
heads had an even harder time trying to placate congressmen
and at the same time keep some control over staffing their
own organizations. The long struggle over the merit system
during these years was also a struggle between President and
congressmen for control of administration.

The second basis of congressional government was the historic one of control of the raising and spending of money.

16 James A. Garfield, "A Century of Congress," *Atlantic Monthly*, vol. 40,
no. 237 (July 1877), p. 61.
17 Leonard D. White, *The Republican Era: 1869–1901* (New York: Macmillan Company, 1958), p. 113.

Although the Constitution had clearly provided that "No Money shall be drawn from the Treasury, but in Consequence of Appropriations made by Law; and a regular Statement and Account of the Receipts and Expenditures of all public Money shall be published from time to time," the Constitution had also provided the President with a broad but vague executive authority. Throughout the first seventy years of the government President and Congress had fought over the actual control of public money. The legislators tried to hold the President and his administrators to specific expenditures at specific times under specific appropriations, but energetic officials wanted discretion. In the decade before the Civil War Congress renewed its efforts to restrict administrative discretion but the exigencies of the Civil War disrupted the uneasy balance and allowed the President wide latitude. At this point, Wilmerding has observed, "Law and practice once more stood in opposition, the one prescribing the extreme of rigor, the other permitting the extreme of laxity." [18]

Following the war Congress systematically went about the job of re-establishing its fiscal supremacy. It prohibited the transfer of funds from one purpose to another and from one fiscal year to the next. It recaptured unexpended Civil War funds that the departments had been happily resorting to when they ran short of money. It forbade any spending in excess of appropriations for the fiscal year, and when Treasury officials desperately tried to gain funds from the proceeds of the sale of government property, such as old military stores, Congress closed off this line of escape too. Most important, the legislators attacked the easy old departmental custom of spending the limited funds appropriated and then going back

[18] Lucius Wilmerding, Jr., *The Spending Power* (New Haven: Yale University Press, 1943), p. 117.

to Congress for a deficiency appropriation to bail the department out for the remainder of the year.[19] This last congressional effort was not fully mounted until 1905, and even then
was not wholly effective.

There was indeed no simple surgical method for concentrating in one body a fundamental governmental power that
the Framers had carefully shared among rival political representatives with separated constituencies. Much depended on
the temperament of the President and on the political power
and administrative resourcefulness of the department and
agency heads. Much depended too on unity and persistence
of congressmen who wished to curb the executive's spending
discretion. Congress itself was not well organized to concen-
trate financial control in its own houses. Committee control
of taxing and spending was divided and subdivided; individual congressmen often conducted their own trading with Administration officials; and often the battle degenerated into
guerrilla warfare, with legislators and officials forming tiny
coalitions in favor of types of spending in which they had a
mutual interest.

The third foundation of congressional power was its basic
authority to frame legislation. Here again, the essential authority had been granted jointly to President and Congress
under the Constitution, or had been established under the
first Presidents; and here again the balance of power oscillated over the years. Still, during these years Congress was
more successful in broadening its actual policy-making power
than in any other extended period in our history. On the
major legislation of the era — reconstruction, currency, tariffs, veterans' affairs, interstate commerce — Congress left a
heavy imprint. The expression of the President's wishes con-
veyed in a message, James Bryce observed, had not necessarily

[19] Wilmerding. *op. cit.*, ch. 6.

any more effect on Congress than an article in a prominent party newspaper. "No duty lies on Congress to take up a subject to which he has called attention as needing legislation; and the suggestions which he makes, year after year, may be neglected, even when his party has a majority in both Houses, or when the subject lies outside party lines." [20]

Congressional supremacy in lawmaking was not extraordinary, given the conditions and attitudes of the day; what was more remarkable was the congressional intrusion into subpolicy-making areas long viewed as under presidential control. Time and again during Hayes' Administration Congress tried to make policy through riders (substantive legislation attached to appropriations bills that the President was expected to find it impossible to veto), and time and again Hayes vetoed the appropriations bill that carried the rider. Congress was more successful in legislating details ordinarily delegated to administrators. The statute book of any session of Congress during this period, according to White, "provides an abundance of raw material to demonstrate the thesis that the legislative branch was constantly making decisions of individual application, both with respect to personal rights, such as pensions and patents, and with regard to administrative operations . . . [Congress] authorized the Secretary of the Treasury to change the name of the steam yacht *Fanny;* it enabled J. H. Schnell to enter a section of public land in California for a tea colony; it gave permission to Robert C. Schenck, United States minister to Great Britain, to employ a private amanuensis; and by formal enactment Congress directed the repair of the enclosure of the cemetery at Harpers Ferry." [21]

20 James Bryce, *The American Commonwealth* (New York: Macmillan Company, 1921), vol. 1, p. 210.
21 White, *op. cit.,* p. 69.

The gravest congressional threat to the integrity of the Presidency did not lie in these rather traditional methods of confining executive power. The Madisonian structure of presidential-congressional relations was adjustable enough to allow the preponderance of power to teeter back and forth and still permit an eventual return to the regular workings of the checks and balances. The gravest threat lay in the possibility that at some point during this period anti-executive elements in Congress would try permanently to upset the Madisonian balance.

There were several near-crises of this sort. If Johnson had not barely escaped conviction, a precedent would have been set for the easy dismissal of a President less on legal grounds than on political. Given the constitutional ambiguity over the division of legislative and executive power between President and Congress, given also the many conflicting precedents and doctrines of previous Presidents and congressional spokesmen, it would always have been possible to impeach an aggressive or intractable President on grounds that he was violating the Constitution or the statutes. Even the threat of impeachment would have been a potent weapon for congressmen. As it turned out, the most unpopular President after Johnson could calculate that if impeachment had not worked under the conditions of 1868, it never would. Impeachment became something like the nuclear arm — a weapon too potent to be used in warfare over limited objectives.

A second near-crisis for the Presidency was the capacity of Congress to override Johnson's vetoes with two-thirds votes; if Congress could continue to mobilize such majorities, there was hardly an executive or legislative power of the President that lay beyond the legislative reach. But Congress was unable to maintain such majorities over a significant period of time with the re-establishment of normal political competition, and has never been able to do so since.

A third threat to the Presidency as an institution was more theoretical but no less serious. This was the attempt to change the actual status and powers of the Presidency through constitutional amendment. One proposal, advanced by Horace Greeley among others, would have limited the President to a single term. Both Hayes and Grover Cleveland (initially) favored this proposal. A less obvious threat to presidential power was the proposal championed both by Republican "Stalwarts" and independent reformers, to allow department heads to sit in Congress. The Pendleton Committee in 1881 recommended that cabinet members be authorized to occupy seats in House and Senate with the right to take part in debate on matters relating to their departments. They would be required to attend twice a week to give information. Praised by reformers as a step toward closer cooperation between President and Congress, the proposal was also intended to bring the department heads more into the congressional orbit and weaken their relation to and dependence on the President. ". . . Either a second term or Cabinet seats in Congress," White concluded, "would have upset the balance of power and . . . would have weakened the President's effective participation in departmental business by increasing the authority of Congress and its committees." [22]

Despite the tenacious and even heroic defense of the Presidency during this period, we must note that it was, after all, simply holding action. The fact that historians almost unanimously judge these three decades to have been the nadir of presidential greatness and influence raises the question, assuming the historians are correct, as to why this particular

22 White, *op. cit.*, p. 109.

period should have been marked by this imbalance in congressional-presidential power.

Some have contended that the main reason lay in the caliber of the men who became President. This was the period when Bryce wrote his famous essay, "Why Great Men Are Not Chosen President." Certainly the historical reputations of Presidents between Lincoln and McKinley do not stand high. Grant and Benjamin Harrison have been dismissed as prisoners of their party, as men who never glimpsed the possibilities of the Presidency. Hayes stubbornly defended his rights as chief administrator but never had any political leverage to influence grand policy even if he wished to do so. James A. Garfield might have been an effective President but was assassinated before he could prove himself. Cleveland was a curious mixture: he could be exceedingly forceful on matters he felt deeply about, such as corruption and the tariff, but he was fatally handicapped by an excessive concern for the separation of powers between the executive and the legislature; essentially he failed as a political scientist, not realizing that the Framers had interwoven powers and responsibilities rather than separating them, and that no President could cast aside his legislative and programmatic responsibilities.

Another reason for relative presidential impotence during this period was the failure of the Presidency to become strongly organized and institutionalized. Lincoln had operated in such a personal manner, and with so little direct help, that he bequeathed only a small executive staff organization to his successors. In his first term Grant was given $13,800 for one private secretary, one stenographer, two executive clerks, one steward, and one messenger. Grant had to borrow three generals from the War Department to help handle his duties. The quality of the staff was often low, for the job of presidential secretary or assistant had none of the prestige of Cabinet membership. Garfield was unable to persuade John Hay to be his private secretary. Over the years there was a moderate expansion of staff, but by the end of the century Congress was still authorizing only a secretary, two assistant secretaries, two executive clerks, and four clerks.

A third reason lay in the absence of crisis — more precisely, of crises that were perceived to be properly within the reach of presidential action. This was a period of panics, depressions, and poverty both in the city and on the farm; it was a period too of desperate strikes and riots and general industrial commotion. But such problems were considered the province of local and state authorities, if indeed government was to intervene at all. And there was no war during this period, except for the brief encounter with Spain. Such crises as did arise the late nineteenth century Presidents, in contrast to the twentieth century ones, did not perceive as reasons — or excuses — for sweeping presidential action. President Chester A. Arthur in his first message to Congress, for example, asked for authority to cope with bands of cowboys who were terrorizing people in the Southwest and even across the border in Mexico. Congress ignored his request. Arthur repeated his request in a special message and then in his second regular message, but without result. Arthur was simply unwilling to act out of that great and undefined executive authority that earlier and later Presidents found so useful for their purposes.

This perception of the role of the President suggests the main reason for the diminishment of the Presidency during this period. The Presidency was not viewed as operating at the center of national affairs; indeed, government itself in the dominant attitudes of the day was a peripheral activity. Politics did not attract men of imagination and creative leader-

ship because government was not seen as a place where such
qualities were needed. In explaining his judgment that "the
proportion of first-rate ability drawn into politics is smaller in
America than in most European countries," Bryce stated that
in America "much of the best ability, both for thought and
for action, for planning and for executing, rushes into a field
which is comparatively narrow in Europe, the business of developing the material resources of the country," while "the
methods and habits of Congress, and indeed of political life
generally, give fewer opportunities for personal distinction,
fewer modes in which a man may commend himself to his
countrymen by eminent capacity in thought, in speech, or in
administration, than is the case in the free countries of Europe." [23]

The national government, and especially Congress, was indeed seen by many as a vast system of trading and bartering,
as one more arena of private enterprise, though a somewhat
tarnished arena. In turning down Garfield's job offer, Hay
said: "The contact with the greed and selfishness of office-
seekers and bull-dozing Congressmen is unspeakably repul-
sive. The constant contact with envy, meanness, ignorance,
and the swinish selfishness which ignorance breeds needs a
stronger heart and a more obedient nervous system than I can
boast." [24] To the delight of reformers and radicals, the Senate
in this period presented the direct and naked expression of
economic interests. Whatever the exaggerations of the muckrakers, Senators did indeed speak for railroad interests, industrial interests, commodity interests as they have never done
before or since. Such naked representation was expected and

[23] James Bryce, *The American Commonwealth*, vol. 1, pp. 77–78.
[24] Theodore C. Smith, *The Life and Letters of James Abram Garfield* (New
Haven: Yale University Press, 1925), vol. 2, p. 1071.

was not frontally challenged by the main guardians of public opinion.

In the deepest sense congressional government was not really government. It was rather brokerage — a place for the adjustment of competing economic interests. The main interest in Congress, Bryce noted, related to the raising and spending of money. And the more the presidency was drawn into the congressional orbit, the less the presidency could be a place for the expression and realization of great dreams, programs, and conflicts.

Theodore Roosevelt and the Modern Presidency

Theodore Roosevelt, a biographer has said, will be remembered as "the first great President-reformer of the modern industrial era." [25] Roosevelt's vigorous and versatile stewardship is one more testament to the remarkable unpredictability and changeability of the Presidency during the nineteenth century in contrast to the general constitutional system within which it operates. Corwin has noted the personalization of the Presidency resulting from its frequent dependence on the accident of personality; Roosevelt is a fitting example. Here was an office that had sunk almost to impotence time and again since the Civil War. Here was the Republican party committed to a policy of laissez-faire. The accident of an anarchist's bullet brought to this office, and to the leadership of this party, a man of enormous and frightening vigor,

[25] William Henry Harbaugh, *Power and Responsibility* (New York: Farrar, Straus and Cudahy, 1961), p. 522.

curiosity, prejudices, and ambitions. He was a metropolitan man, an urban politician, a Harvard graduate, a cosmopolite, widely traveled, broadly read.

Like many of his predecessors, he wanted to be a great President, but unlike many of them, he had a clear idea of how a great President should behave. He had learned from history that the great Presidents were strong Presidents. He consciously tried to model himself on Presidents like Washington and Lincoln — especially Lincoln — and had nothing but scorn for "honorable and well-meaning Presidents, such as James Buchanan," who took the "narrowly legalistic view that the President is the servant of Congress rather than of the people, and can do nothing, no matter how necessary it be to act, unless the Constitution explicitly commands the action." [26]

He had a clear and forthright view of presidential power. He insisted on the theory, in his words, "that the executive power was limited only by specific restrictions and prohibitions appearing in the Constitution or imposed by the Congress under its Constitutional powers. My view was that every executive officer, and above all every executive officer in high position, was a steward of the people bound actively and affirmatively to do all he could for the people, and not to content himself with the negative merit of keeping his talents undamaged in a napkin. I declined to adopt the view that what was imperatively necessary for the Nation could not be done by the President unless he could find some specific authorization to do it. My belief was that it was not only his right but his duty to do anything that the needs of the Nation demanded unless such action was forbidden by the Constitu-

[26] Theodore Roosevelt, *An Autobiography* (New York: Macmillan Company, 1921), p. 395.

tion or by the laws. Under this interpretation of executive power I did and caused to be done many things not previously done by the President and the heads of the departments. I did not usurp power, but I did greatly broaden the use of executive power. In other words, I acted for the public welfare, I acted for the common well-being of all our people, whenever and in whatever manner was necessary, unless prevented by direct constitutional or legislative prohibition. I did not care a rap for the mere form and show of power; I cared immensely for the use that could be made of the substance." [27] This became the famous Stewardship theory of the Presidency, which, Rossiter has said, can be traced back in unbroken line to Hamilton.[28]

Roosevelt was also engagingly frank about his actual conduct of affairs under this theory: "While President I have *been* President, emphatically: I have used every ounce of power there was in the office and I have not cared a rap for the criticisms of those who spoke of my 'usurpation of power'; for I knew that the talk was all nonsense and that there was no usurpation. I believe that the efficiency of this Government depends upon its possessing a strong central executive, and wherever I could establish a precedent for strength in the executive, as I did for instance as regards external affairs in the case of sending the fleet around the world, taking Panama, settling affairs of Santo Domingo and Cuba; or as I did in internal affairs in settling the anthracite coal strike, in keeping order in Nevada this year when the Federation of Miners threatened anarchy, or as I have done in bringing the big corporations to book — why, in all these cases I

27 *Ibid.*, pp. 388–89.
28 Clinton Rossiter, *Alexander Hamilton and the Constitution* (New York: Harcourt, Brace and World, 1964), p. 248.

have felt not merely that my action was right in itself, but that in showing the strength of, or in giving strength to, the executive, I was establishing a precedent of value. I believe in a strong executive; I believe in power; but I believe that responsibility should go with power, and that it is not well that the strong executive should be a perpetual executive. Above all and beyond all I believe as I have said before that the salvation of this country depends upon Washington and Lincoln representing the type of leader to which we are true. I hope that in my acts I have been a good President, a President who has deserved well of the Republic; but most of all, I believe that whatever value my service may have comes even more from what I *am* than from what I *do.* . . ." [29]

This man who so candidly believed in power was an expert manipulator of it. Deeply read in American political history, educated in the political rough-and-tumble for almost a quarter century, he had a fine instinct for calculating his opponents' political power as well as his own. He knew that other political leaders had constituencies to which they must remain faithful, just as he did; he also knew that they had room for maneuver and that he could trade with them, or perhaps outbluff them. Despite his frequent bouts with difficult Senators or party leaders, he understood that they had responsibilities and affiliations that must be included in his calculations of political influence. Despite his unceasing denunciation of his enemies as idiots and fools and criminals, he endlessly bartered with them in the political marketplace.[30]

Roosevelt also accepted the political system within which

[29] Roosevelt to George Otto Trevelyan, June 19, 1908, Elting E. Morison (ed.), *The Letters of Theodore Roosevelt* (Cambridge: Harvard University Press, 1952), vol. 6, p. 1087.

[30] See Roosevelt's revealing letter to Henry Cabot Lodge, September 27, 1902, *Letters, op. cit.,* vol. 3, p. 332.

he had to operate. He wanted — at least during his presidential years — to make governmental institutions work, not to try to change or reform them structurally. He treated congressional leaders and procedure with great respect, at least in his formal dealings with them. When a reformer urged on him in 1905 that a word from him would insure the passage of three bills she desired, he replied testily: ". . . I wonder if you have any idea how much patience it requires not to answer impatiently such a letter as yours. I have done my best for the three bills. I called specific attention to the matters in my message. I am not the legislative body. I am the executive; and if you will read the papers you will see that Congress is very jealous of anything like a usurpation of authority on my part. I simply have not the slightest power to accomplish the end you desire. . . ." [31] He respected "Senatorial courtesy" and faithfully consulted Senators before making appointments. In general he dealt with congressional chairmen with tact and courtesy. And he would not tilt at legislative windmills. "The tariff is of course peculiarly a subject upon which Congress must take the initiative," he wrote Senator William Boyd Allison in 1905, "and the last thing I want to do is to get into such a position as Cleveland got into when he succeeded in forcing tariff revision, only to get a bill so bad that he would not sign it, and yet it became a law, so that the whole proceeding worked great mischief to the people at large and helped split his party in two. When, after all my efforts, I am unable to get even an approach to unanimity of action on such a subject as the tariff with Germany, when the leaders of the House are a unit against touching the tariff at this time, and when of those few members who wish to touch the tariff no two from different localities agree as to what

[31] *Ibid.*, vol. 4, p. 1130.

should be done, I have felt rather at sea as to the possibility of doing anything." [32] Granted that Roosevelt often used congressional opposition as a pretext for not acting, granted too that some of these sentiments reflected reform weariness or simple political prudence, he had a genuine distaste for openly flouting the customary relations between independent agencies of government.

But if Roosevelt was something of a broker among competing interests and something of a conservator of the political marketplace in which the contest took place, he threw his own presidential weight into the balance so forcefully as to change the whole configuration of the struggle. He did this mainly behind the scenes, using pressure, flattery, cajolery, rewards, and all the usual resources of the politician, amid an unending stream of talk, letters, interviews, threats, often in mixtures that defy analysis. His main resource was an inexhaustible supply of Rooseveltian energy. "Let us stand valiantly for what is decent and right; let us strike hard, and take with unshaken front whatever comes, whether it be good or ill," he wrote a friend. "Then the fates must decide what the outcome will be." [33] Unlike certain earlier and later Presidents, moreover, he was willing to spend his personal popularity rather than merely hoard it. He wrote a newspaper editor in 1906: "I have felt a slightly contemptuous amusement over the discussion that has been going on for several months about my popularity or waning popularity or absence of popularity. I am not a college freshman . . . and therefore I am not concerned about my 'popularity' save in exactly so far as it is an instrument which will help me to achieve my purposes. . . ." [34] In this quality perhaps more than any other

32 *Ibid.*, vol. 5, p. 72.
33 *Ibid.*, vol. 5, p. 20.
34 *Ibid.*, vol. 5, p. 170.

he was a truly professional wielder of influence. And in effect he changed the Presidency and presidential-congressional relations without changing the institutional forms.

Roosevelt operated with particular force, shrewdness, and political sensitivity in foreign affairs. He could assess a foreign statesman's latitude of action with the same accuracy and insight as a state politician's. His vigorous intervention in the Russo-Japanese conflict and his adroit effort to lessen tension among the Great Powers over Morocco were instances in which Roosevelt thoroughly understood the princes he was dealing with, such as the Kaiser, and the proud and chauvinistic forces behind them. But he also knew when *not* to intervene; he recognized the limits of American power. Urged to act on behalf of the Jews in Russia and the Armenians in Turkey, and so on, he wrote indignantly that "it is a literal, physical impossibility to interfere in any of these cases, save in the most guarded manner, under penalty of making this nation ridiculous and of aggravating instead of ameliorating the fate of those for whom we interfere. . . . It is therefore necessary to remember how futile, undignified and mischievous it is to use language or attempt interference which would only be justified if, and could under no conceivable circumstances do good unless, there was intention to back up the words by an appeal to arms." [35]

All this was an important side of Roosevelt; but it was only one side. The Roosevelt who shrewdly wielded influence, respected institutions, laws, and traditions, and dealt prudently with foreign powers somehow coexisted with the Roosevelt who abused power, bypassed institutions and laws, upset traditions, and bullied smaller nations. He acted in foreign affairs, Harbaugh says, "with impetuosity and restraint, with bluster and sensitivity, with belligerence and accommoda-

[35] *Ibid.* (April 10, 1906), vol. 5, p. 207.

tion." [36]   He would not intervene to protect far-off Russian Jews and Armenians; he did intervene in the affairs of Latin American nations such as Santo Domingo. He formally respected the prerogatives of Congress but undertook a great deal of manipulation behind the scenes; his caution on the tariff bill, for example, was matched by his Machiavellian boldness on railroad rate regulation legislation. In several cases he simply ignored or overrode ordinary processes of the law — most notably in the Brownsville case, where he summarily gave dishonorable discharges to three companies of Negro soldiers without a military or civilian trial.

How can we explain this dualism in Roosevelt that at times approached schizophrenia? It reflected Roosevelt's lack of an organized, consistent, and principled body of ideas relating his immediate means to his broader ends. He spoke often of his ends — justice, stability, balance, honor, responsibility — but these often lacked content and bordered on the purely symbolic or even ritualistic. They could have meaning only to the extent that Roosevelt drew from these lofty goals an orderly set of principles of personal and governmental action. He was quite specific on his means — regulatory legislation such as the Hepburn Act, conservation, tariff reduction, etc. — but he lacked a set of principles that could have enabled him to marshal these means on the basis of clear priorities. What should be done in any immediate situation often came to turn on Roosevelt's opportunism, his political expediency, and his lofty but fuzzy morality.

Roosevelt so often talked in highly moralistic terms that his exact ends and means became obscured. Blum has concluded that he believed in power and order. "With power he sought to impose order; only with order, he contended, could there

[36] Harbaugh, *op. cit.*, p. 182.

be morality." [37] But the more we examine this morality with Blum, the more it comes down to a question of some kind of proper procedure or due process, which Roosevelt himself often disregarded, or to high-blown objectives of order or justice or morality of so general a content that Roosevelt could and did interpret them most opportunistically.

Consider the basic and simple Rooseveltian concept that justice — justice between men and between groups and between classes — could be achieved through the federal government — meaning in fact the strong executive of the federal government. On the face of it this would seem to be at least an elementary ordering of means and ends. But the "limitations in this position — considered as a political philosophy — are disastrously apparent," Morison has said with great insight. "It has no decent intellectual underpinning; in vain one scrutinizes the scheme to find a logically constructed system of ideas. There is no organized statement of self-evident truths about man and his requirements to provide a direction or a basis for judgment in political action. At anticipated worst this is an acceptance of things as they are; at improbable best this may be only a willingness to reduce inequities to a bearable point so that society may hold together while it edges along the lines of least resistance into the future." [38] Between specific executive action and lofty moralism there was simply no consistent, predictable structure of thought and action.

It is not hard to see why. Roosevelt was living in a period of whirling change not only in the economy but in popular attitudes toward society and government. There was, as he

[37] John Morton Blum, *The Republican Roosevelt* (Cambridge: Harvard University Press, 1954), pp. 106–7.
[38] Elting E. Morison, "Introduction," *Letters, op. cit.,* vol. 5, p. xvii.

said, a "condition of excitement and irritation in the public mind." Roosevelt received clear guidelines neither from the American liberal creed, which was obscure and contradictory, nor from the Republican party platform, which embraced the usual ambiguities and had not made the transition from the canons of laissez-faire to those of modified governmental intervention. His own way of perceiving events discouraged the formulation of coherent principles as guides to action. Life for him, Blum remarks, was strife, "Individuals and societies progressed or retrogressed depending on their ability to fight and to adjust." [39] He viewed life in general, and especially politics, as kaleidoscopic. We "govern in a distinctly haphazard manner," he once commented.[40] He saw government as almost constantly in crisis.

For a man with Theodore Roosevelt's need for personal fulfillment it was a sort of tragedy that he had no war — not even a Whiskey Rebellion. Not only would war have given him immense psychological gratification, it would also have brought his means and ends into better relation. He might then have been spared the traumatic experience of breaking his party asunder in the struggle with William Howard Taft in 1912. He had to use his Hamiltonian and Lincolnian devices for more limited objectives. But he carried on and modernized the Hamiltonian precedents, and his employment of presidential power in the first years of the century sharpened the dilemma of presidential leadership that would face later Hamiltonians dealing with world wars abroad and economic and social crisis at home. This dilemma lay in the coexistence of a highly politicized and personalized President and White House staff along with an increasingly institutionalized executive office in an ever growing federal establishment.

39 Blum, *op. cit.*, p. 25.
40 *Letters*, vol. 2, p. 949.

The Sinews of
Presidential Government

The enormous expansion of the Presidency in the sixty years following Roosevelt I testifies again to the power of that remarkable combination of elements in the development of the American governmental system noted in the preceding chapter: an unplanned executive seated in a carefully planned political structure, both being continually and heavily shaped by economic and social forces.

The sheer expansion itself has been recounted many times — most often by those who have not liked it. Two small facts illuminate the expansion as much as the overall statistics of federal spending and employment: in 1914 President Wilson submitted to the Senate 3418 nominations of civil and military officials; in 1958 President Eisenhower submitted 59,079. In the middle 1890's George W. Vanderbilt established at his ducal estate in North Carolina a program in scientific farming and forestry, the latter under a young man named Gifford Pinchot. The then Secretary of Agriculture, Paul Morton, said of Vanderbilt: "He employs more men than I have in my charge. He is also spending more money than Congress appropriates for this Department." [41]

The two great forces producing this expansion have also been thoroughly explored. One was a set of economic developments that, combined with changing expectations about the role of government, compelled the federal government to assume new responsibilities. The states, with their limited financial means and antiquated governmental arrangements,

[41] Frederick Lewis Allen, *The Big Change* (New York: Harper & Brothers, 1952), p. 30.

were unable to cope with nationwide corporations, trade
unions, transportation problems, conservation, and the like.
The federal government haltingly moved into a political vacuum, and despite the effort of Congress to put much of the
regulatory power under "independent" federal commissions,
the essential responsibility inevitably ended up in the executive branch. The second great expansionist force was the two
world wars. Whether or not war is the forcing house of democracy, certainly it is of bureaucracy. Civilian employment
in the federal government more than doubled between 1916
and 1918, and almost quadrupled between 1940 and 1945.

What concerns us more than the mere growth of the executive department is the actual permanent expansion of the
power, scope, and responsibility of the presidential office —
in short, the institutionalization of the Presidency. Granted
the growth in bureaucracy, who would control it — President,
Congress, or some cluster of leaders with power cutting across
units of the national and state governments? Granted the decline of laissez-faire attitudes toward government during this
century, what power wielders would assume responsibility for
expanded governmental activity? This question hinged directly on the outcome of the struggle for fiscal control, and
secondarily on the capacity of the President to staff his office
so that he could physically handle his heavier responsibilities.

The key fiscal development of the century recalls again the
vagaries of events. The passage of the 16th Amendment in
1913 made possible the enactment by Congress of a graduated
income tax. The constitutional amendment had been proposed to Congress not by Theodore Roosevelt, not by Woodrow Wilson, but by William Howard Taft. The first tax
under the amendment, imposed in Wilson's tariff act of 1913,
was only 1 percent on net income up to $20,000, with a small

surtax on larger incomes. But the power was there, and during the next forty years the graduated income tax became an enormous reservoir of funds for the federal government, especially for financing the social welfare programs of liberal Presidents.

The other great fiscal change, also adopted without a clear understanding of its ultimate impact, was in budgetary procedure. In the early years of this century Congress was still holding jealously to its budgetary powers, but its control was chaotically decentralized throughout its committee structure. A select committee in the House of Representatives found in 1919 that expenditures were not considered in connection with revenues; that Congress did not require of the President any carefully thought-out plans for revenue and spending; that the estimates of spending needs submitted to Congress represented only the desires of the individual agencies; and that "these requests have been subjected to no superior revision with a view to bringing them into harmony with each other, to eliminating duplication of organization or activities, or of making them, as a whole, conform to the needs of the Nation as represented by the conditions of the Treasury and prospective revenues." Not only were the budgetary efforts of the agencies not coordinated, but they competed with one another for influence and funds. Congress, with its separate committees, was in no shape to pull things together.[42]

There was, in short, no national budgetary system and hence little fiscal planning and coordination. But by 1919 the urgencies of World War I had strengthened reform efforts that had been under way for some time. President Taft's Commission on Economy and Efficiency had proposed a na-

[42] *Report* of House Select Committee on the need for a national budget system, 66th Cong., 1st Sess. House Rpt. No. 362 (1919), p. 4.

tional budget system in 1912; states such as Illinois had established integrated budget systems; and the cost of World War I, combined with considerable discretion that had to be vested in the President during the crisis, sharpened congressional interest in budget reform for the sake of economy. Congress passed a measure for a national budget in 1920, only to run into a veto from Wilson, who favored such a budget but opposed one provision that put the newly established Comptroller General beyond the President's power of removal. Harding approved substantially the same measure a year later.

The Budget and Accounting Act of 1921 systematized earlier budgetary legislation that had been widely ignored in practice, and established new machinery. It provided for a new agency, the Bureau of the Budget, and empowered it "to assemble, correlate, revise, reduce, or increase the estimates of the several departments or establishments." Agencies were denied the right to bring direct influence to bear on congressional budget makers except at the request of legislators. Each agency was directed under the act to designate one of its officials as budget officer as a link with the Budget Bureau. The new agency was also given the task of making continuing studies of the needs of efficiency and economy in the federal service. Although many reformers would have preferred to make the Budget Bureau a staff agency directly under the President, Congress, probably acting out of its traditional and benevolently possessive regard for the Treasury, placed the Bureau in that department — though making it directly responsible to the President.

Congress also showed an unusual interest in putting its own houses into order. At long last it abandoned the host of separate appropriations committees that had considered departmental requests individually; it also provided the machinery for integrated congressional budget making. The House in 1920 established one committee on revenue — the Ways and Means committee — and one committee on appropriations. The Senate established similarly integrated committees in 1922.

All these moves were to have an immense effect on government and paradoxically to defeat most of the hopes of their movers. The main congressional motivation behind the Budget and Accounting Act was "efficiency and economy" and while the Bureau doubtless saved a significant amount of money over the years, its main impact on government has not been economy but rather strengthening the President in his budgetary dealings with Congress and with the departments and agencies under him. The congressional effort to integrate its own appropriations activities was largely abortive; especially in the House the new Appropriations Committee spawned subcommittees that operated with almost the same mutual tolerance and independence as had the separate appropriations committees before 1920. Lodging the Budget Bureau in the Treasury Department under its first director, the energetic Charles G. Dawes, did not unduly handicap it, but it was still an awkward arrangement and later had to be remedied.

Yet behind all the false starts and misperceptions, the forces working on the national government were compelling further departures from the makeshift staff arrangements in the presidential office. When Franklin D. Roosevelt entered office in March 1933 the Presidency was still operating without a modern, well-organized staff system. Roosevelt, with his bent for highly personalized and flexible administration, made do with the old arrangements for several years; but even he finally issued a call for help. He appointed a Committee on Administrative Management composed of three authorities on public administration all of whom believed in strong executive direction and responsibility. With some satisfaction Roosevelt reported in 1937 on the committee's findings and recommendations: "The Committee has not spared me; they say, what has been common knowledge for 20 years, that the President cannot adequately handle his responsibilities; that he is overworked; that it is humanly impossible, under the system which we have, for him fully to carry out his constitutional duty as Chief Executive, because he is overwhelmed with minor details and needless contacts arising directly from the bad organization and equipment of the Government. I can testify to this. With my predecessors who have said the same thing over and over again, I plead guilty.

"The plain fact is that the present organization and equipment of the executive branch of the Government defeats the constitutional intent that there be a single responsible Chief Executive to coordinate and manage the departments and activities in accordance with the laws enacted by the Congress. Under these conditions the Government cannot be thoroughly effective in working, under popular control, for the common good. . . ." [43] The committee recommended that the White House staff should be expanded; that the managerial agencies of the government, especially those dealing with the budget, efficiency research, personnel, and planning, be strengthened as arms of the President; and that the whole Executive Branch of the Government be overhauled, the then 100 agencies being consolidated into a few large departments. To strengthen the White House staff the committee recom-

[43] Report of the President's Committee, Administrative Management in the Government of the United States, Washington, D.C., 1937.

mended that the Civil Service Commission, the Bureau of the Budget, and the National Resources Board should be "a part and parcel of the Executive Office."

Changes came on the eve of World War II. Congress passed the Reorganization Act of 1939, under which the President established the Budget Bureau definitely in the Executive Office of the President. With the shifting of other staff operations to this office, the *Executive Office* of the President took on new meaning as a concept. The reorganization was perhaps the most important single step in the institutionalization of the Presidency. Soon the Executive Office began to appropriate office space in the old State-War-Navy building next to the White House.

By 1949 the President's personal staff included three secretaries, an assistant to the President, six administrative assistants, a special counsel, the executive clerk and a number of other aides. But the growth still lagged behind the pressure on the Presidency. The first Hoover Commission recommended that year that an Office of Personnel should be established in the White House under a director who should also be chairman of the Civil Service Commission; that a staff secretary should be added; and that the work of the Budget Bureau be further expanded. It urged that the President be given full authority to organize his own staff and to readjust it as he saw fit.[44]

Under Eisenhower the executive office reached a new peak in organization, numbers, and power. The President's "immediate" staff included the assistant to the President, three deputy assistants, two secretaries, three special counsels, three

[44] Report of the Commission on Organization of the Executive Branch of the Government, "General Management of the Executive Branch," Washington, D.C. (1949), pp. 13–14.

administrative assistants, nine special assistants to the President, four special assistants in the White House office, along with outside advisers, expert consultants, and of course a host of subordinates from the line agencies. Most of the President's assistants had staffs of their own. In addition, three advisory councils established by Congress and a few coordinating Offices or Boards created by the President filled out a growing executive office.

This was the huge establishment that Kennedy inherited in 1961. The new President had misgivings about its complexity and bulk. He expressed some interest in checking the growth or proliferation of the Executive Office, and he abolished the Operations Coordinating Board and Planning Board of the National Security Council, and a number of interdepartmental committees, but the office remained large and complex. Johnson moved into an executive office whose 1500 employees had by now pre-empted all of the huge old State Building west of the executive mansion. It comprised nine main elements exclusive of executive mansion and grounds: the White House Office (376 employees, including the President), Bureau of the Budget (485 employees), Council of Economic Advisers (57), National Security Council (43), Office of Emergency Planning (406), Central Intelligence Agency (no employment figures available), National Aeronautics and Space Council (28), Office of Science and Technology (48), Office of the Special Representative for Trade Negotiations (30).

This super-organization of the presidential office has been accompanied by the amplification, consolidation and exercise of presidential power. The authority that men like Lincoln and Theodore Roosevelt have exercised in times of crisis, real or assumed, has become a stable, dependable, and predictable basis for the exercise of presidential authority. In all their ramifications and precedents these powers would fill a large volume — indeed have done so. They can be summarized here until we have occasion to look at some of them closely. Finer has listed the following as "powers that make for independent strength of tremendous effect:" [45]

1. Control over the entire administrative personnel and operations;

2. Power to act, almost regardless of statute, in any emergency;

3. Power to initiate laws and exercise the power, both positive and negative, of the veto;

4. Budget-making power;

5. Power to conduct diplomacy and make treaties, committing the nation to agreements with other nations, disposing of American troops, etc., in such a way as to court or avoid war;

6. Power as Commander in Chief;

7. Exercise of considerable patronage;

8. Prestige and influence as leader of his party;

9. Glamour as Chief of State, the nation's symbol;

10. Access to the public by means of press conferences, where he alone determines what he shall say and what self-praising excerpts shall be flashed on the screens of television sets and theaters;

11. Access to television and radio to tell his side of any political story, with no equivalent right conceded by the networks to other branches of government, say, the Speaker of the House, the opposition party, or the majority leader of the Senate;

12. Role as the most important source, and object, of news-

[45] Herman Finer, *The Presidency: Crisis and Regeneration* (Chicago: University of Chicago Press, 1960), p. 118.

paper stories; ubiquitous and incessant if compared to other elements of the nation (perhaps with the exception of sports personalities) and far superior to the amount of attention given Congress.

I have quoted Professor Finer's résumé of presidential power because he is concerned, as Corwin was, with the *personalization* of the Presidency, with the fact, as he sees it, that "there is no independent or collective challenge of any real substance to the President's power." I have quoted the résumé at this point hard on the heels of a summary of the institutionalization of the presidential office, because the conjunction of these two aspects of the Presidency poses the question as to whether the Presidency can be characterized by both personalization *and* institutionalization — whether in fact the Hamiltonian tendencies toward opportunistic, manipulative, short-run, even charismatic action are offset by a structure of decision making that makes for stability, continuity, predictability, self-criticism, and principled action — but also for ponderousness, rigidity, and failure to experiment and innovate. Is the Presidency part of, or a threat to, effective government and democratic government?

III

The View Toward the White House

A STUDENT in one of those long college survey courses that run from Plato to Goldwater complained to a friend that he had looked out of the window for a moment and missed the Reformation. This is a book where one can read every line and still miss Presidents and their eras. The reason is that we are not interested in every President, but in Presidents and eras that help us understand the rise of presidential government and its implications for continuing ideas and goals that we value today. We have been looking at models of the Presidency, the way in which a selected group of men have acted as Presidents as compared with these models, and the institutionalization of the office itself. These are parts of the development and analysis of the Presidency, but they are not the whole story.

The whole story must include attitudes *toward* the Presidency and expectations of it. We will never know this whole story, because we will not be able to recapture the attitudes over the years of leaders, subleaders and masses toward the Presidency, except through the crude data of election returns, newspaper editorials, letters to and about various Presidents, and the like.

But the difficulty of the task should not blind us to its importance. The Presidency as a center of a structure of administrative and political powers is inseparable from the President as the center of a shifting pattern of popular loves and hatreds, needs and expectations, hopes and memories. If, as Collingwood insists, we must study the past not as a series of events, but as a system of things known, we must study Americans thinking about the Presidency.[1] We need not be extremist about this and let our subject disappear in a stream of disembodied and overly self-conscious impressions about this very real and eventful office. We must simply grasp as well as we can the relation between the Presidency and ideas about it, keeping in mind that the relation is a two-way affair. Perhaps, indeed, ideas about the modern Presidency have had a greater impact on the office than the Presidency has had on these ideas.

The Presidency
and the Historians

In November 1948 the late Professor Arthur M. Schlesinger of Harvard published in *Life* Magazine the results of a presidential poll of "fifty-five students of American history and government throughout the country."[2] Professor Schlesinger had asked his respondents to evaluate the "greatness" of all the Presidents save James A. Garfield and William Henry Harrison, whose terms had been brief, and Harry S. Truman, who was then in office. What were the tests of greatness used by the fifty-five historians and political scientists? "Not all indicated their criteria," according to Professor Schlesinger, "and it is evident that they could and did use different ones.

[1] R. G. Collingwood, *The Idea of History* (Oxford: Clarendon Press, 1951).
[2] Prof. Schlesinger enlarged on the results in *Paths to the Present* (New York: Macmillan Company, 1949), ch. 5, from which my recapitulation has been drawn.

The quality of greatness, for example, might be regarded as consisting in grandeur of character or in an inspiring advocacy of democracy, in a creative approach to problems of statecraft or in influence wielded upon the long course of history. It could be gauged further by the tensions and urgency of the times and by the incumbent's political skill and his ability to capitalize upon the potentialities of the office. Some Presidents who made poor captains in rough seas might have sailed smoothly in quiet waters, but the great President should obviously be equal to any changes in the weather. Finally, the full measure of the man involves his handling of foreign as well as domestic affairs." [3]

The election returns from this academic constituency went as follows:

"Great": Lincoln, Washington, Franklin Roosevelt, Wilson, Jefferson, Jackson.

"Near Great": Theodore Roosevelt, Cleveland, John Adams, Polk.

"Average": John Quincy Adams, Monroe, Hayes, Madison, Van Buren, Taft, Arthur, McKinley, Johnson, Hoover, Benjamin Harrison.

"Below the Average": Tyler, Coolidge, Fillmore, Taylor, Buchanan, Pierce.

"Failures": Grant, Harding.

Fourteen years later Professor Schlesinger published the results of a similar poll of great Presidents. This time he queried seventy-five "students of American history," including two in English universities.[4] Considering the fact that almost

3 *Ibid.*, p. 95.
4 "Our Presidents: A Rating by 75 Historians," *The New York Times Magazine* (July 29, 1962), p. 12. For an earlier, even more informal poll, see Austin C. Wehrwein, "Historians Paint 'Good President,'" *The New York Times* (January 3, 1960), drawn from interviews with historians attending the meet-

half the participants in the second poll were new voters, the
results of the two polls were astonishingly comparable. Jackson narrowly missed greatness this time, being demoted to the
head of the near-greats. Harry Truman and Dwight Eisenhower, who had never faced each other in presidential elections, now were thrown into competition; Truman won, scor-
ing in the middle of the near-greats, while Eisenhower ended
up toward the bottom of the "average," between Chester
Arthur and Andrew Johnson.

As for the criteria of presidential greatness in the second
poll, Professor Schlesinger stated: "Each participant in the
poll applied his measuring rod in accordance with the relative
importance he attached to the complex factors that helped
make or break the particular Administration. Did the President head the nation in sunny or stormy times? Did he ex-
hibit a creative approach to the problems of statecraft? Was
he the master or servant of events? Did he use the prestige
and potentialities of the position to advance the public welfare? Did he effectively staff his key government posts? Did
he properly safeguard the country's interest in relation to the
rest of the world? How significantly did he affect the future
destinies of the nation?" [5]

The results of Professor Schlesinger's polls not only tell us
important things about the American Presidents. The results
also tell us a great deal about American historians. And because what American historians think about the Presidency is
important — because of their near-monopoly of the writing of
high school and college textbooks, the influence they have on
the political and cultural leadership of the nation, the final

---

ings of the American Historical Association; those interviewed, according to
Wehrwein, "were in general agreement that they preferred a 'strong President' and that the Presidents called great in history books were of that sort."
  [5] *Ibid.*

word they are supposed to have in a nation where people like to settle arguments by "leaving them to the verdict of history" — the historians are a profoundly important constituency indeed. It could be argued, of course, that Professor Schlesinger carefully chose this clutch of historians. But anyone going through the two lists published with the articles would agree, I think, that the fifty-five and the seventy-five form a good cross section of the influential academic writers about American political history — a good representation of whatever we have in the way of a historical Establishment.

The fact that these men, otherwise so diverse in party affiliation, university, age, and geographical background, could agree so closely in their evaluations suggests a basic agreement on their criteria of greatness as well as on the way in which various Presidents individually fit into the five slots. I do not challenge the results; indeed, I was a member of the second poll and broadly agree with the results. What seems to me important is the agreement over criteria.

What were these criteria? From extensive reading of the work of many of these historians, I believe that the criteria set forth by Professor Schlesinger represent the criteria of the great preponderance of the respondents. And these criteria seem to boil down to one crucial characteristic — strength in the White House. The great Presidents were the strong Presidents, and by "strong" the historians meant their mastery of events, their influence on history, their shaping of their country's destiny, their capacity to draw talented men to their side, their ability to magnify their own department, and their own powers, at the expense of the other branches.[6]

These criteria of leadership will probably come as no sur-

[6] For some of the methodological and intellectual difficulties implicit in comparing presidential "greatness," see Curtis Arthur Amlund, "President-Ranking: A Criticism," *Midwest Journal of Political Science*, vol. VIII, no. 3 (August 1964), pp. 309–15.

prise to the reader because the chances are that he has been
brought up to accept them. But they do not form the only
conceivable legitimate test. Another test could be "how representative was the President?" Another could be a President's character — for example, whether or not he stuck to his
basic principles in the face of political pressures, especially
threats of election defeat. A third could be whether the President had the sense not to interfere too much in events, especially in economic events, but let things take their natural
course.

Under the first of these criteria Harding and Coolidge
might rank as "greats" and Wilson, at least in his second term,
as below average. Under the second criterion Herbert Hoover, who resolutely stuck to his principles of laissez-faire in
the face of heavy pressures on the national government,
might rate among the greats for courage and honesty. Under
the third criterion we might rate Presidents like Cleveland
very high and activists like the two Roosevelts very low. I do
not happen to rank these particular criteria very high; but
anyone rating Presidents — or any other historical figures —
must be self-conscious about the basis of selection. And he
must be equally aware of the basis for selecting the evaluators.
Presumably a cross section of another influential group —
such as small-town newspaper editors or the selectors of statues or portraits that are put in various halls of fame — would
have designated different criteria, and hence produced different presidential greats.

Historians are supposed to be unprejudiced in their professional activity, of course, and Professor Schlesinger suggests
that in this poll they were "admonished by their professional
consciences against partisan bias." But there was a deeper
bias that we must consider before evaluating the impact of
the historians on the Presidency. The nature of their criteria

suggests that the historians had two major premises: that Presidents *can* influence history significantly, and that they *should* do so in a generally liberal, humanitarian, egalitarian, reformist direction.

What lies behind these beliefs that so powerfully influence historians and their histories and hence our memories of the past and our expectations of the present? The answer lies in part in the nature of American history and the nature of American historians.

The writing of American history in the nineteenth century had a heavily political emphasis. Eminent historians like George Bancroft, James Ford Rhodes, and John W. Burgess dealt intensively with political leaders, groupings, and institutions. A number of leading historians followed Bancroft's example of taking an active part in politics and public service. Imbued with a genteel nationalism, caught up in the political movements of the time, influenced by their Germanic training with its emphasis on the State, many of the chroniclers made their history turn on the doings of statesmen and party politicians, somewhat at the expense of adequate attention to other, less visible, forces in history.[7] Implicit in these histories was a belief in the need and a faith in the possibility of political leadership. It is not surprising, given this emphasis in historical writing, that the hero in America has tended to be the political leader, especially the great President.[9]

[7] See generally, G. P. Gooch, *History and Historians in the Nineteenth Century* (London: Longmans, Green and Company, 1952); Herman Ausubel, *Historians and Their Craft: A Study of the Presidential Addresses of the American Historical Association, 1884–1945* (New York: Columbia University Press, 1950); Michael Kraus, *The Writing of American History* (Norman: University of Oklahoma Press, 1953).

[8] Cf. Marvin Zetterbaum, "Tocqueville: Neutrality and the Use of History," *The American Political Science Review*, vol. 58, no. 3 (September 1964), pp. 611–21.

[9] Dixon Wecter, *The Hero in America* (New York: Charles Scribner's Sons, 1941), pp. 2–3 and *passim*.

American historiography has changed a good deal since the last century, especially in its greater concern with economic, intellectual, social, and other forces. Yet this shift has taken place with little apparent diminution in the belief in the central and critical role of the President in influencing history and bringing about change and progress. As late as 1948 a historian commented to his profession on the continuing historical perception of presidential politics and issues as the center of the sythesis of American history and the perception of the central government as having the primary role in our historical development. "From Theodore Roosevelt on," according to this historian, "presidential administrations and national political issues, including wars, again become the center of the narrative." [10] If this speculation is correct, there has been a kind of cultural lag among some American historians. It is noteworthy that Charles A. Beard, with all his emphasis on basic economic and social forces and his belief (with some waverings) in historical relativism, imputed to Franklin Roosevelt a crucially influential role in the entrance of the United States into World War II.

A second cause of the historians' preference for strong Presidents was the intellectual and psychological environment of academic and other professional groups late in the last century. Many academic historians were among the political mugwumps who revolted against the commercialism and coarseness of the self-made men who were triumphing on the business scene in the 1880's and 1890's. "In a score of cities and hundreds of towns," Hofstadter has said, "particularly in the East but also in the nation at large, the old-family, college-educated class that had deep ancestral roots in local commu-

[10] Thomas C. Cochran, "The 'Presidential Synthesis' in American History," *American Historical Review*, vol. 53, no. 4 (July 1948), pp. 748–59.

nities and often owned family businesses, that had traditions of political leadership, belonged to the patriotic societies and the best clubs, staffed the governing boards of philanthropic and cultural institutions, and led the movements for civic betterment, were being overshadowed and edged aside in the making of basic political and economic decisions. In their personal careers, as in their community activities, they found themselves checked, hampered, and overridden by the agents of the new corporations, the corrupters of legislatures, the buyers of franchises, the allies of the political bosses. . . . Their conception of statecraft was set by the high example of the founding fathers, or by the great debating statesmen of the silver age, Webster, Sumner, Everett, Clay and Calhoun. Their ideal leader was a well-to-do, well-educated, high-minded citizen, rich enough to be free from motives of what they often called 'crass materialism,' whose family roots were deep not only in American history but in his local community. Such a person, they thought, would be just the sort to put the national interest, as well as the interests of civic improvement, above personal motives or political opportunism. And such a person was just the sort, as Henry Adams never grew tired of complaining, for whom American political life was least likely to find a place." [11] Lawyers, editors, ministers, writers (including many novelists) shared in the revolt of the mugwumps.

At the start the protest of the intellectuals and professionals was not economically or socially radical. They were calling not for social reform or economic egalitarianism; they were turning against the pecuniary corruption of all major sectors of society, including government, against the dominance of

[11] Richard Hofstadter, *The Age of Reform* (New York: Vintage Books, 1955), pp. 137, 140.

the *nouveaux riches* and their trading and money-making mentality, and against the transfer of political influence from the statesmen of old to the millionaires who managed the economy and who ran Society. In the governmental sphere the Mugwumps attacked the spoils system, urban bossism, and the alliances between sordid commercial and political interests. And the men of their time who embodied national symbols of political integrity were not senatorial gladiators but Presidents. Hayes, Cleveland, and Theodore Roosevelt not only fought the spoils system but built their careers in large part on their willingness to attack the unholy alliances between businessmen and bossism.

During the last decade of the nineteenth century and the first decade of this, the protest of the intellectuals and many professionals took on a more radically economic and social note. As Hofstadter again has suggested, a large creative minority of university professors supported the reform cause and came to be virtually a brain trust for the Progressives. These men looked to the Presidency for political leadership rather than to Congress or the courts. Roosevelt and Wilson not only represented the kind of men they wanted in public office, but each of these Presidents turned to intellectuals for advice and thus elevated their psychological and professional status. Both these Presidents also personified the third great cause that occupied the mugwump and progressive movements — internationalism. Roosevelt by his conciliation of warring nations and advocacy of arbitration treaties, and Wilson by his fight for the League of Nations aroused intensive support among the intellectuals for their specific policies, and incidentally demonstrated the enormous potential in the Presidency as an institution.

Doubtless there were other causes for the historians' hunger for presidential leadership: for example, the tendency deep in the historical discipline to look for men who personify or pattern or simplify complicated historical causations and sequences; or perhaps the tendency of historians ideologically to belong to the moderately liberal, or presidential, wings of the Democratic or Republican party (in which case, however, we would have to look for the direct cause of that tendency). But the main causes, I suggest, lie in the politically rooted historiography of most leading American historians during the nineteenth century and their social and psychological situation.

One can think of examples: T. D. Woolsey, merchant's son, student at three German universities, a historian and political scientist who stressed the role of political parties; Richard Hildreth, minister's son, political historian who also wrote a campaign biography; John Bach McMaster, banker's son, biographer and author of best-selling primary school and high school texts; Henry Cabot Lodge, son of a wealthy merchant and ship owner, Congressman and Senator, biographer of Washington, Hamilton and Webster; Herbert Baxter Adams, student at Heidelberg, who organized the Johns Hopkins Historical and Political Science Association and taught Woodrow Wilson; Henry Jones Ford, merchant's son, author of a classic political history that stressed the interrelation of party organization and governmental structure; even Henry Adams, diplomat's son, who was skeptical about many things but gave ample attention to the ways and wiles of political leaders; and later historians like Charles A. Beard.

But perhaps the best example is one man who combined a number of the tendencies — Theodore Roosevelt, philanthropist's son, a partisan with mugwump tendencies, foe of political corruption, son of parents of established wealth who looked down on the millionaires, a political leader who moved steadily toward economic and social reform — and a man who became president both of the United States and of the American Historical Association.

The Presidency and the Political Scientists

The influential teachers of political science in the late nineteenth and early twentieth centuries shared the historians' assumptions about the state of, and the need for, political leadership. Political scientists and historians were, indeed, closely allied; many university and college departments embraced both subjects, and many scholars, such as John W. Burgess, Woodrow Wilson, Henry Jones Ford, and Charles A. Beard, produced works in both fields. Wilson and Beard were chosen head of both the American Historical Association and the American Political Science Association.

This recognition of the role of government and of leadership within government was sometimes explicit, sometimes buried in a host of assumptions about the good society and polity. Francis Lieber, the German-born political scientist who had a critical influence on the emerging discipline in this country during the mid-century, viewed the State as the central and most influential association among many others in the pluralistic society of the United States. Burgess, the main architect of graduate study in political science at Columbia, drew from his Hegelian philosophy a belief in a purposeful pattern in history and a theory — or at least an ideology — of the supreme power of the state. Other political scientists, more heavily influenced by British political theory and institutions, stressed the active role of parliamentary and party leadership. Relatively few shared the prevailing popular attitudes in favor of laissez-faire, with its implications favoring a sharply restricted sphere for government, or in theories of history that stressed impersonal forces, social or economic or geographic or ideological. Some political scientists were influenced both by their grounding in Germanic theories of the all-encompassing state and by their admiration for British parliamentary and party forms; they emerged with theories of the sovereignty of parliament under law. These theories in turn underlay various governmental reforms that political scientists advocated.

Lieber and Burgess both favored a strong national government, but Lieber saw a central role for political parties and Burgess believed in a powerful (but stable and generally conservative) form of "presidential government." Woodrow Wilson, in his earlier years, favored some form of cabinet government; A. Lawrence Lowell saw an indispensable role for political parties in large-scale democracies; Henry Jones Ford also believed in political parties, but saw their effectiveness depending on presidential leadership. Herbert Croly advocated strong executive leadership, especially at the state level. Most later political scientists favored variations or combinations of these alternatives. While political scientists differed in the institutional machinery they preferred, they agreed that a democratic form of government required strong leadership, that such leadership could be exerted through the executive branch or through political parties that coordinated the executive and legislative branches of government, and that representative assemblies in general, and Congress in particular, were obstacles to leadership in a democracy. Paradoxically, nineteenth century liberals who feared strong governmental intervention despised Congress for its corruption and

its obsequiousness to "vested interests," while those who favored radical social reform through government, such as Walter Weyl, saw Congress as a barrier to the expression of social
protest and to political and economic reform.

No one better exemplified the political scientists' predilec-
tion for political leadership than Woodrow Wilson, and no
one's views in the end were more important. Son of a schol-
arly Presbyterian preacher, he was brought up on a heavy diet
of English and American political history and biography.
Perhaps the first book he read was Parson Weems' admiring
and semi-fictitious *Life of Washington;* he avidly followed
British politics through the *Edinburgh Review* and the New
York *Nation;* his hero was William Gladstone, prime minister, party leader, and splendid orator. Entering the legal profession as a carefully planned step towards politics, he was
bored and appalled by the trivial content and vulgar commercialism of the law. Its practice "for the purposes of gain,"
he decided, was "antagonistic to the best interests of the intellectual life," [12] and he quit his idle law office for Johns Hopkins and the academic world. He came under the intellectual
influence of the English publicist, Walter Bagehot, whose
career had anticipated his own; Bagehot too had studied law
but found it intellectually cramping; had looked to politics
for great leaders who could orate and act in terms of grand
principles; and had criticized the American system for elevating incompetents to office and for the rigid system of checks
and balances that "weakens the whole aggregate force of government." [13]

These early influences were clearly evident in Wilson's first

[12] Quoted in Arthur S. Link, *Wilson: The Road to the White House* (New
York: Harper & Row, 1947), p. 10.

[13] Walter Bagehot, *The English Constitution* (New York: D. Appleton &
Company, 1908), p. 91.

book, *Congressional Government*. Just as Bagehot had criticized the American governmental system from a distance,
Wilson had never seen Congress at firsthand before writing
his classic condemnation of it.

On the face of it, Wilson's *Congressional Government* was
an examination of the supremacy that Congress had established over the other two branches, of the fragmentation of
power in both the Senate and the House, of the petty trading,
logrolling, and commercial attitudes that dominated legislative life, and of the resulting erosion of political and moral
responsibility. Behind all this, and commanding his whole
approach to American institutions, was a deep yearning for
leadership and nobility in American politics. Wilson was not
overly disturbed by the naked representation of interest
groups in Congress or by the measures that were enacted, or
failed of enactment. What distressed him most was that men
of principle and intellect could find no footing in the system.
He looked vainly for anything like the great debates that elevated British politics — the flashing oratory, the government
and loyal opposition cleanly arrayed against each other —
above all, for the Gladstonian statesmen who commanded
the political stage and were responsible to their party and nation. His severest criticism of Congress was less in what it did
than in how it did it. He was appalled that great national
issues such as the tariff should be split into pieces and secretly
disposed of in the trading and brokerage of the committee
rooms.

Perhaps the most remarkable aspect of the book, as we return to it today, was its depreciation of the Presidency as he
then observed it. "The President," wrote Wilson, "is no
greater than his prerogative of veto makes him; he is, in other
words, powerful rather as a branch of the legislature than as

the titular head of the Executive." [14] The President was not really Chief Executive, even in this sector reserved to him by the Constitution. "In so far as the President is an executive officer he is the servant of Congress; and the members of the Cabinet, being confined to executive functions, are altogether the servants of Congress." [15] Here again power was splintered, "cut up into small bits," with individual members or committees of Congress controlling parts of the administrative machinery. In these views Wilson shared the preconceptions of other political scientists writing during the post-Civil War drought in presidential leadership.

Because Wilson viewed the Presidency as in such low estate, and because he centered his hopes of improvement on cabinet government, it has been said that he had strangely forgotten the role of the great Presidents of earlier times. But he had not. He was simply measuring the current dearth of leadership against leadership during three great stages of national growth, each of which, he said, had created a distinct class of political leaders. "In the period of erection [of new governmental structure] there were great architects and master-builders; in the period of constitutional interpretation there were, at a distance from the people, great political schoolmen who pondered and expounded the letter of the law, and, nearer the people, great constitutional advocates who cast the doctrines of the schoolmen into policy; and in the period of abolitionist agitation there were great masters of feeling and leaders of public purpose." [16] Now, in the mid-1880's, "we are

[14] Woodrow Wilson, *Congressional Government* (Boston: Houghton Mifflin Company, 1885; New York: Meridian Books, Inc., 1956), p. 173. Page references in this and subsequent footnotes are to the Meridian paperback edition, which contains an Introduction by Walter Lippmann.

[15] *Ibid.*, p. 177.

[16] *Ibid.*, p. 139.

left to that unexciting but none the less capitally important business of everyday peaceful development and judicious administration to whose execution every nation in its middle age has to address itself with what sagacity, energy, and prudence it can command. It cannot be said that these new duties have as yet raised up any men eminently fit for their fulfillment." [17] There could be no great leaders without great causes.

Wilson remained pessimistic for some time about the prospects of the President becoming once again a great leader of government or party. As late as 1897 he was complaining that the national government was leaderless, that "the President cannot lead" and had "as little power to originate" as the Queen of England; that the convention system had weakened the Presidency by separating Congress from it; that the original system of checks and balances had given way to a "government without definite order"; that affairs were not conducted on the basis of meaningful principle; and that the executive and legislature must be drawn more closely together.[18]

Wilson's low estimate of the Presidency was shared by a number of his fellow political scientists. It was in 1888 that Bryce published his book with the chapter on "Why Great Men Are Not Chosen Presidents." Bryce had a kind of crisis theory of the Presidency. "In ordinary times," he said, "the President may be compared to the senior or managing clerk in a large business establishment, whose chief function is to select his subordinates, the policy of the concern being in the hands of the board of directors. But when foreign affairs be-

17 *Ibid.*, p. 141.
18 Woodrow Wilson, "Leaderless Government" (an address before the Virginia State Bar Association, August 4, 1897), in Ray Stannard Baker and William E. Dodd, *The Public Papers of Woodrow Wilson*, vol. 1 (New York: Harper & Brothers, 1925), pp. 336–59.

come critical, or when disorders within the Union require his
intervention, — when, for instance, it rests with him to put
down an insurrection or to decide which of two rival state
governments he will recognize and support by arms, everything may depend on his judgment, his courage, and his
hearty loyalty to the principles of the Constitution." [19] But
the 1880's were a calm period and Bryce did not think too
highly of the office or of its recent incumbents. In 1900 Professor Goodnow, of Columbia University, could publish a
study of American politics and administration that paid little
attention to the President other than in his narrowly administrative role.[20]

Within a decade of his indictment of "leaderless government" in 1897 Woodrow Wilson almost completely changed
his estimate of the Presidency. What brought about the reversal?

Walter Lippmann has theorized that Grover Cleveland's
rise in prominence in the summer of 1884 had caused Wilson
to lose full confidence in a fundamental reform — cabinet
government on the British model as described by Bagehot —
that he had publicly favored not long before. Cleveland, according to Lippmann, was the first American political leader
in Wilson's own lifetime who aroused his interest in the presidential office.[21] But it is doubtful that Cleveland was showing
in the summer of 1884 much leadership that was relevant to
Wilson's views of the potential of the Presidency, and Wilson
had completed his manuscript and submitted it to Houghton

[19] James Bryce, *The American Commonwealth* (London: Macmillan and
Company, 1890), p. 62.

[20] Frank J. Goodnow, *Politics and Administration* (New York: Macmillan
Company, 1900).

[21] *Congressional Government, op. cit.*, Introduction by Walter Lippmann,
pp. 13–14.

Mifflin in Boston by October 1884, well before the election. Moreover, as late as 1897, as I have noted, Wilson was saying that the President could not lead. Cleveland's eight years in the White House had not made much difference in his thinking.

It was not Cleveland but Theodore Roosevelt who mainly educated Wilson in the potentialities of the American Presidency. The book in which Wilson's changed view was most evident, *Constitutional Government,* appeared in 1908, the last year of Roosevelt's Presidency. To be sure, Wilson's attitude toward leadership must have been influenced by his own struggles as President of Princeton during these years, and by the reformist pressures during this decade of the muckrakers. Admittedly too, there is little specific reference to Roosevelt in the book, even less than to Cleveland. But the whole description of the revived Presidency seems to be distilled from Roosevelt's strenuous leadership, and it was not surprising that Wilson, as a Southerner and Democrat, might not wish to give Roosevelt personally much credit. He suggested, indeed, that it was the war with Spain that had put the Presidency at the front of government.

But as a believer in political leadership Wilson could not but admire the éclat and imagination with which Roosevelt had carried off his role. Certainly the office he described was a Rooseveltian one, and the phrases seem to bring Roosevelt to life.

"Greatly as the practice and influence of Presidents has varied," Wilson wrote in *Constitutional Government,* "there can be no mistaking the fact that we have grown more and more inclined from generation to generation to look to the President as the unifying force in our complex system, the leader both of his party and of the nation." Of the national convention, of which he once had been so critical, he now wrote: "In reality there is much more method, much more definite purpose, much more deliberate choice in the extraordinary process than there seems to be. . . ." Soon after came the sentences that have been so often quoted ever since:

"He cannot escape being the leader of his party except by incapacity and lack of personal force, because he is at once the choice of the party and of the nation. He is the party nominee, and the only party nominee for whom the whole nation votes. . . . He is not so much part of its [the party's] organization as its vital link of connection with the thinking nation. He can dominate his party by being spokesman for the real sentiment and purpose of the country, by giving direction to opinion, by giving the country at once the information and the statements of policy which will enable it to form its judgments alike of parties and of men.

"For he is also the political leader of the nation, or has it in his choice to be. The nation as a whole has chosen him, and is conscious that it has no other political spokesman. His is the only national voice in affairs. Let him once win the admiration and confidence of the country, and no other single force can withstand him, no combination of forces will easily overpower him. His position takes the imagination of the country. He is the representative of no constituency, but of the whole people. When he speaks in his true character, he speaks for no special interest. If he rightly interprets the national thought and boldly insists upon it, he is irresistible; and the country never feels the zest of action so much as when its President is of such insight and calibre. . . ."

Most of the Presidents, he granted toward the end of this essay, had taken their duties too literally and had attempted the impossible. "But we can safely predict that as the multitude of the President's duties increase, as it must with the growth and widening activities of the nation itself, the incumbents of the great office will more and more come to feel that they are administering it in its truest purpose and with greatest effect by regarding themselves as less and less executive officers and more and more directors of affairs and leaders of the nation, — men of counsel and of the sort of action that makes for enlightenment." [22]

It is symptomatic of the unplanned growth of the Presidency that a President-by-chance should have shaped the thinking of one of the leading academic exponents of political leadership, who in turn would become a brilliant practitioner. And Roosevelt influenced other political theorists, most notably Herbert Croly, who glimpsed the powerful direct link that could be forged between an ebullient chief executive and public opinion. Still, if theorists learned a good deal from practitioners, Presidents — especially Theodore Roosevelt and Wilson — had been greatly influenced by nineteenth century intellectuals who yearned for great political leadership while disagreeing on the means of achieving and institutionalizing it. So the chance elevation of Theodore Roosevelt was not decisive in the long run; the quest for leadership was already under way. If Bagehot influenced Wilson and Wilson influenced scholars like Henry Jones Ford, and if Roosevelt and Wilson established presidential images and precedents that later Chief Executives could imitate and exploit, and if, finally, the practitioners and professors could learn so much from one another, all this was a clear indication of the deep hunger for leadership that lay among men of action and of thought around the turn of the century.

[22] Woodrow Wilson, *Constitutional Government in the United States* (New York: Columbia University Press, 1961), pp. 60, 63, 67–68, 81.

The Quest for Leadership

During the seeming nadir of presidential leadership under Grant, intellectuals and reformers, writing in such journals as the *Nation,* had deplored the decline or absence of great political statesmanship, and this criticism has continued with varying degrees of intensity ever since. The call for leadership was strongest during the last three decades of the last century, but even during "strong" Presidencies — even under both Roosevelts and under Truman and under Kennedy — the intelligentsia complained of excessive caution and compromise in the White House. The restiveness under Eisenhower undoubtedly had a significant effect on the presidential campaign of 1960, when Kennedy again and again promised to get the country moving again.

But all this tells us little about the great number of less articulate Americans. Have they too been hungering for some kind of political leadership? Of what type? From whom? The President? Congress? State or local officials? From nongovernmental leaders? Data for answering such questions are unhappily so limited that we must be rather speculative.

Of course the people have their own way of registering their feelings about leadership. They do this most immediately and effectively by endorsing or rejecting strong leaders in national elections. In the past century all "strong" Presidents, as defined by the historians, have been re-elected. Of course, these Presidents may be considered strong because they were re-elected, rather than having been re-elected because they were strong, but some men who were re-elected —

notably Coolidge and Eisenhower — are not considered strong Presidents. In general, the electoral record would indicate heavy popular favor for the man who tried to exercise political leadership.

People have other ways of "voting" on leadership. They put up statues to some leaders and not to others; they elect heroes to Halls of Fame and name schools for them; they read popular biographies about some men and not others; they visit the White House or Congress or the Washington Monument or the Lincoln Memorial; they write letters to men they believe wield some influence. Senate leaders — notably Henry Clay, Daniel Webster, and John Calhoun — were political heroes to many Americans during the last century. The enormous sale of books by Horatio Alger, Jr., indicates something of the stature of business and industrial leaders toward the end of the century. Generally, though, as Wecter has suggested, our most powerful hero epics have centered about political leaders. But we know little about the structure and political significance of attitudes toward political leadership in the nineteenth and early twentieth centuries.

In the last two or three decades public opinion surveys have provided us with somewhat more substantial information on attitudes toward presidential leadership and power. At the beginning of 1946 a cross section of Americans were polled on the question: Which of these four United States Presidents do you think was the greatest — Washington, Lincoln, Wilson, F. D. Roosevelt? (A comparable cross section was asked the question with the names in reverse order.) The results:[23]

[23] American Institute of Public Opinion, January 3, 1946, Hadley Cantril (ed.), *Public Opinion 1935–1946* (Princeton: Princeton University Press, 1951), p. 590.

Washington	15%
Lincoln	37
Wilson	5
F. D. Roosevelt	39
Don't know	4

Considering that Franklin Roosevelt had died only eight months before and hence had an advantage in this popularity contest, the results are of limited use, though they do suggest the relative position of Lincoln and Washington as heroes. A better constructed poll ten years later is more revealing. The question: What three United States presidents do you regard as the greatest? The national sample was 1385.[24]

Eisenhower	468
Truman	180
F. D. Roosevelt	891
Hoover	83
Coolidge	42
Wilson	177
Theodore Roosevelt	136
McKinley	13
Lincoln	864
Jefferson	93
Washington	648
Other	44
No answer — don't know	106

These popular returns show a remarkable resemblance to the results of the historians' balloting. Lincoln, Washington, and Franklin Roosevelt are at the top in both polls; the order is the same except that Roosevelt outballots Washington and Lincoln in the popular poll — a result doubtless influenced by the close personal memories of the World War II Presi-

[24] American Institute of Public Opinion, Survey No. 558, January 4, 1956.

dent. Eisenhower's relatively low vote — considering that he
was in office when the survey was conducted — might suggest
that the people, as well as the historians, placed him somewhere in the middle ranks. Three other Presidents rate high
both with historians and people: Wilson, Theodore Roosevelt, and Jefferson. The most striking difference is that the
historians place Jackson among the "greats" and he is barely
mentioned in the popular balloting, but the different structures of the two questionnaires make comparison difficult beyond this. Truman had not achieved the standing in the
popular view that he later won from Professor Schlesinger's
historians.

If we can make the reasonable assumption that people remember Lincoln for his successful conduct of the Civil War,
his emancipation of the slaves, and his political leadership,
and remember Washington for his solidity and patriotism
(and for his dogged generalship), the results of the popular
poll suggest that the people admire strength in Presidents.
The disparity between Franklin Roosevelt's votes and Hoover's and Coolidge's, is revealing; so is that between McKinley and Theodore Roosevelt. In the popular mind as well as
the historical, the great Presidents are the "strong" Presidents.

But other polls taken during this period indicate a deep
fear of power. In July 1937 the American Institute of Public
Opinion asked a sample of 2843: Do you think the President
of the United States should have more or less power than he
has now? [25]

More	18%
Less	35
About the same	47

[25] *Ibid.*, pp. 589–590.

Broken down into political affiliation:

Republican:
More	3%
Less	71
About the same	26

Democratic:
More	27
Less	16
About the same	57

Broken down into economic status:

	More	*Less*	*About the same*
Average-plus	8%	52%	40%
Average	12	40	48
Poor-plus	17	32	51
Poor	25	27	48
On relief	39	21	40

That Republicans should fear Roosevelt's power is not surprising. The increasing confidence in Rooseveltian (or presidential) power as one moves down the economic ladder is notable, though it could be explained in part by the increasing Democratic strength at the lower economic levels, and in part by long observed authoritarian tendencies in the working class. The division among the Democrats as to how much power the President should have is perhaps more significant.

This poll was conducted during Roosevelt's effort to "pack" the Supreme Court and may reflect atypical fears of presidential power. But later surveys indicate a strong current of apprehension about executive authority. A survey early in 1938 posed the question: "Do you believe the President of the United States should have the power of a dictator over the country in time of war?" [26] Almost three times as many respondents answered a strong no to this rather loaded question as gave a strong yes. Shortly afterwards respondents were asked: "Do you think the President of the United States should have more power or less power than he now has?" Sixteen percent answered "more," 38 percent "less," 39 percent "the same," and the rest had no opinion or did not answer.[27]

The responses may be somewhat more meaningful when the question is put less abstractly — for example, when the question of the extent of presidential power is posed in relation to the extent of congressional power. On Harry Truman's elevation to the Presidency in April 1945 the question was asked: "Some writers believe that with Truman as President, Congress will have more importance and power than it had under Roosevelt. Do you think this would be a good thing or a bad thing for the country?" [28]

	Good Thing	Bad Thing	No Opinion
National total	65%	16%	19%
BY EDUCATION			
College	84%	9%	7%
High school	70	16	14
Grade school or less	57	18	25

There is a good deal of ambiguity in these attitudes. Only a few months after this poll respondents answered as follows to the question: "Do you think President Truman should

26 *Ibid.*, p. 590.
27 American Institute of Public Opinion, Survey No. 558, Jan. 4, 1956.
28 American Institute of Public Opinion, May 14, 1945, cited in Cantril, *op. cit.*, p. 888.

take a stronger stand in trying to get Congress to carry out his recommendations for things that need to be done in this country?" [29]

	Yes	*No*	*No Opinion*
National total	52%	21%	27%

There was no major difference between Democrats and Republicans who answered this question.

Ambiguity toward presidential strength and power is reflected also in attitudes toward the 22nd Amendment, which forbids presidential third terms. In the same year that voters elected Franklin Roosevelt to a fourth term by a decisive majority, 57 percent of a national sample said that they favored a constitutional amendment preventing any President from serving more than two terms.[30] Eight years after passage of such an amendment 58 percent of a national sample stated that they would like to vote for Eisenhower if he could run for a third term, but in this same poll 64 percent stated that they favored an anti-third term amendment.[31] Sampling registered voters in Detroit shortly before the presidential election of 1960 as to their attitudes toward the amendment, investigators found that a great majority favored a two-term limitation and that fear of power and its abuse was the most frequently offered reason. "The fear is overwhelming that a President would become too powerful if continuously reelected, that such concentration of power might lead to monopoly of power and possible dictatorship." [32] The authors

[29] *Ibid.,* cited in Cantril, *op. cit.,* p. 931.

[30] American Institute of Public Opinion, cited in Mildred Strunk, "The Quarter's Polls," *Public Opinion Quarterly,* vol. 15, no. 2 (Summer 1951), p. 395.

[31] *Public Opinion News Service,* March 1, 1959.

[32] Roberta S. Sigel and David J. Butler, "The Public and the No Third Term Tradition: Inquiry into Attitudes Toward Power," *Midwest Journal of Political Science,* vol. 8, no. 1 (Feb. 1964), pp. 39–54, at 44.

speculate: "Perhaps we are confronted not so much with fear of power as with ambivalence toward power. Such ambivalence towards power runs like a red thread through American history and politics. We have managed to *admire* strong men who knew how to use power well and have *suspected* them of wanting to become autocrats, tyrants, and dictators. It is as though 'the public has rather ambivalent attitudes towards power and powerholders. In the case of the President, it wants to endow him with very full powers while he is in office. . . . But . . . [it is also] genuinely concerned over a possible abuse of power and hence [prefers] a time limit set on the exercise of power.' What seems like a paradox at first now acquires logic. Limited tenure is the device by which to keep strong power from becoming irresponsible power." [33] This popular logic is the same that Theodore Roosevelt used in rationalizing his self-conscious use of power, but since a power-mad President could do a great deal of harm in one or two years, this logic does not dispel the ambiguity in either popular or presidential attitudes.

Robert Lane, analyzing intensively a small group of men in New Haven, explored attitudes toward President and Congress during the Eisenhower administration. He found that at the time Congress was more important, and the President less important, than he had expected. But:

> Speaking of the past, the men speak of Presidents, not Congresses. Speaking of the recession, they are hurt that Eisenhower has been so delinquent, rather than angry that Congress has been so slow to act. Speaking of elections, they speak of presidential elections, not congressional or senatorial elections. Speaking of their surprise and wounded feelings over the American failures in rocketry, they discuss the defective intelligence, foresight, and action of the "Administration,"

[33] *Ibid.,* pp. 53–54.

not the Congress. Perhaps one can reconcile their views of the current power of Congress with these other phases of their image of government in two ways. One is to allocate time periods differently: past time is for the Presidency; contemporary time is for Congress. Another is to separate responsibility for initiative and responsibility for decision: the President must initiate, the Congress must decide.

Congress, it appears, is an "oral" agency — the congressman's job is one of talking and listening, often quite informally. He is rarely pictured in debate on the floor of the Senate or the House; rather he is seen meeting the folks from back home streaming endlessly through his office; he is answering his mail, traveling to see his constituents. He seems to receive his information and advice directly from the common man, the people. Not so the President. He *studies* matters, something he can do alone. When he is with others, he *tells* them; he does not listen. . . .

Congress is responsive; the President is more autonomous. This follows, in a way, from the idea that Congress has an ear cocked for the voice of the people, while the President listens to inner voices. It also follows from the idea that the President proposes, the Congress disposes. . . .

Congress looks inward toward the nation; the President looks outward to the world. Congressmen have special duties to their home districts; they are custodians of popular welfare. The President is custodian of popular safety, national destiny, the conscience of the people. Congress expresses the impulsive immediate needs; the President has a longer view. Congress offers "secondary gain"; the President offers a chance to fulfill the life goals of the nation. Perhaps this is the reason that in normal times they write to their congressmen, if they write at all. In times of national emergency (major depression, conscription, humiliation, as in the missile lag) they write to the President. . . .

The President . . . is a strong arm against the outside world; he is a national protector, and has the stature to be one. He does not have this soft side, this slightly lovable venality — hence reinforces the voice of the superego; he calls for a higher morality; he is a protector against our weaker natures — the side of ourselves that might cut taxes when we should keep them high to pay for defense. He cares deeply about what happens to the nation and the people and the values for which this country stands. Part of what makes congressmen so appealing is that they are not so seriously committed in this way; they are more human. But what makes the President appealing is that he is not "all too human" like the rest of us; while not quite a hero, he is supportive of whatever small heroic qualities we have in us, at the very least, of our moral selves. Perhaps it will be misunderstood, but in a figurative sense Congress is the group-adjustment leader; the President is the task leader; Congress is the mother, the President the father.[34]

So we find, on balance, a mixed set of popular attitudes toward presidential power, but with a strong element of combined fear and respect, shifting in content from administration to administration, from crisis to crisis. We also find a seeming paradox: at any one time people may regard the current strong President with fear and suspicion; but over time they give a tremendous vote of confidence — as do the historians — to the strong Presidents in history. In this seeming paradox lies a clue as to the future of presidential government.

[34] Robert E. Lane, *Political Ideology* (New York: Free Press of Glencoe, 1962), pp. 148–49, 152.

The Three Models Reconsidered

At the close of the eighteenth century the Washington-Hamilton administration had been followed by a Madisonian type of President in John Adams and a Jeffersonian type in Thomas Jefferson. Doubtless by pure chance the same sequence occurred at the start of the twentieth century in Theodore Roosevelt, William Howard Taft, and Woodrow Wilson. This sequence under more recent political conditions makes possible a closer view of the three types of Presidency in action. Happily for our purposes, these three men had more coherent and articulate theories of presidential power and its limitations than any other Presidents in this century.

The *Madisonian* model, in this century, has embraced these concepts:

1. *Checks and balances.* Each branch of the federal government possesses some kind of veto power over the two other branches. At a minimum each branch must protect its own independence arising from its unique constitutional powers and bolstered by its special constituency and method of recruitment. Even the so-called weak Presidents of the latter nineteenth century made gallant, and eventually successful, efforts to protect their powers as chief executives, notably their appointive powers. The widest power and the broadest duty of the President, Taft once observed, was the constitutional provision that "he shall take care that the laws be faithfully executed." [35]

2. *Minority rights.* The chief purpose of checks and bal-

[35] William Howard Taft, *Our Chief Magistrate and His Powers* (New York: Columbia University Press, 1916), p. 78.

ances is the protection of minority rights. Because, as Madison noted so brilliantly in the 51st Federalist Paper, ambition must be made to counteract ambition and the "interest of the man must be connected with the constitutional rights of the place," each major constituency in the nation — each major interest or region or ideology — had its "own" branch or sector of government that would protect its interests. Note, however, that this was the expression of minority rights *against* federal power; this theory did not grapple with the question of the achievement of minority rights *through* government.

3. *Anti-majoritarianism.* By the same token, the Madisonian formula quite deliberately aimed at thwarting popular majorities from getting control of government and turning it toward its own ends — usually seen as "tyrannical" or "despotic" ends. The great fear was that a majority would get control of all the branches of government, for the accumulation of powers in the same hands — even hands as numerous as majority control would imply — was considered the "very definition of tyranny." So various barricades were erected against majority rule through the mechanisms of automatic stabilizing devices, such as the presidential veto and (implicitly) judicial review, powered by separate and mutually conflicting sources of political energy in the various constituencies supporting the House, Senate, and President.

4. *Prudent, limited government.* The major inarticulate premise of the Madisonians was a belief in deliberate, circumscribed government, at the national level especially. They feared rash governmental action; they feared above all that government might succumb to the mob. They did not propose that government be deadlocked indefinitely — after all, they saw the need *to be governed* — but they preferred that

government wait until such a popular consensus was built up in favor of some action that all the separate interests and constituencies would have been brought into agreement.

The Madisonian model required that each branch of government observe constitutional limitations and proprieties. Nobody has expressed this point of view better than Taft in a passage from his *Our Chief Magistrate and His Powers* that was clearly designed as an answer to Theodore Roosevelt's Stewardship theory: "The true view of the Executive functions is, as I conceive it," said Taft, "that the President can exercise no power which cannot be fairly and reasonably traced to some specific grant of power or justly implied and included within such express grant as proper and necessary to its exercise. Such specific grant must be either in the Federal Constitution or in an act of Congress passed in pursuance thereof. There is no undefined residuum of power which he can exercise because it seems to him to be in the public interest. . . . The grants of Executive power are necessarily in general terms in order not to embarrass the Executive within the field of action plainly marked for him, but his jurisdiction must be justified and vindicated by affirmative constitutional or statutory provision, or it does not exist. There have not been wanting, however, eminent men in high public office holding a different view and who have insisted upon the necessity for an undefined residuum of Executive power in the public interest. . . ." [36]

The *Jeffersonian* model embraces somewhat antithetical concepts: [37]

[36] *Ibid.*, p. 138.
[37] For further development of the Madisonian and Jeffersonian concepts and practices see Robert A. Dahl, *A Preface to Democratic Theory* (Chicago: The University of Chicago Press, 1956), especially ch. 1, "Madisonian Democ-

1. *Unified political system.* A united group of political leaders and government officials overcome the checks and balances (while leaving the constitutional provisions intact) through party control of the machinery of government. This party control depends on the existence of a coherent and disciplined party that won office at the last election on a meaningful and principled party platform and hence can claim a popular mandate. The leaders act as a team — usually through some such body as a Cabinet.

2. *Collegial leadership.* The party leader becomes President and governs through his party. His main responsibility in policy and programs is to the party and majority that elected him. He is a "team man" in office as well as out of office: that is, he governs with at least the passive consent of his fellow party leaders, who have some independent power. While the President as party leader can operate within fairly wide limits, ultimately he is governed by party purpose and limited, as well as supported, by the other national party leaders. In practice his leadership cuts across all sectors of government and politics, except perhaps the judiciary, but in style he may be much more the undramatic corporate leader, like Baldwin, Attlee, or Macmillan in Britain, than the heroic type.

3. *Majority rule.* Government can act on the basis of a mandate endorsed by a majority of the voters, who have judged the competing platforms and candidates. Once granted power on this basis, the party leaders can govern subject to only two basic limitations: free criticism protected by the Bill of Rights and other constitutional safeguards; and free elections within a limited span of time. Otherwise the

racy"; and James M. Burns, *The Deadlock of Democracy* (Englewood Cliffs, N.J.: Prentice-Hall, Inc., 1963), esp. chs. 1 and 2.

leaders can override traditional institutional and political restraints on action, even to the point of changing machinery
(such as congressional procedure or administrative organization). According to theorists believing in majority rule, ma-
joritarianism would not be tyrannical or despotic because any
candidate who must win the support of the majority of people
in a pluralistic and socially stable nation must hew to the center of the political spectrum, and so many of the various interests of the nation would be represented in any majority,
that minority rights would be protected. The system, moreover, can positively protect minorities who wish to defend or
expand their rights through government, rather than against
government. While majority rule could operate on behalf of
a laissez-faire majority, the thrust of the doctrine is toward a
more energetic and productive government.

4. *Minority opposition.* The Jeffersonian model assumes
that the opposition party will maintain a vigorous and vocal
opposition to the party in power. The opposition party can
declare certain issues, such as "bipartisan" foreign policy, outside the arena of party rivalry, but this is the right of the opposition, not the government. The opposition party is compelled to criticize the government responsibly, and with some
moderation, however, because as the alternative party it is always on the brink of gaining office and governing and hence
would imperil its own tenure in office if it had made reckless
and vainglorious promises.

The *Hamiltonian* model is much harder to define than
either of the above models, because at its core there lies a
large element of opportunism and expediency. Indeed, this
kind of presidency can be and has been justified on the
ground that it is flexible and resourceful enough to meet a
variety of political situations. At its most limited, the Hamil-

tonian model could be described simply as Madisonianism plus a vigorous and versatile President; at the other extreme a Hamiltonian might use party machinery and serve as national party leader, at least for a time, in much the same style as a Jeffersonian. Still, key elements can be found in it:

1. *Heroic leadership.* The President must be more than administrative chief or party leader. He must exert great leadership in behalf of the whole nation. He must not be unduly restricted by his party; when necessary (as he sees necessity) he can ignore it or even desert it. In practice he both uses party and "rises above" it. Heroic Presidents have some of the qualities of the hero in modern setting: they cut an impressive figure on the hustings and before the television camera; they have style; they speak movingly and even passionately; they seem to establish a direct connection with the mass public. And they are invested by the press and the people with even magical qualities: they are physically inexhaustible, it is said; they can read with lightning speed; they have total recall; and so on.

2. *Personal organization.* The President depends less — and is committed less — to the party as a whole than to his personal organization built up over the years. This personal organization is far more centralized, disciplined, and efficient than the general party organization. It is bound directly to the leader by ties of intense personal loyalty and hope of reward. Its relation to the regular party is ambiguous and changeable; the personal organization is ascendant during the presidential campaign, especially in the convention fight for the nomination, but cannot control the vast and diffused regular party that has its roots in scores of state and local organizations. Both Hamilton and Theodore Roosevelt maintained personal organizations; under Lincoln the Republican party

was transmuted into the Union Party, which served as a vehicle for mobilizing support for Lincoln and the war effort.

3. *Expedient use of power.* It is in this respect that the Hamiltonian model differs most sharply from the Jeffersonian. A President with the backing of a strong party enjoys a relatively assured basis of power; he may still have to marshal influence, but the building of the party and the success of the party in winning executive and congressional office at the preceding election provides the President with a reservoir of power that he can draw on from day to day. The Hamiltonian President has no such reservoir; he must employ every weapon that he has — his own reputation, his prestige, his patronage power, his political friendships — to achieve the results he wants. He must constantly fill, draw on, and replenish his own store of political credits. He depends more on personal influence than on party influence. He deals with opposition party leaders, as Theodore Roosevelt did with Senator Benjamin R. "Pitchfork Ben" Tillman in winning railroad legislation, to muster support for his policies. Because he is not obligated to a great political party, he can "rise above" party when he wishes and pose as leader of all the nation. Although the power arrangements within which he operates are somewhat institutionalized, he has far more leverage in manipulating personal and presidential power than if he were the responsible leader of a unified and disciplined party.

4. *Disorganized opposition.* The freedom of the President from party obligation and control gives him a latitude of political tactics and governmental decision making that in turn complicates the role of the opposition party leadership. The "out" party needs a clear target to shoot at, but it sees only a constantly moving one. The President may even make

off with some of the opposition's leadership, as in 1940, when Franklin Roosevelt enlisted Henry Stimson and Frank Knox to his cause on the eve of the Republican nominating convention. By flirting with the opposition the President can seem to lift certain issues above partisanship. The opposition party is tempted to become opportunistic too, to attack the President from opposite and conflicting positions, but in doing so it loses face as a party cohesive and clear-minded enough to govern.

Woodrow Wilson and Franklin D. Roosevelt are tangible examples of the latter two presidential models. Brought up in the belief that the best politics was a mighty forensic battle between two organized and principled parties over meaningful differences in platform and policy, Wilson acted as a strong party leader both as governor of New Jersey in 1911–1912 and in his early years as President. Despite the grave weaknesses in the national Democracy of 1913, he used his party expertly to marshal opinion behind his program, and to put it through Congress. He worked closely with party and committee leaders; used the caucus to unify the congressional party behind his proposals for tariff reduction and a federal reserve system; and borrowed the influence of his fellow partisan and Secretary of State, William Jennings Bryan, to push his program through. He acted, in his own term, as "the responsible leader of the party in power." But Wilson knew that party leadership meant more than cleaving to the dead center of the party; it must be a leadership that moved with changing circumstances and popular attitudes. In 1916, with the Progressive Party of 1912 crumbling, and with much of the old Democratic party agenda enacted or irrelevant, Wilson reoriented his party toward urban needs and claims. In that year, Link says, Wilson became "almost a new political creature, and under his leadership a Democratic Congress enacted the most sweeping and significant progressive legislation in the history of the country up to that time." [38] He led his party to victory in 1916, tried (and failed) to win a Democratic congressional majority in 1918, and made the League of Nations fight mainly a party struggle.

Contrast the political leadership of Franklin D. Roosevelt, a liberal Democrat who also had to re-orient his party toward urban economic needs, internationalism, and war. Taking office during economic crisis, he assumed the role of nonpartisan leader as he urged the nation to attack depression as though it were a foreign foe. As the election of 1936 neared, he assumed the posture of party leader and conducted, at least in the final stages, one of the most militant party campaigns the nation had seen. In 1938 he took his party leadership so seriously that he tried to purge conservative members of Congress from the party. As the European crisis grew he reverted to his nonpartisan role, which he adhered to through much of the war. He had to fight the campaign of 1944 as a Democrat, however, and in the last year of his life he was apparently contemplating the possibilities of party realignment that would shift liberal Republicans into the Democratic party and bring about "two real parties — one liberal and the other conservative." [39]

Roosevelt was a Hamiltonian in more than his party leadership. He was the gay, ebullient President who overcame economic and military crisis. He seemed to have magical personal and political gifts. He was flexible, resourceful, versatile, manipulative — even Machiavellian — in his employ-

[38] Arthur S. Link, *Woodrow Wilson and the Progressive Era* (New York: Harper & Row, 1954), p. 225.

[39] Samuel I. Rosenman, *Working with Roosevelt* (New York: Harper & Row, 1952), ch. 24.

ment of power. He developed and managed a highly personal political organization. He disorganized the opposition. And he had a clear and self-conscious desire to govern in the tradition of Hamilton, Lincoln, and Roosevelt — though often for Jeffersonian and Wilsonian goals.

But Franklin Roosevelt more than any other President exemplifies the central problem of this book. He made the Presidency essentially his personal instrument and he used it brilliantly to experiment, innovate, and establish important reforms. But he failed during his first two terms to realize the main goal for which he had been elected — overcoming depression. He greatly enhanced the power and reach of the presidential office, but failed to develop a political base that could have provided sustained and dependable support for long-run programs. Partly for reasons outside his control, he was unable in the end to bring into productive relation his ultimate goals, his instrumental ends, and his means; on the other hand, by his dexterous employment of presidential power he helped set the stage for the more purposeful action to come.

★ PART TWO ★

PRESIDENTIAL GOVERNMENT TODAY

IV

The Central Decision Makers

To some Americans the aspects of the Presidency stressed so far in this book — Hamiltonian opportunism, the rise of a powerful presidential bureaucracy, and the yearning of both intellectuals and masses for strength in the White House — form a volatile and dangerous combination in a democracy. Domineering Presidents, it is feared, can act in an expedient, unprincipled manner, subordinating the federal establishment to their own ends and banking on history to vindicate their use of power no matter how serious their excesses or failings. Much of the criticism has centered on the alleged problem of one-man rule. Over the years, as the President came to exert extensive legislative and political as well as administrative powers, critics and reformers have hammered away at the whole concept of the single executive. John Calhoun proposed two Presidents. Academic critics like Woodrow Wilson, as we have seen, wanted the President established in a strong cabinet. Later reformers preferred some kind of parliamentary government under which the President would share his powers, as a prime minister does, with legislative leaders. Still others have favored stronger party government that would sustain the President as Chief Executive and Chief Legislator but would make him subject to the collegial restraints of a top party council.

A number of political scientists have been especially critical of the single-headed Presidency. Not many have shared the fears of a French observer that the presidential office had come to be endowed with "powers of truly Caesarian magnitude."[1] But as noted, an eminent student of government, Edward S. Corwin of Princeton, feared that the Presidency had become "dangerously *personalized*" in two senses: "first, that the leadership which it affords is dependent altogether on the accident of personality, against which our haphazard method of selecting presidents offers no guarantee; and, secondly, that there is no governmental body which can be relied upon to give the President independent advice and which he is nevertheless bound to consult."[2] Corwin proposed a stronger cabinet to stabilize and institutionalize presidential power. C. Perry Patterson contended that the President could not supply vitally needed continuity of leadership, could not possibly handle by himself the mammoth job of running the huge executive department, and could not be head of a responsible government; Patterson proposed the creation of a congressional cabinet.[3]

These two critiques could be discounted somewhat on the grounds that the authors were cool to the trend toward bigger national government with its vast regulatory and social welfare programs and hence to the office that had been so instrumental in the broadening of federal responsibility. But three recent critiques of the Presidency come from men who do favor heavier federal responsibilities and are simply worried over the spectacle of one man trying to cope with the swollen

---

[1] Amaury de Riencourt, *The Coming Caesars* (New York: Coward-McCann, 1957), p. 6.

[2] Edward S. Corwin, *The President: Office and Powers* (New York: New York University Press, 1941), 2nd ed., p. 316. Corwin modified his views on this matter in the 1957 edition of this book.

[3] C. Perry Patterson, *Presidential Government in the United States* (Chapel Hill: The University of North Carolina Press, 1947), ch. 10.

executive branch and its huge demands. Professor Hyneman expresses doubt that the President could "personally consider and decide anything like all the questions that are involved in giving the administrative departments and agencies the political direction and control which they require" and at the same time exercise his broader responsibilities. "The supposition that a single official, even though occupying the most exalted position in the land, can be trusted with the dominant political authority overlooks the importance of spreading power among a number of individuals and the importance of dividing the power to select those men among different sectors of the nation." [4] Hyneman proposed a Central Council of administrators and legislators to formulate and execute the government's program. Professor Finer sees the physical burden of the office as too great for one man, the range of responsibility beyond the reliable power of his decision. We are "left with a single man who, to a frightening degree, is alone in his decisions on what he believes the Constitution permits him to do; and what he believes to be his responsibility — immersive and bold, conceiving and constantly constructive, or permissive, quiescent, passive-postfacto in his conduct of the office — and a man with a fixed term, shielded by the glory of being the nation's representative, not subject to account to anyone but himself, not, at any rate, through the conveniently and flexibly operating criticism of a loyal opposition with independent authority to force him to take notice." [5] Finer calls for sweeping structural reforms, including the election of eleven Vice-Presidents with the President who would form a powerful cabinet. And Rex-

4 Charles S. Hyneman, *Bureaucracy in a Democracy* (New York: Harper & Brothers, 1950), pp. 171, 569.

5 Herman Finer, *The Presidency: Crisis and Regeneration* (Chicago: University of Chicago Press, 1960), p. 198.

ford Tugwell, a man of vast public experience and of strong "executive impulse," has wondered whether the Presidency is equal to the demands upon it.[6]

Other political scientists — for example, Pendleton Herring, Wilfred E. Binkley, Richard E. Neustadt, Clinton Rossiter, Arthur N. Holcombe — have taken a far more confident view of the effectiveness and responsibility of the President. But the attack has been advanced so long and so effectively that any assessment of the presidency today must deal with it. The relevant questions are:

1. Has there been a tendency toward more centralized control in the executive branch?
2. Does more centralized control mean more "one-man" control of the executive branch?
3. Is there an inevitable dichotomy between stronger presidential control and the kind of collective decision making most appropriate for a democracy?

The Executive Impulse

The answer to the first question is a categorical yes. The Framers of the Constitution made the cardinal decision for a single executive, and an impulse toward unity has pulled the Cabinet, the Vice-President and other parts of the executive branch more centrally into the orbit of presidential direction and influence.

Like other Americans before and since, the Framers

[6] Rexford G. Tugwell, *The Enlargement of the Presidency* (New York: Doubleday & Company, Inc., 1960), p. 14.

wanted executive firmness and leadership at the same time that they feared one-man rule. They tried to overcome this ambivalence by making the President supreme within the executive branch while surrounding the executive with countervailing pressures from men and institutions outside the department. But even on the Framers' terms, as embodied in the Constitution, the President could not be confined to administration. From the start he pushed — or was pulled — into the full orbit of national life. "It may be interesting for the President to consider . . ." Hamilton wrote Washington in March 1794, "whether there ought not to be some Executive impulse. Many persons look to the President for the suggestion of measures corresponding with the exigency of affairs." [7]

The Framers debated at some length whether the President should be a single executive or a collective one. The New Jersey plan in the 1787 convention proposed a weak plural executive chosen by Congress; Edmund Randolph, according to Madison's notes, "strongly opposed a unity in the Executive magistracy. He regarded it as a foetus of monarchy." Hamilton and others favored a single executive. The "idea of three heads," James Wilson noted, promised neither vigor nor tranquillity; such an executive had been set up in none of the thirteen states. In the end the Hamiltonian conception — the idea of a single, strong, independent chief executive — carried the day; such an executive could administer the national government with "energy, despatch, vigor and promptness." The President was not even saddled with an executive council or cabinet holding independent constitutional power.

The theory of executive unity was thus established under

---

[7] John Hamilton (ed.), *The Works of Alexander Hamilton* (New York: John F. Trow, 1850), vol. IV, p. 508.

the Constitution, but the practice of unity developed more slowly. The cabinet was long an arena of centrifugal and centripetal forces. Washington ruled his cabinet with a fairly firm hand, although there were sharp divisions that did not take long to come to the surface. Adams presided over a group of strong-minded men who clashed over policy and politics; Adams could not govern them effectively. The extent of cabinet unity under presidential direction has varied since these beginnings. Jackson experimented with cabinet combinations, sacking the dissidents until he gained the unity he wanted. Lincoln had to forge a coalition in his cabinet out of the tumultuous forces unleashed in the late 1850's. "For the most part . . ." Hendrick has said, "Lincoln's councilors were forceful men, with their own programs, their own ambitions, their own vanities, jealousies, obstinacies, and defects of temper. Each had his set of ideas and his personal following, and on few matters had any two agreed." [8] Midway in his term Lincoln had to cope with a serious conspiracy against his leadership on the part of cabinet members allied with Senators and other politicians.

The balance of cabinet unity and disunity under the President has wavered in this century too. Wilson's selection of William Jennings Bryan for Secretary of State suggested the President's willingness to establish in his cabinet a political leader with his own separate basis of power, a willingness which meant in turn that Wilson might pay the price of intra-cabinet dissidence in order to obtain Bryan's political backing for his own administration. Later on, however, Wilson was able to let Bryan go without great political damage. Franklin Roosevelt tolerated such diverse types as Cordell Hull, Har-

[8] Burton J. Hendrick, *Lincoln's War Cabinet* (Boston: Little, Brown and Company, 1946), p. 369.

old L. Ickes, and Jesse Jones in his cabinet; since Roosevelt had a penchant for highly personal administrative leadership and often deliberately kept his agency heads separated and uncoordinated in order to maximize his own influence, the Cabinet was hardly an instrument of unification. Still, when the chips were down, Roosevelt was able to overcome Hull and Jones despite their independent power bases.

The Cabinet has been, in short, a kind of battleground of forces working on, and out from, the President. It has been both an extension of presidential authority and a block to it. In recent years, however, the Cabinet has shown signs of settling into an agency of more predictable harmony and unity than has been the case often in the past. While it still is not a body of primary importance and probably never will be — as compared with the British Cabinet — to the extent it has influence, the Cabinet tends to be more dependent on the President and less dependent on outside political forces. The "clientele" departments such as Agriculture, Labor, and Interior continue to speak for their interest groups through the department heads, in cabinet meeting or outside, but not to the point of significantly opposing the President. It may well be that the age of the great department chief, with his image, political power base, and program conspicuously separated from those of the President, is over. This does not mean that the Cabinet will be reduced to a group of technicians and organization men, as some have feared. It means simply that the Cabinet as a policy-influencing group will be even less important than it has been in the past.

The issue of presidential coordination is not so much an issue of the Cabinet as an entity as of individual department heads. "In matters of prestige, partisan politics, and legislative relations alike," Fenno has summed it up, "the Cabinet as a collectivity has only a symbolic value, a value which readily disappears when the need for action supersedes the need for a show window. . . . The political help which the President receives comes not from the group but from individual Cabinet members, who can and do augment the President's effectiveness in his leadership roles." [9] Thus the broader question is not whether one formal group called the Cabinet has strengthened or sapped presidential leadership, but whether the leaders of the whole executive establishment, representing even more varied interests, have done so.

But even in this broader executive sphere we can see major unifying forces at work. The most immediately important of these has doubtless been the impact of the establishment of the Executive Office of the President and hence of a tighter, more unified staff organization around the President. In institutional terms we are dealing with two concentric rings here. The outer ring is composed of the Executive Office of the President, as described in Chapter II, with the exception of the White House staff. The inner ring is the President's personal staff, the White House group, the "inner circle." Actually the two rings often crisscross, for the heads of the Budget Bureau and the Council of Economic Advisers may make themselves almost as single-minded instruments of presidential direction as the immediate White House staff. I say "almost" because even the disinterested budget chief may have to respond to pulls from the group of experts and technicians that he himself leads.

It was with a gift not only for a vivid phrase but also with keen administrative insight that the Brownlow Committee in 1937 called for six presidential aides with a "passion for ano-

[9] Richard F. Fenno, Jr., *The President's Cabinet* (Cambridge: Harvard University Press, 1959), p. 247.

nymity." The committee knew that presidential aides could not be anonymous; the voracious Washington press corps would prevent that. What the committee wanted was a personal presidential staff that would be given a privileged sanctuary under the President's wing against the kinds of political and organizational pressures that played on the more conspicuous men around the President. These aides would be appointed solely by the President, without requirement of confirmation by the Senate; they would serve wholly at the President's discretion; their duties would be determined solely by the President, who would have power to shift them around in the staff hierarchy and assignment of duties; their responsibility and loyalty would be wholly and only to the President, to the extent that organizational arrangements made this possible. Such staff people have virtually no independent source of power except that derived from the President.

This close interdependence between President and personal staff does not convert his aides into exact and automatic executors of the President's "will" — a matter that we will return to shortly. But where the President's organizational and political interests diverge from those of agency heads, the White House staff and other elements of the executive office powerfully assist the President in coping with the administrative forces playing on the two innermost rings of the executive branch.

The most important of these forces is the great array of "line" departments and agencies that carry out the operations of the government and make up the bulk of the executive establishment. The major department heads convene fleetingly as the President's council, but they spend most of their time as the political heads of executive departments that are in many respects simply holding companies for scores of bu-

reaus and offices that administer specialized programs. We do
not have enough hard data to know for sure whether departmental chiefs have been brought more centrally within the
orbit of presidential command. But it can be hazarded that
one result of the recent era of stronger Presidents and of bigger presidential staffs is that top policy making in the executive departments and other presidential agencies has been
unified more closely with that of the President. Much depends on the President's political strength, as we will note in
the next chapter.

The chain of decision-making command between the President and final administrative action can be broken in many
places. Heads of agencies may fail to overcome the parochial
interests operating in their subordinate units, especially in
long-existing bureaus that have developed close and mutually
satisfactory relations with well organized clientele groups. In
this event, a department head can fall back on the President's
political strength to cope with groups pressing for decisions
and programs not in accord with the President's program.
More often the chief may try to mediate between presidential demand and the pressures of his bureau and clientele.
Here in particular the President benefits from his executive
office staff, which is elaborately enough organized to deal
with the sometimes subtle and half-concealed forces that
can frustrate presidential interests. The Budget Bureau, for
example, is divided into five divisions — Commerce and
Finance, International, Labor and Welfare, Military, and
Resources and Civil Works — that not only coordinate presi-
dential-departmental decision making but also the development of policy between departments.

As noted in Chapter II, the growth of the Budget Bureau and its secure lodgment in the Executive Office of the

President have put the single most important executive function — budget making — firmly under the President's wing. The Budget Bureau affords another practical example of the institutionalization of the presidential office. Especially significant here is its system of central (i.e., White House) control of stands taken on legislation by line and independent agencies. Originated under President Harding, this central legislative clearance by the Budget Bureau is one more example of the unplanned presidency, for Harding did not see the implications of this kind of clearance for presidential power over decision making, except perhaps for economizing. Actual Budget Bureau control of the agencies' legislative positions slowly took root despite the anguished complaints of the agency heads. It survived the transition from Republican to Democratic administrations in 1933; and it also survived Roosevelt's flair for fragmentized administrative arrangements and Truman's underappreciation early in his administration of its potential utility for presidential control of the executive branch. Its survival was due in part to its formal placement in the Budget Bureau, described by Neustadt as the "oldest, toughest organism in the presidential orbit. The making of the budget is still the prime general-purpose, decision-and-action-forcing process yet institutionalized in the executive. The budget process, as it stands, is so firmly a fact of governmental life, so thoroughly assimilated in legislative and administrative practice and expectation, that its continuation goes unquestioned. . . ."[10] The fact that a small agency established mainly to save the taxpayer's dollar should become, both in budget making and regulation of agency pol-

---

[10] Richard E. Neustadt, "Presidency and Legislation: The Growth of Central Clearance," *The American Political Science Review* (Sept. 1954), vol. XLVIII, no. 3, p. 669.

icy, a bastion of presidential control attests to the centralizing tendencies within the executive branch.

An important ingredient of presidential power in this sphere is the Chief Executive's control over the organizational structure itself. Congress has long resisted giving the President *carte blanche* to organize and reorganize departments as he saw fit, even though this power is vital to an executive who wishes to be in full command of his establishment. Largely in the name of economy, however, the Congress has grudgingly granted the President limited powers to reorganize. Today the President can submit reorganization plans to Congress that become effective in sixty days unless either chamber by majority vote disapproves them. While this power is limited by the pluralistic forces operating through Congress, it has been used for such major organizational achievements as the establishment by President Eisenhower of the Department of Health, Education, and Welfare.

There is, finally, an "outer" ring of agencies around the President that are specially designed to be more immune to presidential control. These are the independent regulatory agencies. In general the organization of federal departments and agencies has followed the Hamiltonian model of executive unity and singlemindedness. At the age of twenty-three Hamilton wrote: "A single man, in each department of the administration, would be greatly preferable. It would give us a chance of more knowledge, more activity, more responsibility, and, of course, more zeal and attention. Boards partake of a part of the inconveniences of larger assemblies." [11] But strong legislatures usually prefer administrative boards as a protection against arbitrary or hasty executive action and as a

11 **Hamilton** (ed.), *Works, op. cit.*, vol. I, p. 154.

means of protecting legislative influence. In general the Hamiltonian concept has won out in our national administrative establishment (just as the collective board concept has won out in many states). The great exception at the federal level has been the establishment, beginning in the late nineteenth century and running up to recent times, of the multi-headed independent regulatory commission combining administrative, legislative, and judicial responsibilities.

The usual rationale for creating such agencies is that under our constitutional system of checks and balances, agencies combining such powers should be made somewhat independent of President and Congress. So many important policy-making and judicial powers have been lodged in "line" agencies directly under the President, however, that this cannot be the paramount reason. A more important motive of Congress has been to segregate sensitive and important governmental decisions from direct presidential control. By giving commission members staggered terms overlapping the presidential span, by limiting the President's power of dismissal, and by fostering both the law and myth of necessary independence, Congress has placed such agencies relatively beyond the President's reach. The Supreme Court has backed up the Congress in this respect; when Franklin Roosevelt tried to remove a highly conservative member of the Federal Trade Commission, the Court upheld the right of Congress to restrict his power to remove, and more recently the Court ruled that the President lacks power to dismiss board members unless Congress has specifically authorized him to do so.

But even in this area there has been a tendency toward unity of policy between President and agency. Board members cannot ignore a strong President who has won some kind of mandate that cuts across their field. The President's staff can follow and even intervene in the legislative rule making of independent agencies, especially where the decisions relate closely to those of line agencies. The President can establish competing agencies, perhaps even in his own executive office, when he wants badly to bypass the existing commission; this was a favorite device of Franklin Roosevelt. Finally, the board member can be no more resistant than other policy makers to a strong President's prestige, standing in the country, influence with Congress, and power to control countless awards and deprivations — for example, major appointments — for a long time to come.

One other office has been drawn into the presidential orbit — the Vice-Presidency. The Throttlebottom conception of the Vice-President has in the past so dominated the office in fact and fiction that we long ignored the Vice-President's capacity to disregard, resist, or even harass the Chief Executive. But the Presidents have not ignored it. They have traditionally left their running mates out of the center of presidential affairs because the Vice-President was usually not equipped by experience to have a central administrative role, because he was essentially a Senate man in background and orientation, or because he represented a different faction or alignment in the party from the President's. Recent Presidents seem to have overcome some of these obstacles. Roosevelt gave important tasks to Henry Wallace, Eisenhower to Richard Nixon, Kennedy to Lyndon Johnson, and Johnson to Hubert H. Humphrey. Presidential candidates have been selecting running mates either close to them politically or clearly adaptable to major administrative roles. Nixon sometimes served Eisenhower in virtually a staff capacity, as Johnson did Kennedy. Vice-Presidents occupy offices in the White House, as well as on Capitol Hill; they increasingly delegate

their task of presiding in the Senate; they serve less as spokesmen for the Senate or Congress as a whole, less even as medi-
ators between Congress and President, and more as agents of
the President.

Two recent developments will plant the Vice-Presidency
even more solidly in the presidential structure. A new amendment to the Constitution on presidential succession would in
effect transfer from Congress to the President the power to
name the next person in line of succession. For many years
presidential candidates have had power to designate their
running mates; now Presidents will have a comparable power
to choose Vice-Presidents if a vacancy occurs. Secondly, Lyndon Johnson went to new lengths to elicit from Hubert Humphrey explicit assurances that if Humphrey became Vice-
President, he would not differ with the President publicly,
that he would clear his speeches with the White House, and
that once decisions were made he would support the President. Acceptance of such an understanding will doubtless become a test by which future Vice-Presidents are chosen.

All these developments combined represent a virtual can-
cellation of the no-third-term amendment. It has been widely
feared that the ban on a third term would weaken a President
in his second term, as watchful politicians moved out of the
presidential orbit and built new political fences elsewhere.
But if from now on the President can choose his own man
and make him part of his political and policy-making establishment, the President can also ensure through his control of
the convention that his man will become the party's next candidate. His heir apparent would be cautious about seeking support outside the presidential party. Thus the Vice-
Presidency is one more power center previously separated
from the Presidency, and even competitive with it, that now

has been integrated into the structure of presidential power and decision making.

The Structure of Presidential Decision Making

In considering the issue of "one-man" or "dangerously personalized" presidential power, we must think in terms of: (1) the President; (2) staff advisers and immediate subordinates in the White House Office, in the Executive Office of the President, and at the top of the departmental pyramids — the presidential politicians and administrators who closely identify with the President, whom I will call here "central decision makers"; (3) policy makers throughout the executive branch somewhat less dependent on the President and more responsive to congressional, clientele, ideological and other forces, whom I will term "exterior decision makers"; and (4) the administrative officials responsible for directing the more routine, settled, and specialized operations nearer the "action" end of government, whom I will designate, in the technical and noninvidious sense of the term, "bureaucratic decision makers."

I use these terms to suggest patterns of likely behavior on the part of these administrative types, not to try to pigeonhole people. Indeed, the ultimate impossibility of pigeonholing people is a vital consideration in the whole problem of presidential control. An army lieutenant dealing with village politics in Vietnam or a county agent in Iowa could well be "closer" to presidential policy than a presidential staff adviser. Could be — but given the structure involved, usually is not. We are dealing with infinitely variegated decision makers across the line — but decision makers operating within definite contexts. The interrelationships between the President, central decision makers, and exterior and bureaucratic decision makers have organizational, intellectual, and psychological components; let us begin with the organizational.

The distinguishing feature of the central decision maker, in an organizational sense, is that he has little administrative or political power outside the orbit of the President himself. While his actual independence of the President may vary considerably, the member of the inner White House circle is ordinarily wholly dependent on the President's patronage. Perhaps he has been recruited from some government agency or business corporation or university or foundation, but he has largely severed his ties. He is useful to the President because of his skills and loyalty, but these give him little independent power. To be sure, there is the subtle possibility of withdrawing his services — but he knows and the President knows that a replacement can always be found. His tenure in the White House or at the top levels of an executive department or agency is not likely long to outlast his chief's even if the new President is of the same party and general political ideology.

The sad fate of a number of central decision makers in the immediate White House circle attests to their almost exclusive dependence on the President. The governmental careers of men such as Colonel House and Sherman Adams virtually collapsed after they lost the confidence of their chiefs. Adams had built up a tremendous standing with Eisenhower; he virtually controlled access to the President; he was respected or feared by the Washington professionals for his influence over appointments, White House decisions, presidential recognition, and much else. Adams insisted that he had influence only in the name of the President, but quite rightly this explanation did not satisfy those who suspected that there might be a Sherman Adams personality separable from the Dwight Eisenhower personality. Certainly there was a degree of independence; for some reason still hard to comprehend fully, Adams felt in some way obligated to, or dependent on, one Bernard Goldfine. Once Adams fell from Eisenhower's grace, there was no political foothold to sustain him. He had been so much the instrument of Eisenhower's purpose, as Adams defined it, that he had been unable, even if he had wished, to build separate bases of support. He had taken out no organizational (or political) insurance policy. Hardly a congressman or administrator or political figure tried to help him.

Outside the narrow group of White House advisers are the key leaders of the Executive Office of the President. These men too are largely dependent on presidential grace and protection, but organizationally their situation is a bit different. A few boss presidential agencies with several score to several hundred employees, and hence are subject to organizational pressures and claims that might pull them a bit outside the narrower White House circle. A man like the Director of the Budget or the chairman of the Council of Economic Advisers has some standing with the public, or at least with the observant part of it; a budget director may symbolize economy, the chairman may be known for his expansionist bias in economic policy. Such men may have a professional standing with professional organizations, formal or informal, that they wish to guard. They are recruited by the President and can be quickly dismissed, but their departure is likely to arouse speculations about changes in administration policy or about tension or differences in the White House — speculations that a Chief Executive might prefer not to arouse.

Outside the Executive Office but close to the President are the political executives who run the major departments and agencies. Their physical distance from the Oval Office may not affect their organizational dependence on the President. Many of them may have come into office as leaders of the President's party. They are dependent on the President for public recognition, political support, budget support, policy decisions. Their terms are likely to be coterminous with his; symbolically, they submit their resignations to him at the end of his term whether they wish to retire or not. They meet often with the President and at other times communication can be almost instantaneous. The President can grant or withhold administrative responsibilities and jurisdictional rights to them, as Franklin Roosevelt did to Harold Ickes and Henry Wallace. But the two organizational orbits do not wholly coincide. The big-agency chief, whether a cabinet member or not, establishes a standing with the press, the clienteles he serves, and with the voters. He may have a strong political base in some section of the country or among some group, such as farmers or conservationists or internationalists; indeed, it was this very support that may have influenced his appointment in the first place. To the extent that he has such political support independent of the President he has an actual or potential organizational independence, as we will note more fully in the next chapter.

To attempt to spell out these interrelationships systematically is to risk ignoring the subtleties of the situation. The big-agency chief in practice will show neither full independence of the President nor full dependence on him. To some extent he acts as a mediator between presidential demands and the perhaps more pluralistic or parochial forces operating on him. His relation with the President is bound to be a

somewhat uneasy one. Unless he is, say, Secretary of Defense
during wartime, he can hardly expect that the President can
give him the political and financial support that he may feel
he deserves. He cannot be sure of continued presidential favor and patronage in the endless jockeying that surrounds the
White House. He is subject to shifts in the political winds,
changes in presidential policy and program, chance political
or public-opinion calamities as a result of which the President
may consider him expendable or may not come to his rescue if
he runs into trouble. In general, though, the big-agency
chiefs and their staffs will place their main political reliance
on the President; he is often the most stable and predictable,
as well as the most powerful, of the few fixed points to which
they can hold fast amid the swirl of forces operating around
them. Hence they are part of the central decision-making
group.

It is the gap between big-agency chief and his bureau or
division head that often marks most sharply the organizational outer limits of dependable presidential influence. For
here we enter the world of the "exterior decision makers"
who operate nominally under presidential direction but actually in response to many other influences. Typically these decision makers run agencies or bureaus that have existed for
many years or even decades, hold close relations of support
and dependence on clientele groups, work closely with committees or blocs in Congress, and are relatively free from departmental control. Their chiefs rarely see the President,
who may have selected them formally but without actually
having much choice. The agency's functions are often protected by statutes from excessive interference from the President. They may be protected in law or in fact from presidential reorganization. They have to cope with the power of the

Budget Bureau but even here they may have an effective right of appeal to Congress or interest groups.

The classic and extreme example of such independence is the Federal Bureau of Investigation, whose director has built up such prestige and standing in Congress and country that only a foolhardy President or Attorney General would threaten his organizational independence. Indeed, Presidents have leaned on the Director's prestige. But more typically a bureau holds a position of quasi independence from President, Congress, clientele group, and public, and of quasi dependence on them; as best he can the agency chief works out his own "mix" of organizational alliances and independencies.

Finally there are the "bureaucratic" decision makers who administer the more established, less controversial service functions of the federal government. Postmen follow their accustomed rounds; the Veterans Administration grinds out checks; Forest Rangers range the forest — and so on, through the hundreds of routine occupations that make up the action end of government. It is here that we find the classic features of bureaucracy in the neutral sense — the systematic organization of persons and positions into the most efficient instruments for accomplishing repetitive tasks. The hallmarks are specialization, impersonality, discipline, an elaborate structure of formal and informal regulations, a "maximum calculability of rules" [12] and of expectations. The duties of these agencies are ordinarily so uncontroversial, traditional, and indispensable that they fall far outside the range of presidential interest or interference. But they can become of great concern to a President when a major blunder occurs, when a

12 John M. Pfiffner and R. Vance Presthus, *Public Administration* (New York: The Ronald Press Company, 1953), 3rd ed., p. 41.

seemingly parochial issue is projected into the public consciousness and hence into the White House, or — most of all — when the President wishes to bring innovations to some bureaucratic routine.

It was doubtless the ways of both exterior and bureaucratic decision makers that prompted Franklin Roosevelt's most acid remarks about the line departments:

"The Treasury is so large and far-flung and ingrained in its practices that I find it almost impossible to get the action and results I want — even with Henry [Morgenthau] there. But the Treasury is not to be compared with the State Department. You should go through the experience of trying to get any changes in the thinking, policy, and action of the career diplomats and then you'd know what a real problem was. But the Treasury and the State Department put together are nothing compared with the Na-a-vy. The admirals are really something to cope with — and I should know. To change something in the Na-a-vy is like punching a feather bed. You punch it with your right and you punch it with your left until you are finally exhausted, and then you find the damn bed just as it was before you started punching." [13]

The Unstable Equilibrium

The structural context in which presidential decisions take place is important because those decisions are affected by the organizational perspective, the administrative group affilia-

[13] Quoted by Marriner S. Eccles, *Beckoning Frontiers* (New York: Alfred A. Knopf, 1951), p. 336.

tions, the communications circuits of the decision makers. The more administrative relationships become systematized, durable, predictable, and closely organized — in short, the more they are institutionalized — the heavier influence they will have on executive decision making. One need never have even been in the offices of the F.B.I. or the Department of Agriculture or even the Bureau of the Budget to have a good feel for the kind of perspectives and tendencies that will affect decision making there.

The closer one moves to the central decision-making processes in the White House, however, the more one confronts a dilemma. With the possible exception of the staff arrangements of organization-minded Presidents such as Eisenhower, the White House circle is informal, inchoate, nonroutinized, unpredictable. After spending three years in the White House office under Kennedy, Arthur Schlesinger, Jr., concluded that "the historian tends in retrospect to make the processes of decision far more tidy and rational than they are; to assume that people have fixed positions and represent fixed interests and to impose a pattern on what is actually a swirl if not a chaos. I think the historian doesn't realize the opaqueness of the process." [14] The political scientist, who shares the temptation to inflict patterns on disorderly political processes, may also underestimate the almost anarchic nature of decision making among a group of men without established relationships meeting perhaps in a crisis amidst a stream of murky information in order to grapple with the shifting activities and plans of rival politicians or foreign leaders. Hence the dilemma: the closer the observer approaches the center of de-

---

[14] Henry Brandon, "Schlesinger at the White House," *Harpers Magazine*, vol. 229, no. 1370 (July 1964), p. 56. See also Arthur Schlesinger, Jr., "The Historian and History," *Foreign Affairs*, vol. 41, no. 3 (April 1963), pp. 491–97.

cision making, the more his understanding of the process is frustrated by the very nature of the decision making.

But the dilemma is not a hopeless one. We know enough from the long history of relations between Presidents and presidential decision makers to have some grasp of the kinds of interrelationships that arise and the interpersonal harmonies and tensions that develop. We have learned enough from studies of small groups — even as informal and apparently fluid a group as a street-corner gang — to know that meaningful continuities are likely to arise in the relationships between members of the group, especially the relations between the leader and his immediate followers.

To be sure, the relations between a President with his special authority and complex array of powers and his staff can hardly be compared to those between a foreman and a team of workmen, or between an African chief and his tribe. On the other hand, the very fact that the President does have such special status gives us in the course of time a decent chance to generalize. Insiders and outsiders — Presidents, presidential advisers, cabinet members, journalists, and historians — have provided information even on the more intimate relationships of President and members of the inner circle. A pattern is not always decipherable but perhaps some untidy generalizations are permissible:

1. No matter how loosely organized the presidential staff may be, no matter how informal and fluid the relations among President and staff and department heads may seem to be, the interrelations of these central decision makers will develop continuities and expectations about division of labor, status and hierarchy, specialization, and effective channels of communication, and hence will take on some structure. It is said that Kennedy hoped to develop a freewheeling staff ar-

rangement that would discourage fixed assignments and organizational rigidities, and certainly he altered White House arrangements visibly from the rather formal line-and-staff system that Eisenhower had established. But considerable specialization, an informal communications network, and leadership structure quickly developed among Kennedy staff members considered equal in status. Even in the case of Franklin Roosevelt, who liked to contrive competitive and fluid relationships among his staff, a hierarchy of leadership and status developed; first Louis M. Howe, later Thomas G. Corcoran, and finally Harry Hopkins had a clearly commanding position, and other presidential decision makers had to channel much of their effort through them. As relationships among executive decision makers become more settled, men "farther" from the President will turn to men "closer" to the President for dependable means of access to, and influence with, their chief. The President will learn the capacities and specialties of his advisers and come to depend on them; he will learn something of their intellectual biases, organizational commitments, unofficial relations with and personal obligations to other decision makers and to outsiders.

2. In this rough and rather plastic structure, an unsteady equilibrium will develop between the somewhat more diverse forces operating on the President and on the central decision makers from outside (i.e., from the exterior decision makers in the executive branch and from external forces impinging on the executive branch) and the more unitary forces that influence decision making in and near the White House. The interrelations of the central decision makers attain some stability as a result both of some continuity in the delegation of assignments from the center — presidential recognition, access, and interest — and also as a result of the patterning of

initiatives, influences, and pressures from outside. Exterior decision makers in the executive department come to depend on certain kinds of access to the President; some channels of influence are found ineffective and discarded; certain men around the President are found to be responsive and helpful at least for arranging access. This process may develop to the point that a staff member will come to be known as some agency's "man" in the White House. He may become less the instrument of the President in dealing with the agency than the reverse; ordinarily he becomes at least a communications channel and perhaps even a mediatory force between President and exterior decision maker. But such a relationship sets off reverberations; in the competition for presidential accessibility and support other agencies will turn to other central decision makers so that they can have their own more protected route to the Oval Office. The President is not a wholly stable factor here; his own interests will shift, he may seek to disrupt the pattern if it becomes overly rigid, he may rearrange assignments and redistribute recognition. But no matter how independent of fixed arrangements he tries to become, inevitably — given the flow of problems and obligations streaming into the White House and the interrelationships of a large number of decision makers — a structure will develop that establishes some balance between unitary and pluralistic tendencies. This balance deserves closer inspection.

3. The greater the central decision makers' dependence on the President, the greater the President's power to channel communication through himself, initiate action, and control decision making. The nature of this dependence can take many forms. As a minimum a staff member or department head may need the President's support for the job he holds

and all the satisfactions, recognitions, and other rewards that go with it. But ordinarily, at least within the inner circle, there is a strong psychological factor in this dependence. The decision maker wants presidential recognition for reasons that go far beyond holding a good job. He has made the President's cause his own; his own prestige and self-esteem are mixed up with presidential success and failings; he needs presidential assurances to help him in a highly competitive situation, as so many of Franklin Roosevelt's aides did.

Sometimes the dependence is almost complete. Shortly after Wilson's re-election in 1916 he solicited the resignation of Joseph P. Tumulty, his secretary since Wilson's early days in New Jersey politics. Tumulty's reply is a study in anguish and sense of rejection:

". . . I had hoped with all my heart that I might remain in close association with you; that I might be permitted to continue as your Secretary, a position which gave me the fullest opportunity to serve you and the country. To think of leaving you at this time when the fruits of our long fight have been realized wounds me more deeply than I can tell you.

"I dread the misconstruction that will be placed upon my departure and its reflection upon my loyalty which hitherto had been unquestioned, for I know, as you probably do not, that rumors have been flying thick and fast in the past few months as to the imminence of my removal and even as to the identity of my successor. But despite these regrets, I feel that I cannot do otherwise than leave you, if you really wish it.

"You do not know what this means to me and to mine. I am grateful for having been associated so closely with so great a man. I am heart-sick that the end should be like this." [15]

15 Quoted in John M. Blum, *Joe Tumulty and the Wilson Era* (Boston: Houghton Mifflin Company, 1951), p. 121.

This kind of dependence gives the President great potential power over the men around him and hence over the personal relations among the central decision makers. He can exercise this power in subtle ways: by offering or refusing access, by granting or withholding authority, by the distribution of assignments and responsibilities from day to day, by giving or withholding private or public credit for work done, by "extracurricular" favors such as invitations to state dinners or the chance to go on a fishing trip with the President. Of course, a President may decide not to use his power to manipulate these rewards and deprivations. Or he may even delegate much of this potential power, as Eisenhower did to Adams. It was access to Adams, and recognition by Adams, and support from Adams that other presidential decision makers vied for, just as American politicians and foreign emissaries used to stream into Colonel House's little apartment on Manhattan's East Side in Wilsonian days. But such a delegation of presidential power is revokable, and both Eisenhower and Wilson in the end revoked it.

4. The less the central decision makers' dependence on the President (or on a subordinate clearly designated by him), the more the relations among the decision makers will be characterized by bargaining and reciprocity, rather than by central control and hierarchy. Presidential policy makers may carve out separate sectors of policy making for themselves; or, where policies must cut across jurisdictional lines, they may clear and adjust their decisions with their colleagues. In either case there is a bargaining relation; there must be give and take, mutual forbearance, a willingness not to "appeal" decisions to higher authority (because higher authority may not exist). The bargaining may not be on equal terms, of course; much will depend on the exterior dependen-

cies and loyalties of the bargainers, as well as on their sheer finesse at bargaining. Some influence will always gravitate to the man who simply understands influence.

The lessened dependence of a central decision maker on the President also tends to enhance the bargaining relation between those two. The classic examples are of course cabinet members: Wilson and Bryan; Roosevelt and Hull or Jones; Truman and Secretary of Commerce Charles Sawyer; Eisenhower and Secretary of Labor Martin Durkin or Secretary of Agriculture Ezra Taft Benson. Almost always the presidential preferences overcome the cabinet member's, but usually the President would prefer to mediate the difference in order not to pay the administrative or political price of a total immediate victory. But decision makers who are organizationally closer to the President also may have bargaining power. Lewis Douglas, Roosevelt's director of the budget, resigned over the issue of New Deal spending despite Roosevelt's efforts to conciliate him. Douglas had an ideological bent for budget balancing, strong factional support in Congress (where he had served), political backing from conservative Democrats and from business and financial groups.

5. Paradoxically, the structure of presidential decision making attains stability and durability from intrinsic qualities of flexibility and informality. Arrangements among central decision makers — work assignments, presidential access and appeal, communications channels — can be adjusted readily because there is little protocol, legal or procedural obligation, or even public or political scrutiny. If the presidential office required the kind of formality, red tape, lengthy clearance that we associate with the Court of Versailles, the structure would indeed be brittle and might fly apart under pressure. But pressure is precisely what the presidential office

can absorb, as it bends and re-forms under the blast of events.
Moreover, the channels of action and of human relationships
are greased by a special kind of lubricant. Men build up
credit with one another. If an aide fails on one assignment,
the President can give him another. If one assistant gets presidential recognition that seems excessive and even undeserved
in the eyes of another, the latter will await his own turn. If
the President fails to come through on a project enthusiasti-
cally sponsored by a department head, the latter can try again
and hope for better luck. As long as one discerns a reservoir
of loyalty in the other he can wait. But of course credit, like
reservoirs, can eventually run dry unless it is replenished —
unless an equilibrium is maintained.

The Lonely President?

I do not pretend that the above generalizations are anything more than speculations about tendencies to be found in
presidential decision making. We would have to know a good
deal more than we do about subtleties and nuances in White
House interrelationships to infuse such generalizations with
more exactness and relevance. For example, one presidential
aide has noted the occasional tendency of some presidential
advisers to take the *opposite* position from what would be expected on the basis of their ideology or interest, perhaps with
an eye to impressing the President with their objectivity and
selfless devotion to him rather than to some cause of their
own.[16] While a discerning President might catch on to such

[16] Theodore C. Sorensen, *Decision-Making in the White House* (New York:
Columbia University Press, 1963), pp. 62–63.

perverse role taking just as this presidential aide did, one must grant that it would be an inspired theory indeed that could generalize about individual behavior as subtle as this.

I do contend that as a result of the development of the presidential office, and as a result of tendencies to be explored in later chapters, the Presidency has developed settled processes of decision making that embody and reflect the kinds of interactions among the President and central decision makers that I have described. There is, in short, some pattern, some continuity, some predictability, some structure in the executive impulse in the modern Presidency. This conclusion runs counter to two important views, one intellectual, one popular.

The first view, held most notably by historians, is that the Presidency is too nearly a unique institution, its incumbents too varied and impenetrable as persons, the stream of forces impinging on it too tumultuous, mixed, and unpredictable, the whole political, social and ideological context too inchoate and changeable, to permit significant generalizations about presidential decision making. Presidential personality alone — the tremendous contrasts between a Hoover and a Roosevelt and a Truman and an Eisenhower and a Kennedy and a Johnson — would thwart any effort at systematic theory. All of us — including historians — actually do generalize about Presidents. Indeed, the theory of strong Presidents is a vitally important generalization in itself, as we have noted. But effective theory seeking to penetrate much below the level of such simplicities or pieties is hopeless, it is said.

This view stems of course from a certain view of history; it stems also — as it applies to the Presidency — from the era of Hamiltonian Presidents who have exercised great powers but in an unstable executive, political, and ideological environment. Presidents have been dependent on a small circle of advisers subject to sudden shifts in membership and attitude. It is only natural that a historian studying the Roosevelt administration would come away from it with a sinking sensation (or perhaps with a feeling of relief) that Roosevelt and his decision-making methods were so harum-scarum as to be ultimately inscrutable. He could react in the same way to seemingly more fixed relations between a President and one adviser. Wilson's relation with Colonel House was so intimate (they even used a private code in telephoning), so mutually dependent, and so informal and unofficial as to seem indestructible. That relationship had much of the quality of a man's relation to his mistress; its very lack of formality was both a strength and a weakness. Certainly it would be hard to generalize about such a relation — except to note that in the end it collapsed, as did that between Roosevelt and Corcoran, and that between Eisenhower and Adams.

But it is precisely here that the office — and the capacity to generalize about it — has changed. The modern President is less dependent on single outside advisers or on haphazard staff arrangements. The collective decision-making processes that have been built up in the Presidency are so strong in their own right, so durable, so rooted now in governmental and administrative practice, that the Presidency itself has come to be more bureaucratized (in the sense of routine, specialization, interdependence). Clearly there will be occasional Presidents who will suppress or distort the usual pattern of presidential decision making. But the continuing tendencies will be strong, and generalizations all the more permissible.[17]

This view, however, runs counter to a second, more popu-

17 Lester G. Seligman, who has done pioneering work on the institutionalization of presidential leadership, states: "The position of the President in this microcosm [of his relationship within the leadership structure] should give us significant insights into his leadership behavior in the macrocosm of his relationship — the public, Congress, organized groups, the bureaucracy, po-

lar conception of the Presidency. This is the notion of "the lonely President" — the man who, though surrounded by many other men, is ultimately alone with his thoughts and his decisions. Immersed in his problems and the squabbles of his advisers, ultimately he rises, steps out of the Oval Office through one of the French doors, and paces up and down in the Rose Garden as he — very much alone — comes to the Final Decision.

This is a good scene for novels about the Presidency but a long way from reality. The President is never alone. He would not be President if he did not incorporate within himself the hopes, attitudes, policy preferences, interests, and goals of scores of central decision makers and of a host of interested politicians and voters outside. To be sure, there are some decisions that call for personal intervention from him, that may arouse greater conflicts within himself, that threaten to strain the bonds between him and men he may esteem and need. But in such situations he will be leaning all the more heavily on other advisers or interests or publics — or on future historians. Loneliness as such is impossible in such a situation of interdependence — the concept is analytically meaningless.

It is also a misleading concept. For the more we are led to think in terms of the "lonely President," the more we bolster the fears of those alarmed about "one-man" presidential power, just as we bolster the case of the historians who conclude that the Presidency is impenetrable. If the great deci-

---

litical parties, foreign relations" (in "Developments in the Presidency and the Conception of Political Leadership," *American Sociological Review*, vol. 20, no. 6 [December 1955], p. 711). I will contend that, even more, the forces in the microcosm and macrocosm are congruent and reinforce one another. See also Lester G. Seligman, "Presidential Leadership: The Inner Circle and Institutionalization," *The Journal of Politics*, vol. 18, no. 3 (August 1956), pp. 410–26.

sions — including the decisions about life and death — in the
end are made by lonely Presidents wrestling with their consciences in the dark, then indeed we could share, for example,
Professor Hyneman's fears about a "single individual with
dominant political authority." No democrat would want his
future, and his country's, settled by some unpredictable decision maker responding to inscrutable forces in some normless
void. No democrat could tolerate a political institution so divorced from the expression of popular attitudes and choices,
from constitutional machinery and safeguards, and above all
from the advice and consent of the men immediately around
him.

Thus I conclude that more centralized control has not
meant more "one-man" control of the executive branch. The
real danger, it seems to me, is just the reverse — whether we
have created such an institutionalized Presidency that the
President will be smothered by the machinery, whether he
will lose the vitality, independence and inventiveness necessary for creative leadership. The question is whether the executive impulse, in helping to produce the modern Presidency, has begun to sacrifice the qualities that Hamilton
wanted in the executive. We can dismiss the concept of the
lonely President as a myth. But there is another, equally popular concept of the Presidency — "the President is many
men." This notion is true — and embraces the real problem.

The executive impulse in the American Presidency has become collective. But the executive impulse is not the only
one that flows through the Chief Executive. He is also a party
leader and a spokesman for American and for Western consensus. These roles, and the forces impinging on them, must
be considered before we can evaluate the President as follower, as an active broker, or as a leader.

V

The Presidential Politicians

Is the Presidency an intrinsically personalized office — haphazard, contingent, ultimately inscrutable? Or has it taken on some qualities of stability, routine, and order; in short, has it become somewhat institutionalized? We have examined this question in a central but narrow context, the executive impulse, and hence we have begged a major part of the question. For the executive decision makers are exposed also to pressures from party and legislative leaders, group interests, world-wide ideologies, foreign leaders; they are caught in the glare of publicity, and buffeted by the stream of events — most of the events taking the form of crisis problems or they would never have come to the White House. And the central decision makers are not inert receptacles of these pressures. They respond to some and not to others and hence change the political environment within which the decision-making process takes place. The presidential office truly is a crucible in which the political elements are transformed.

Once we take into account all these broader political forces we sharpen the question as to the extent to which the presidential office has been, can be, or should be, institutionalized. For each of these forces has seemed in many respects wayward, inchoate, unstable, and unpredictable.

To begin with the broadest contextual force, the American ideology has appeared formless and fluid. Historians of American ideas long have noted that we neither inherited nor shaped in the last century a solid or coherent system of values. We had a belief in egalitarianism that legitimized enormous inequality in fact, a belief in individual liberty that excluded millions of Americans from it. American liberalism has embraced doctrines that range across almost the whole continuum of American thought; from extreme laissez-faire and "rugged individualism" to radical collective action and governmental responsibility. Our conservatism has been especially disjointed, embracing the economic development goals of Hamilton, the natural aristocracy of Adams, the radical individualism of Sumner and Carnegie, the erratic anti-governmentalism of Barry Goldwater, the racism and reaction of Southern Citizens Councils. We have of course shared, as Myrdal has suggested, an "American Creed" of humanitarianism, equality of opportunity, individual liberty, but we did not have during the formative decades an enduring and stable set of relatively explicit political principles that could link this kind of ideology with governmental institutions and public policies.

Our political structure too has seemed plastic and disorganized. Ultimately, some politicians say, it is every man for himself, and it could be argued that power in the last analysis is divided so broadly and minutely, among so many politicians and then subdivided among so many of their followings, as to defy any attempt at patterning. But this would be to ignore the coalitions that channel political influence into a relatively limited number of camps in the national political arena. Congressional candidates with almost opposite views support the same presidential candidate because they will need friends in the White House. But these same congressional candidates must protect their congressional security and affiliations on Capitol Hill — especially their ties with the opposite congressional party. The upshot is that party affiliation can be used to mobilize partisan votes for a President and for a congressman, in the same party but hostile to him, all at the same time. Party affiliation is no less important for this reason. It still sets boundaries for leadership discretion. But its importance must be assessed with an eye for the way in which politicians can exploit party names and symbols and yet retain tremendous latitude in policy making. And they have this latitude, of course, because each party has embraced, for historical and structural reasons, such widely discordant points of view.

In this context of a hazy ideology and loose political parties the political attitudes and affiliations of the American people have varied widely in direction and quality. Some sectors of public opinion are characterized by intensity, others by superficiality. Some are stable, others volatile, some latent, others in an almost permanent condition of mobilization. Fads come and go; celebrities rise and fall; issues wax and wane. If the United States had a highly stratifed class system, political attitudes toward policies and issues might show more stability and durability, but our class structure too is inchoate.

Our interest groups have seemed to fortify the tendencies toward a volatile politics. They have not been closely tied to enduring ideology or party or class; for years the major group associations such as labor and business and medicine have self-consciously played nonpartisan politics and hence tried to protect their "independence." Leaders of group interests try to keep access open to both political parties. Within the large national organizations competing factions tie in with shifting clusters of leaders; the coal miners, for example, have flirted with both major parties, and today the teamsters' unions at times favor the Democrats and at times the Republicans but always the teamsters. Smaller interest groups might pursue a somewhat more even political course and work out lasting alliances because of the very clarity and particularity of their objectives, but the larger groupings constantly have tried to adapt to a shifting political environment. The internal political life of many organized interests has been characterized by unstable factional relations, disorganized leadership structures, and wavering membership allegiance.

Of all these fluid and pluralistic forces in American parties, our political parties have seemed to be the most inchoate. Except in occasional moments of high-blown and rather synthetic oratory, national party leaders have shrunk away from ideological commitments and involvements. In order to win majorities the two national parties have each had to embrace sharply differing sectional and local interests and attitudes, and hence they have often sacrificed coherence in national policy and program. Since political factions and parties tend to organize around candidates and officeholders, the parties have been heavily federalized and decentralized in response to our constitutional structure. Essentially our national parties have been aggregations or coalitions of personal parties reflecting economic and social interests, but they have had to deal with foreign policy issues and "qualitative" or "way-of-life" issues — with Prohibition, women's rights, conservation, morality in government, the relation of church and state — that have strained and twisted party lines built around traditional divisions over economic and social matters.

Despite all these pluralistic and even atomistic tendencies, we can discern a structure of presidential politics that stabilizes much of the activity of American government today.

The Structure of Presidential Politics

Within the broad confines of the national parties, political leaders have built their personal organizations in order to win office and to mobilize support in office. It is these personal organizations in both parties, existing in a state of unstable equilibrium with one another, that provide considerable continuity and stability to the party system. By far the most important and most durable of these candidate or officeholder organizations are the presidential parties. The presidential party in power is headed by the President, his political staff, his Cabinet and other politicians; it embraces much (but usually not all) of the regular party organization; it has its own leadership cadres in the states and cities. Collectively these people comprise the "presidential politicians" who supply relatively firm political support for the President and the central decision makers. The presidential party out of power is technically headed by the previous presidential candidate and by his colleagues; but it lies inert within the "regular" national party until a new presidential candidate is chosen.

The historic origin of the presidential parties is obscure. Presidents have always had to build personal followings in order to win office, and they have maintained their organizations in order to gain re-election and to protect themselves politically against the competitive pressure of other officeholders in the party, especially of congressional leaders. Presidents are expected to be "party leaders" but rarely do they lead the whole party. They cannot respond to all the forces in the sprawling party structure and still run a government that demands at least a general direction, coherence of policy, and administrative consistency. And some sections of the party will be in open rebellion, as many Southern Democrats were against Truman and Kennedy, and as the McCarthy wing was against Eisenhower.

In this century the presidential parties have emerged most clearly, as might be expected, under the activist Presidents. In the muckraking years of the new century, Theodore Roosevelt mobilized the old reformist and "conscience" elements of the Republican party, organized them behind himself and his Square Deal, and built a personal coalition of progressive Republicans, independents, labor and farm leaders, and southern Negroes. This coalition, cutting across the boundaries of the regular party, ensured his presidential nomination in 1904. In the face of accusations that he was trying to form a "Roosevelt party" in Congress, Roosevelt tried to maintain friendly relations with the regular party leaders, but the relations were often marked by suspicion. It was his personal party, headed by the former presidential politicians that he had gathered around himself in his Administration, that summoned him back to political combat in 1912. It was significant that while President Taft was strong enough with the regulars to win renomination at the 1912 convention, Roosevelt's own party was widely enough based to muster more popular votes than Taft was able to gain.

Woodrow Wilson too created a presidential party and he did so in an even more unyielding environment, amid the ancient and diffused Democracy. Having won the nomination against splintered Democratic opposition, and then the election against the sharply divided Republicans, he sensed immediately that he had to establish bases of personal support within and outside the traditional party. For a time before his Inaugural he contemplated reconstructing the Democratic party and aligning it with liberal-minded independents and Republicans. Shortly after his Inauguration he explained to Albert S. Burleson, his Postmaster General and patronage dispenser, that on appointments he was simply not going to "advise with reactionary or standpat Senators or Representatives." [1] Burleson warned him that if he wanted to get his reform program through he had better let the congressmen have the "little offices" in Paducah. In the end Wilson gave way, and he got his program through Congress, but in the long run every political concession he made to potentially competitive officeholders simply strengthened the latters' independent political power, and hence threatened Wilson's own. Late in his first term, as he faced the need of creating a new personal political coalition to overcome the now reunited Republicans, he once again turned to the task of infusing new blood into the party. He supported labor and farm legislation, and he even departed from the conventional wisdom of the Democratic party to furnish some protection for American business overseas. Wilson, said Walter Lippmann, was "temporarily at least creating, out of the reactionary, parochial fragments of the Democracy, the only party which at this moment is national in scope, liberal in purpose, and effective in action." [2] But Wilson's maneuver was not simply in pursuit of new policies or lofty aims. He was very much the practical presidential politician who recognized the inadequacies of the existing national party for *him* and his reelection.

Harding, Coolidge, and Hoover were less activist Presidents than Roosevelt or Wilson and hence could co-exist

[1] Arthur S. Link, *Wilson: The New Freedom* (Princeton: Princeton University Press, 1956), p. 159.
[2] "The Case for Wilson," *The New Republic*, vol. 8, no. 102 (Oct. 14, 1916), p. 263.

more easily with the regular national party. Even so there were strains and tensions. Republican progressives and internationalists felt isolated from the White House. Men like Charles Evans Hughes and Herbert Hoover held cabinet positions, but the old reformist impetus withered amid the complacency and anti-governmentalism of the 1920's. The three Republican Presidents of course maintained something of a presidential party. Indeed, Coolidge could not have won the presidential nomination in 1924 unless he had quickly buttressed his personal power in the party. But widely and strongly based presidential parties were not needed because the White House during the 1920's supplied relatively little leadership as to policy or program.

It was the next activist President, Franklin Roosevelt, who built the most formidable presidential party up to that time. Coming into office during the pressures and uncertainties of the economic crisis, Roosevelt turned for help wherever he could find it to put through his emergency measures of 1933 and the enduring reforms of the "second Hundred Days" in 1935. To make it easier for Republicans to support him, Roosevelt played down ordinary partisanship. "I am trying to get across the idea that if we have the right kind of people the party label does not mean so very much," [3] he told newsmen off the record. By 1936 he had built a personal coalition that stretched far outside the old Democracy; it included farm and labor groups, ethnic leaders, old Bull Moose progressives, Jeffersonian and Wilsonian liberals, along with the twin bastions of traditional Democratic strength, the city bosses and the southern Democrats.

Roosevelt's tremendous re-election victory of 1936 was at

[3] Quoted in James MacGregor Burns, *Roosevelt: The Lion and the Fox* (New York: Harcourt, Brace & Company, 1956), p. 202.

least as much a personal as a party triumph. "There's one issue in this campaign," he had told Raymond Moley. "It's myself, and people must be either for me or against me." [4] Such a broad coalition, bound together by one man and lacking clear principle and grass-roots organization, was bound to show internal fissures. Defeated on his court-packing bill and other reform measures, Roosevelt tried to purge the Democratic party in the 1938 primaries. The outcome was a revealing measure of the boundaries between Roosevelt's personal party and the regular national party. Roosevelt lost in the South; got mixed results in the border states; and won a significant victory in the North. As New Dealers such as Robert Jackson, Thomas Corcoran, Henry Wallace, Harold Ickes, and Harry Hopkins won increasing influence in the presidential party, true-blue regulars like national Democratic chairman James A. Farley became increasingly distressed. When Farley wrote later that "White House confidence on politics and policies went to a small band of zealots, who mocked at party loyalty and knew no devotion except unswerving obedience to their leader," he was venting the complaint of many a national chairman who has tried to represent the whole national party while the presidential politicians have pursued their somewhat separate interests. [5]

With the coming of war in Europe Roosevelt reorganized the presidential party so that he could assume a "nonpartisan" stance on foreign and military policy. But as the war drew to a close, and as he faced in 1944 a re-election campaign that would turn in part on postwar plans and issues, he once again had to contend with the weaknesses of the Democratic

4 Raymond Moley, *After Seven Years* (New York: Harper & Brothers, 1939), p. 343.
5 James A. Farley, *Jim Farley's Story* (New York: Whittlesey House, 1948), p. 68.

party and the limited reach of his personal party. Once again
he considered realigning his party so that he could attract the
liberal and internationalist elements among the Republicans.
He conducted discreet preliminary negotiations with Wen-
dell Willkie, but Willkie was dubious about Roosevelt's in-
tentions, and he died in 1944 before the negotiations could
make much progress.

Willkie was suspicious partly because he too had had a taste
of the ever simmering conflict between presidential parties
and national parties. He had invaded the Republican party
in 1940 as a former Democrat, a moderate on social welfare
legislation, and an internationalist. Knowing that the G.O.P.
could not possibly win against the master campaigner and
coalition-builder in the White House unless it immensely
broadened the range of its appeal, he had established a host of
personal organizations — Willkie clubs and the like —
through which he had run part of his campaign. Inevitably conflict had risen between the regulars and the "amateurs" or "volunteers" or "citizens," as they were variously
called, and much of the party's regular leadership had turned
against Willkie after his defeat.

It was in part this conflict between party regulars and party
volunteers that underlay the struggle between Dwight Eisenhower and Senator Robert A. Taft in 1952. Henry Cabot
Lodge and the other Eisenhower managers knew that the
General's wartime popularity in itself was not enough to ensure victory. Nonpartisan support had to be mobilized and
organized. Citizens for Eisenhower appealed to independents, dissident Democrats, and previous nonvoters. The fight
at the 1952 convention was waged between the regulars, especially in Congress, who had dominated the structure of the
national party and a group of Republican governors and

other officeholders who mobilized amateurs and volunteers in the presidential primaries. Citizens for Eisenhower helped notably in rolling up the big presidential majority of 1952, but what was to be their fate after election? When the Taft Republicans on Capitol Hill killed or stalled some of Eisenhower's key legislative proposals, the General toyed with the notion of building a new party of Democrats and Republicans who were middle-of-the-road in domestic matters and world-minded in foreign policy. But he lacked the conviction, tenacity and political skill to pull off a feat that had baffled abler political leaders in the White House, and the Administration jogged along trying to maintain the Eisenhower organization, including its citizens' groups, at the same time seeking to preserve peaceful relations with the party regulars ensconced in the congressional power structure.

In the face of Eisenhower's personal appeal and citizen support the Stevensonian Democrats too tried to enlist citizen groups. Volunteers for Stevenson had blossomed in 1952 and soon demonstrated that many political amateurs could be far more professional than the regular "pros" in practical election work. The Volunteers could not stem the Eisenhower tide in either 1952 or 1956, but they had a lasting impact on the Democratic party, for in some states many of the Stevenson citizens stayed in the party and added a dash of ideology and verve in the elections that followed. They were able to help John Kennedy in 1960, but Kennedy also had his personal organization that had been built up prior to and during the hard-fought presidential primaries in the early months of 1960. The Kennedy organization, one of the most expertly led, well-manned, and generously financed personal organizations in history, virtually swallowed the regular Democratic organization during the battle with Richard Nixon.

Barry Goldwater organized a somewhat different type of personal party in 1964. During his preconvention campaign he mobilized two major groups. One consisted of party organization men, some of whom were not much enchanted by Goldwater's ideas but wanted to try a different style of candidate after years of losing with moderates. The other was composed of ideological conservatives who had been active in right-wing groups and who now moved into Republican party organizations, many of which, especially in the West and South, they captured for their leader. The Goldwater leaders purged much of the national party apparatus after their convention victory. If Goldwater had won the Presidency in the fall, he would have completed this purge in Washington, but he still would have had to contend with the "Governors' party" — the moderate elements headed by Rockefeller, Scranton, Romney, and the like — in the large industrial states. Once again a presidential party would have existed uneasily with opposition elements — with the curious difference that the presidential party would have been the conservative one. This indeed was implicit in Goldwater's strategy, but this strategy was a hopeless one for 1964.

The fact that presidential parties are essentially personal organizations formed around Presidents suggests that they have a fluid and impermanent quality. This is true to an extent. But over the years important continuities have developed in the make-up of the successive presidential parties. From Theodore Roosevelt to Dwight Eisenhower one can trace the life careers of men who have been somewhat independent of the regular Republicans at the state and local level but who have been available for service to moderate and liberal Republican presidential candidates. Major continuities in personnel could also be found between Wilson's,

Franklin Roosevelt's, Stevenson's and Kennedy's presidential organizations. The presidential parties have recruited their top and middle-level leadership from somewhat similar sources: from universities, law schools, foundations, and large metropolitan law and banking firms, especially in the Northeast and on the West Coast, and the more established business and industrial corporations. Men like Elihu Root, Gifford Pinchot, Henry Stimson, John Foster Dulles in the Republican party, and Newton D. Baker, Felix Frankfurter, Dean Acheson, Averell Harriman, James Forrestal in the Democratic party not only have been leaders of presidential parties; they have drawn into the presidential orbit a host of younger men who in turn have recruited others.

Four-Party Coalitions

The presidential politicians in power hold a commanding position in the vast political arena. The White House is a superb command post from which to conduct day-to-day presidential politics. It is also a "bully pulpit" from which Presidents can hurl political thunderbolts and moral judgments. Day after day the nation's politicians, legislators, group leaders, and free-wheeling VIP's troop into the west wing as steadily as the tourists trudge through the east wing and the mansion. The White House is a round-the-clock, round-the-year campaign headquarters.

Its political resources are enormous. Even aside from the President's constitutional power in determining "who gets what, when, and how," he has a reservoir of specific favors

that whet any politician's appetite. The host of appointments, including the most prestigious such as ambassadorial
ones, are only the more obvious kind of favors. The presidential politicians can grant access to the President, obtain a letter or photograph from him, and arrange special forms of recognition, such as an invitation to a state dinner. An interest
group can be favored with a special White House conference
on a problem it wishes spotlighted. Presidential commissions
can be established to focus attention on an issue, and membership on the commission is another form of patronage.
Presidential acceptance of invitations to speak is an important kind of patronage. Such presidential favors may seem to
the outside observer to be rather freely and loosely distributed; actually there are few given out that are not schemed
and struggled for, and they are granted only after the presidential politicians have carefully calculated the advantages to
the President.

The presidential party at the center is a highly centralized
and disciplined political organization. Political decisions are
made on the basis of one criterion: what is best for the political standing, prestige, reputation, and re-electibility of the
President. The Chief Executive's almost absolute control
over his staff is as crucial politically as it is administratively.
Anyone below the President is expendable. Men must be
willing to take the gaff for errors; they must be able to cope
with the disappointed politicos who may be left out of presidential favor and who vent their wrath on "the White House
gang" or the "inner circle" which, they feel, have cut them off
from the President.

Under activist Presidents the presidential party extends far
beyond the White House. The Vice-President has come to be
a political as well as executive and legislative aide and deputy

of the President. The national chairman of the party has become wholly absorbed into the presidential orbit. There was a time when national chairmen felt responsible for the whole party and hence somewhat independent of the White House. But the "strong" President today considers the national chairman his own man. It has become definite practice that the newly nominated presidential candidate chooses his own national chairman, who then takes over the whole national party organization. It is odd that the organizational apparatus of a great, historic national party, with its own wide interests and obligations, should so completely subordinate itself to the man who is able to win the nomination, as in the case of Goldwater's convention victory in 1964. But this situation illustrates the relation between the presidential candidate's personal organization and the regular national party — and it suggests the relative weakness of the latter. James Farley's influence and security, as long as he was Roosevelt's man in the national chairmanship, illustrates the reach of presidential influence, and also its limitations; once Farley ceased being only Roosevelt's man and tried to speak for other elements in the party he lost Roosevelt's confidence, and soon broke with his chief.

Almost always the presidential politicians control the national convention lock, stock and barrel. Here again the proud historic party — Democratic or Republican — humbly submits to its leader, and does so under the gaze of the nation and the world. In the last century, conventions occasionally repudiated the President and chose a rival, but this is almost unheard of today. Harry Truman, despite deep defections from his party, easily won the nomination in 1948; almost from the moment of Lyndon Johnson's accession it was certain that he would have his party's nomination nine months

later. And choosing a running mate has become almost a humorous presidential sport. While the convention waits, the
President plays with his little secret; trots out various possibilities; and finally springs the news when he pleases. The delegates would go along with almost any reasonable presidential
choice, however much they might grumble privately. There
was only a passing wavelet of resistance to Kennedy's choice of
Johnson in 1960 on the floor of the Democratic convention,
and many delegates to the 1964 convention were still a bit
uncertain of Johnson's selection until the very end of the
speech when the President uttered Hubert Humphrey's
name. Eisenhower chose Nixon in 1952 without opposition,
and could have dumped him in 1956 if he had been so
minded. Adlai Stevenson tried the audacious experiment in
1956 of throwing the vice-presidential race open, but such a
gamble will rarely be repeated.

The presidential party reaches its greatest influence and
degree of activity during the presidential campaign. The
presidential politicians in the White House work closely with
the President's men throughout the nation. These men may
or may not be the "regulars"; often the state and city chairmen and their organizations are bypassed or given the barest
possible recognition. The presidential politicians in the
states are more often the men who have been close to the
President, who are interested almost exclusively in his candidacy, who know how to reach the influential leaders in the
area, who can appeal to citizens' groups and clubs as well as to
the regulars. The presidential politicians will of course depend on local bosses where the bosses can predictably deliver
the vote, as Roosevelt depended on Mayor Hague of Jersey
City, and Kennedy and Johnson on Mayor Daley of Chicago.
But such city machines are limited in number and effective-

ness, and the Presidents must reach out through their own men to other sources of support.

One of the most convincing tests of the relative power of the presidential party and the regular national party is fundraising. Again and again the money men have discovered that it is far easier to raise funds for *candidates* — especially incumbents — than for parties. People prefer to give money to a man than to a vast organization. Especially they prefer to give to Presidents, who can do so much to reward the donor. Partly this preference may be a prudent wish to know something of the party's candidates and policies before giving; but mainly it is a desire to incur an obligation on the part of a man, or of a smaller group with a definite leader, rather than on the part of a huge party that cannot easily be held accountable or that is not well organized to honor the obligation at a future date. Political operators are known to speak frankly of "buying a piece" of a candidate; it is easier to buy a piece of a man than a piece of a national party.

Despite all this, the power of the presidential party is not unlimited. On the national scene it has had to coexist with three other parties that have grown up around national candidates and officeholders: the opposing presidential party and two congressional parties.

The scope of the presidential party's appeal is sharply limited by the fact that it has responsibility for policy and must in the long run shape relatively coherent programs. It is limited by the President's commitments and promises as a candidate, by scarce fiscal and other governmental resources, by the pressure of time and circumstance. A President may range back and forth between the broad policy alternatives of his party, avoiding definite commitments to ideology or program, as Franklin Roosevelt did for two or three years, but eventually he must make some kind of commitment. And given the pluralistic nature of the entire Democratic and Republican parties, he will inevitably leave some groups dissatisfied.

But the main opposition to the presidential party within the overall national party is not simply a cluster of interests, leaders and party groups that have been left out. The main opposition comes from chiefly rural and conservative voters, represented by politicians organized around the legislative committee leadership in the national House and Senate. In their efforts to win fiercely competitive national elections, the presidential parties in this century have had to arouse and respond to the waxing city and suburban vote across the nation. They have had perforce to support liberal social and economic programs. The presidential "gerrymandering" and "winner take all" arrangement of the electoral college, as a result of which the presidential candidates tend to vie for the big, closely contested, heavily urban states with their big labor unions and ethnic groups, has forced both presidential parties to the left. This shift has opened a vacuum in both national parties that has come to be filled by two congressional parties playing rearguard politics.

The two congressional parties have been relatively small in voting strength, since they have largely rested on the narrow electoral base of one-party states and districts. But they have achieved tremendous power on Capitol Hill, especially in blocking legislation. They have benefited from their solid strength in one-party districts; from the extra representation they receive as a result of gerrymandered and malapportioned congressional districts; from the seniority their leaders attain in Congress and the extraordinary influence granted to seniority in the committee organization and procedures of Congress; from special blocking devices such as the right to filibuster in the Senate and the control of parliamentary action by the Rules Committee in the House. All these arrangements have long been praised and condemned; we must see them here as the indispensable elements of a congressional party system.

Try as they might, the presidential politicians have not been able to overcome the congressional parties' bases of power. In great sweeps such as Roosevelt's in 1936 and Eisenhower's in 1952 the presidential candidates seemed to bring in scores of congressmen on their coattails, and it appeared that in these cases the presidential party had submerged and overcome the congressional. But once the election was over and the legislative leaders were established in their independent positions of power on Capitol Hill, the old rivalry asserted itself. Within a few months of his 1936 triumph Roosevelt was struggling on even terms with Democratic Senators over court reform and other second-term measures. After Eisenhower won in 1952 he found Taft and other conservative Senators willing to work with him but only from somewhat independent positions. His relation with them was one of bargaining rather than that of leader and follower.

The only way that the presidential parties could effectively overcome the congressional parties would be through attacking the basis of their political power. This Roosevelt tried to do in 1938 through the sudden, improvised and highly personalized "purge." As we have noted, his success was limited. After John Kennedy had experienced congressional intransigence over his major legislative proposals in 1961 and 1962, some urged him to try a "purge in reverse" — that is, to build the presidential party more strongly in a number of key congressional districts, recruit able congressional candidates, provide them with ample presidential recognition, expert advice, and funds, and seek to overcome the entrenched courthouse rings and party factions supporting Old Guard congressmen. While Kennedy never gave signs of endorsing this plan as a basic strategy, before his death there appeared to be some tentative endeavors in this direction with considerable (though unacknowledged) White House backing. President Johnson had neither the time nor perhaps the inclination to carry out such a strategy during the 1964 campaign. It is possible, however, that the presidential parties are overcoming the congressional as a result of other developments that will be explored in later chapters.

The weakest of the four parties is the presidential party out of power. Once a presidential candidate is beaten, he becomes titular leader of the national party — which means in fact that he moves over and the congressional party leadership assumes command. These leaders — for example, Senator Everett Dirksen, minority House leader Charles Halleck, and Senator Barry Goldwater during the Kennedy-Johnson administration — had their own party organization, such as it was: a press conference (dubbed the "Ev and Charlie Show" in the case of Dirksen and Halleck); prominent rostrums in the House and Senate; their own sources of party funds; their own ties with interest groups, often through Washington lobbyists; and their own electioneering organizations, the House and Senate campaign committees.

For any presidential party that has recently vacated the White House, coexisting with the now dominant congressional party is a frustrating experience, as the Stevenson Democrats discovered after 1952. A number of old presidential party leaders — including Harry Truman, Stevenson, Herbert Lehman, Eleanor Roosevelt, Averell Harriman, Hubert Humphrey — established an Advisory Council to serve as a focus of opposition to the Eisenhower Administration. Lacking institutional support, the Council had little influence, and it was boycotted and largely ignored by the leaders of the Democratic congressional party. Later the Republican presidential party experienced its own frustrations. A year and a half after Nixon's defeat in 1960 Eisenhower Republicans established the Republican Citizens Committee under the honorary chairmanship of the General, and with a Critical Issues Council composed in part of high-ranking officials of the Eisenhower administration. The Council put out a number of admirable position papers espousing moderate Republicanism, but along with the rest of the presidential Republican party it was run over by the congressional party at the 1964 Republican convention in San Francisco. Following Goldwater's defeat in November Republican leaders continued to debate party image and organization. Many wished to reestablish a council that could "speak for the whole party" (i.e., the moderates). Others proposed an annual or biennial national convention to refurbish the party's program, or even a top-to-bottom reorganization of the party. In general, congressional party leaders wanted to strengthen — or at least protect — their own leadership institutions, while the presidential party leaders demanded more representation in national party circles for the governors, urban interests, intellectuals, and the old volunteer elements. Eisenhower even proposed abolition of the House and Senate Republican campaign committees, which had long been part of the election-waging apparatus of the congressional party.

The existence of four national parties with separate bases of power has had a crucial effect on policy making, especially domestic. Typically action could not be taken except as a result of bargaining and coalitions among at least two of the four parties. On the face of it such a multi-party system might appear likely to produce the mercurial alignments and fleeting marriages of convenience characteristic of European parliamentary systems. In practice there has been considerable continuity and stability in our four-party alliances. The two presidential parties, despite their quadrennial battles for control of the White House, have long maintained a quiet alliance on foreign policy and on certain domestic policies. Thus Theodore Rooseveltian, internationalist Republicans in 1920 supported some kind of League of Nations even though they spurned Wilson's League. Franklin Roosevelt gave access to and made use of internationalist Republicans, most notably in his selection of Stimson and Knox (the latter a Teddy Roosevelt Bull Mooser of old) in his cabinet during the European crisis in 1940. There were major continuities in foreign policy and personnel between the Truman, Eisenhower, and Kennedy-Johnson administrations. The rhetorical note of the foreign-policy coalition was the cry that "party politics stops at the water's edge," but it was really only *presidential* party rivalry that was adjourned.

Each presidential party has coalesced with its "own" congressional party on matters that bound the two together — for example, on foreign policy under Franklin Roosevelt and on attempts to curb federal spending under Eisenhower. Some of the most productive alliances have been those between the two parties close to the center of the domestic policy spectrum, the presidential Republicans and the Congressional Democrats. Eisenhower got some of his major bills through Congress after 1954 as a result of a more or less covert working relation with Senate Majority leader Lyndon B. Johnson. Both Kennedy and Johnson gained legislative support from a small number of presidential Republicans in the House and Senate.

The Framework of Voting

This review of presidential party organization suggests that despite the tremendous discretion and apparent personalization of the President and his fellow presidential politicians, they work within a relatively stable framework of administrative, legislative, and party restraints. But we have been mainly discussing the interrelations of the national leaders — the presidential decision makers and their counterparts in the congressional parties and in the out-of-office presidential party. Now we must broaden the focus and consider the total political environment within which the presidential politicians, their allies, and their adversaries operate. Ultimately these parties depend on electoral sanctions. Is voting for national office in the United States characterized mainly by shifting and even erratic decision making in the election booth? Do opinions relevant to national policy and personnel jump crazily about, showing neither pattern nor predictability nor apparent logic?

The great weight of evidence indicates that where opinion is relevant to, and influential with, presidential decision making, it is characterized more by viscosity than fluidity. Some find this conclusion hard to swallow because they want to think of a free people as independent in thought, ready to shift political opinions in the light of changing facts, and capable of piercing through the smog of vested ideas, propaganda, and apathy that surrounds them. But people create their own smog to protect themselves against unwelcome ideas; they inherit their own lenses through which to view political events. Voters are products of families that have previously learned and transmitted set attitudes toward political parties, issues, and ideologies. They associate in groups that, subtly or not, maintain sets of attitudes toward external events, sometimes as the price of maintaining group solidarity. They have occupations that largely dominate their opinions, often on the basis of rational self-interest. All this creates a stable framework for political attitudes.

It is easy to find specific cases or areas of volatile, fast-shifting opinion. Social psychologists like to point to the aftermath of the broadcasting of Orson Welles' "Invasion from Mars" because people reacted to this electrifying and terrifying pseudo-event in a variety of remarkable and hardly predictable ways. But that is just the point: the invasion was an unprecedented, strange, and shattering "event" to which people reacted in illogical ways precisely because they could not fit it into a pattern or tradition.

In the context of relatively settled and deep-rooted political attitudes, on the other hand, voting on national offices shows impressive comparability from state to state and considerable continuity over time. We tend to underestimate the stability of the vote because in competitive constituencies (including the presidential one) the pendulum can swing only a few degrees and overturn a party. Between 1936 and 1964, for example, the party split of the presidential vote showed great stability despite two shifts in presidential party control. The Democratic share of the two-party presidential vote in Detroit in the five elections from 1940 through 1956 was never greater than 64.7 percent or less than 59.3.[6] Even electoral "landslides" show only marginal changes in many constituencies; the landslide was not really in voting but in the electoral college or in the party control of Congress. Of

---

[6] Samuel J. Eldersveld, *Political Parties: A Behavioral Analysis* (Chicago: Rand McNally & Co., 1964), p. 31.

course "realigning elections" take place, with all sorts of implications for party change in the future, as in 1896, but such elections seem to have been rare in this century.[7] And even such elections may only be measures of slower, long-gathering change; it has been suggested that we might better think in terms of realigning electoral *eras* rather than realigning elections.[8]

At the core of this stability in voting is a remarkable durability in party identification. Contrary to Gilbert and Sullivan's remark about the astonishing tendency for every little boy or girl alive to be born Liberal or Conservative, people are not born Democrats or Republicans, but the great majority are born *into* these parties. In the 1950's, Key notes, "the proportions of persons regarding themselves as strong Democrats or as strong Republicans or as partisans in some other degree remained remarkably constant." [9] And as Key suggests, basic, deep rooted, strongly structured party attitudes act as an anchor for views toward candidates and issues. The party, as I have suggested elsewhere, serves as a kind of "instant ideology" for those who need some quick, easy and familiar yardstick for measuring changing and often obscure political events.[10] People may desert their party candidate, or they may shift specific political opinions, but they ordinarily do so only by rationalizing that their new candidate choice or opinion fits their party identification. And to the extent a voter has to rationalize his new decision in this way, party

7 V. O. Key, Jr., "A Theory of Critical Elections," *Journal of Politics* (Feb., 1955), vol. 17, pp. 3–18.

8 Angus Campbell, Philip E. Converse, Warren E. Miller, Donald E. Stokes, *The American Voter* (New York: John Wiley & Sons, Inc., 1960), p. 535.

9 V. O. Key, Jr., *Public Opinion and American Democracy* (New York: Alfred A. Knopf, 1961), p. 244.

10 *The Deadlock of Democracy* (Englewood Cliffs, N.J.: Prentice-Hall, Inc., 1963), p. 208.

loyalty is serving as a dampener on the volatility of his political behavior.

How does this strong and continuing identification with the Democratic or Republican parties relate to the four-party structure of leadership, coalitions, and policy making? The answer lies in the intervening variables, or linkage, between the great number of voters with their simple partisan affiliation, and the organization of power in the national government. Two links are especially important: the patterning of opinion by the leadership structure, and the organization of the news and editorial media in Washington.

On the face of it, two large armies of partisans stretching across the nation would seem cause for a relatively clean and meaningful split between a set of national party leaders in power and a set of "outs." This would be the case if the machinery of government leant itself to capture by one party (as it does in Britain). But our machinery does not; it was designed to fragmentize power. While ultimate constitutional authority is divided among President, several hundred legislators, and nine judges, power has tended to polarize in rival camps within each major party, which I have called the presidential and congressional parties.

For many years each presidential party and its sibling congressional party has been evoking the same party name, party myths, party heroes, and party symbols, while meaning something quite different in party platform and governmental policy. Democratic congressional candidates in Detroit or New York have exhorted the party faithful in behalf of social welfare programs and civil rights, while other Democratic congressional candidates in Alabama or Arkansas have begged *their* party faithful for votes in order to oppose these same programs. Republican congressional candidates in suburban areas of Connecticut or New Jersey have been calling for internationalist foreign policies while their colleagues in Ohio or Illinois or Colorado have been promising to cut foreign aid and safeguard American industry. These are old and familiar contradictions. They are sustained, as we have seen above, by two parallel and competing structures in each overall party — by a congressional structure of power anchored in overrepresented rural districts, voting tendencies in congressional elections, and congressional procedures and leadership, and by a presidential structure rooted in public attitudes toward the Presidency, voting tendencies in presidential elections, the mechanics of the electoral college, the national convention, and the presidential establishment in Washington. The result is a four-party system and the various party alliances without which the system would be hopelessly deadlocked.

The Presidential Press

The four-party pattern that emerges out of these attitudinal, electoral, and institutional forces has influenced the organization of news processing in Washington, and has been affected by it. That processing is not, of course, entirely neutral. Presidents and their subordinates have been accused of trying to "manage" news — and they do try — but reporters, editors, and other participants are not wholly neutral in reporting events. They exercise discretion in how they report "facts" and in what facts they consider worth reporting. Wire men, make-up men, headline writers, press services — all, to varying degrees, "manage" the news. The question is

whether this management has any pattern; that is, do those
who influence the processing of news make their day-to-day
decisions in a persisting context that helps shape those decisions, or do they act as independent individuals influenced by
random and discrete forces?

Much of the discussion of this problem has been couched in
the dialogue — or the diatribe — about the "one-party" press.
Democrats have complained that the great bulk of the press
has favored the Republican presidential candidate; in 1948,
for example, an *Editor & Publisher* survey indicated that 65
percent of the nation's daily newspapers supported Thomas
E. Dewey, compared to 15 percent for Truman. Yet the 1952
preconvention presidential contest saw an interesting variation on the old refrain. After Senator Robert A. Taft's defeat
in the Republican convention by Eisenhower, Taft wrote in a
memorandum that "four-fifths of the influential newspapers
in the country were opposed to me continuously and vocifer-
ously and many turned themselves into propaganda sheets for
my opponent . . . supplemented by the violent support of
every New Deal and so-called independent paper." [11] The
contests since then within the Republican party — and to a
lesser extent within the Democratic party — have been fea-
tured by contentions that the conservative wing of the party
(i.e., the congressional party) was getting short shrift from
the large metropolitan newspapers and weeklies. This feeling
rose to a pitch in 1964 during the Goldwater campaign and
erupted in catcalls and fist-shaking directed at columnists and
television commentators covering the Republican convention
in San Francisco. Like Taft before him, Goldwater attrib-

[11] Quoted in Paul T. David, Ralph M. Goldman, and Richard C. Bain,
The Politics of National Party Conventions (Washington, D.C.: The Brookings Institution, 1960), p. 556.

uted his defeat in the fall largely to bias and distortions in the "one-party" press. What has happened to the conservatism of the press that we were hearing so much about only a few years ago?

We can understand the nature of the collective bias of the press if we grasp the social composition and working environment of the Washington correspondents. First consider their social recruitment. In the mid-1930's Leo Rosten conducted a detailed and probing survey of 127 Washington correspondents. Since words are the journalist's tools, he wrote, "it would seem a defensible hypothesis that newspapermen are drawn from a psychological environment which placed a premium upon articulateness. One would expect more reporters to be the children of parents who handled ideas rather than things: teachers, clergymen, lawyers, or editors, rather than farmers or industrial workers. One would expect newspapermen to have been exposed to the attraction of talk, particularly talk about social and political affairs, in homes with literate preoccupations. And one would expect them to have middle class origins. . . . In the light of this approach it is not wholly fortuitous that out of 123 Washington correspondents who supplied information on this point, 97 (76.3 percent) are children of Professional, Proprietary, or Clerical groups, according to the occupational categories of Professor William F. Ogburn, the so-called 'white-collar' class. Fifty five (44.7 percent) correspondents' fathers were members of a profession. . . ." Rosten concluded that the correspondents came from families which had incomes considerably above those on the average for the country's wage earners as a whole. Out of 127 members of the press corps, 65 (51.1 percent) were college graduates possessing a four-year college degree, and 36 others had attended college but received no degree. There was a goodly sprinkling of Phi Beta Kappas and Rhodes Scholars.[12]

"Scratch a journalist and you find a reformer," Rosten observed. Forty-four of the fathers of his respondents were Republicans, 41 Democrats, and the rest were self-styled independents, liberals, socialists, progressives, radicals, labor, or "no-party." Rosten concluded that the large number of fathers who were nonaffiliates of either major party represented a marked divergence from the general political pattern of the electorate. As for the correspondents themselves, of the 84 returns, 54 of the Washington correspondents supported Roosevelt in early 1936, while the combined vote for all the possible Republican candidates was 26.[13]

It seems likely that the factors in social recruitment analyzed by Rosten have continued to exert at least as much influence on the Washington correspondents as in the past. Probably there is an even heavier incidence today of college and graduate education. Certainly the correspondents continue to be heavily liberal and Democratic. In a follow-up poll of Washington correspondents 25 years later, 32 percent styled themselves Democrats, 10 percent Republicans, and the rest independents. More than 55 percent of the correspondents called themselves liberal, 27 percent conservative.[14] Perhaps the most revealing figure here is the number of correspondents in 1963 who refused to state their affiliation with either of the regular parties but who called themselves liberals or conservatives — mainly the former. My impression from this and other scattered evidence is that a large majority

[12] Leo C. Rosten, *The Washington Correspondents* (New York: Harcourt, Brace and Company, 1937), pp. 153, 156, 159.

[13] *Ibid.*, pp. 157–58, 348.

[14] William B. Dickinson, Jr., "Politicians and the Press," *Editorial Research Reports*, vol. II, no. 9 (Sept. 2, 1964), pp. 658–59.

of the Washington press corps today would identify themselves attitudinally with the moderate elements of either or both of the two regular parties — that is, would generally support the two presidential parties. If this is correct, there exists a community of attitudes and opinions between key members of the press corps and the presidential politicians.

Another factor that strengthens the links between Washington news processers and the presidential parties is the focus of the reporters in their work. In general, news processing is organized around the major decision-making agencies, for the leading press, television, radio and other news-purveying organizations assign men to gather news at these posts. Thus a recent assignment sheet of the Associated Press had eleven reporters assigned to Congress, five to the Supreme Court, eleven to the White House and the major departments and regulatory agencies.[15] This may seem an obvious pattern, but it is well to note what is *not* regularly covered — for example, the Democratic and Republican national chairmen.

The presidential and congressional politicians are not passive objects of news processing. They organize themselves, of course, to project the image of themselves that they want the world to see. The President has his press conference, Congress its House and Senate press, television, and radio galleries, the agencies their sizable information offices. The power of the President to use or manage news through his press conferences or televised messages or stump speeches — above all by making news and being news — has long been noted. But every major policy maker in Washington is trying to adapt news processing to his own purposes. It is not only the White House that goes in for calculated leaks, carefully planned

---

[15] Douglas Cater, *The Fourth Branch of Government* (Boston: Houghton Mifflin Company, 1959), p. 5.

briefings or unattributable "backgrounds," the timing of news releases, trial balloons, strategic denials and the other methods of propaganda. The reporter is submerged in a torrent of documents emanating from all decision-making points, as well as from the headquarters of interest groups represented in Washington.

The President's press conference deserves special note both because of the wide public attention it commands and because the press conference, like so much of the news-making process in Washington, has become heavily institutionalized. Roosevelt ran his press conferences in a highly informal, idiosyncratic, and almost intimate manner. By the time Truman left office, according to Elmer Cornwell, who has made the closest study of the subject, "the highly informal, personalized, almost casual press conference of the past had become an increasingly routinized, institutionalized part of the presidential communications apparatus. Preparation became elaborately formalized, as did the conduct of the meetings themselves in their new setting, with a growing array of electronic aids. Finally, the nature of the meetings as private encounters between the Chief Executive and the newspaper representatives was rapidly changing into a semi-public performance (soon to become completely public) whose transactions were increasingly part of the public record." [16] Under Eisenhower the press conference became increasingly formalized and "staffed out." Kennedy took the inevitable and ultimate step of making the first live telecast of a presidential press conference. Although Kennedy, like the two Roosevelts, preferred informal exchanges with reporters, the press conference had become too much of an epic projection of presidential image and policy to be reconverted to its earlier

[16] Elmer E. Cornwell, Jr., *Presidential Leadership of Public Opinion* (Bloomington: Indiana University Press, 1965), p. 175.

status. Staff preparation increased; the attendance of reporters grew; the President's stance on an elevated stage made him seem more remote from the reporters; he made long opening statements; questions were planted; and many millions of people watched on television. Lyndon Johnson has followed a more informal and less regularized procedure, but it seems likely that the organized, formal press conference has become a permanent part of presidential government.

But the journalists — whether they attend the conference or watch it on television — still report and interpret it in printed form. Cater has aptly called the Washington press establishment the "fourth branch of government" — a useful term if we consider this and the other three branches not as autonomous power centers but as clusters of decision makers intensively interacting with one another — that is, as politicians of various sorts with relations marked by mutual access, reciprocity, bargaining, coalition and competition. Certainly the interaction between press corps and decision makers has assumed a good deal of continuity. Reporters, like politicians, develop lines of access, networks of connections and friends, balance sheets of credits and obligations, along with their usual assignments and responsibilities. For example, a political correspondent will have an old acquaintance in the White House; he will turn to that acquaintance for access to White House information; the acquaintance will in turn use *him* for floating trial balloons, for information, and for journalistic favors. The fact that some columnists have been able to unearth "inside" security information year after year is not due to a peculiar knack at eavesdropping but to an informal but dependable communication channel through which many types of political information and favors flow in both directions.

But again, this is not a random process. Just as the executive establishment, and to some extent the legislative, is characterized by bureaucracy — by elaborate organization, specialization, routine — so is the news processing industry in Washington. Stable relationships develop between parts of these bureaucracies, but not without a partisan or ideological bias. While any judgment must be in part impressionistic, the bulk of the Washington press does seem to be organized around, and to hold a community of attitudes and interests with, the presidential party in power and with the leaders of the out-of-power presidential party. This seeming partiality of influential elements of the Washington press corps for the presidential parties results from the largely similar social origins of the two groups, their ideological community of interest, the organization of their different tasks, and the sheer output of news in the executive branch.

Reporters have even closer relations with the presidential establishment abroad. The information officers of American embassies and consulates in foreign capitals and major cities provide the press with news material, background briefings, and often with facilities for transportation and communication. Foreign correspondents and "stringers" are free to get information where they wish, of course, but under the conditions of foreign reporting, especially outside Europe, they are heavily dependent on American officials. There is no institutional representation of Congress or the opposition party to challenge the announcements or official line of the local Ambassador or other representative of the President. There is no collusion or conspiracy here, but a community of interest and a practical need to cooperate on the part of men who broadly share similar social and economic backgrounds and similar commitments to liberal, internationalist foreign policies.

These tendencies in the Washington press and overseas re-

porting are reinforced by the differences in editorial view-
point of the major newspapers. The old, simple division between Democratic and Republican newspapers has been
breaking down. Many newspapers that earlier had proudly
identified their regular party affiliation have forsaken it in the
last decade or two. The *New York Times,* once Democratic,
is independent. The *Herald Tribune,* once solidly Republican, is now independently Republican. The *Chicago Daily
News* endorsed Republicans in seven straight presidential
elections but then switched to Johnson in 1964. The *Washington Post* has long since rejected formal party affiliation or
support. *Time* and *Life,* magazines born in more recent
times, have never identified formally with a political party.

But all the newspapers listed are in effect supporters of one
or both of the presidential parties. They generally opposed
Taft in 1952 and Goldwater in 1964. They have somewhat
the same relation to the Presidency that the *Times* of London has to the Government: broadly and strongly supportive
over all though critical in details. They not only generally
praise presidential program and policy; they admire and even
venerate the Presidency as an institution. They not only criticize the congressional parties for their conservatism and neg-
ativism but attack the very foundations of congressional party
strength. The *New York Times* and the *Washington Post,* for
example, have long criticized the committee seniority system;
obstructionist devices, and "inequitable" representation
(gerrymandering and other forms of malapportionment)
that shore up the congressional parties.

The congressional parties of course have some media support. The New York *Daily News,* the *Chicago Tribune,* the
Hearst newspapers and numerous smaller newspapers in the
rural towns and small-city areas predictably line up behind

the congressional Democrats and Republicans; these are the papers that dependably denounce presidential "usurpation" and the heavy hand of the "gigantic bureaucracy" in Washington. The congressional parties also benefit from the electronic media. The radio programs regularly subsidized by H. L. Hunt's conservative organization, Facts Forum, emanate from stations heavily concentrated in the South, the Rockies, and the rural Midwest. A host of right-wing publications, some extremist, some evangelical, provide ideological ammunition for the congressional parties.

But the heavy editorial guns are with the presidential parties. This may seem odd, in view of the fact that Presidents are notoriously sensitive to the press, especially to the big-circulation dailies and weeklies. Presidents are rarely agitated by opposition in Congress or in the out-of-power presidential party, but they have been known to explode over even slight criticism in a *Times* column or *Life* report. The paradox is only superficial. It is precisely because these journals *are* basically friendly that censure from them is hard to take. As always, it is easier to withstand the infidels than the heretics.

What can we conclude about the effect of presidential politics — of the presidential politicians, parties, coalitions, voters, and press — on the Presidency? The main effect has been to place the office more firmly in a set of continuing and relatively stable political processes and forces. The party tendencies that seem intensely pluralistic and inchoate turn out to be more durable and coherent when we see the President's power as anchored in his presidential party rather than in the general party. The American ideology may seem hazy and thin, but the President does not interact with some ethereal ideology; he interacts with public attitudes that are shaped by, and are in part channeled through, a visible system of news managing on the part of public officials and private news processers alike. Voting, which at times seems fitful and capricious — especially when it overturns men long in office — shows remarkable continuities in its basic pattern and regularities, especially in elections for President. All these tendencies toward political institutionalization of the Presidency sharpen the question as to whether the President can lead with vigor and imagination — the question to which we now turn.

VI

Collective Leadership

As we near the heart of the problem of the Presidency, a short pause is in order. What perspective have we established on this famous and unique institution? The Presidency was originally established as an unclearly defined and inadequately empowered department in a relatively well planned constitutional structure — a structure that in turn embodied basically Lockean assumptions of the late eighteenth century. Under Washington the office began to gain weight and dignity and — with Hamilton's indispensable aid — executive force. Under Jefferson it acquired for a time a broad ideological direction and a strong political base. Jackson, Lincoln, and other nineteenth century Presidents exploited some of the early precedents and powers, but for about a hundred years after Jackson the power of the President turned largely on contingent developments, such as presidential opportunism and personality and the existence of crisis.

The twentieth century has brought several interrelated developments. As an executive organization the Presidency has become heavily institutionalized. As a political organization it has found in the presidential party a firm and durable base of political power. This base provides the President with assured support; it also stabilizes and somewhat focuses the exercise of his powers. Hence the office is less dependent on personality and crisis for the maintenance of presidential control and leadership. At the same time, as we noted in Chapter

III, expectations of the Presidency on the part of both opinion shapers and the general public seem to have been greatly enhanced. Today presidential power is both magnified and channeled by executive organization, political agencies, and a combination of high expectations and old fears about the office. The Presidency, in short, has been both strengthened and institutionalized.

How much scope, then, is left the President for innovation, new directions, creative leadership? Even though he is at the center of the web of presidential structure and power, is he so checked and stabilized by the forces working through and around him that he cannot free himself for new departures? Is he so anchored in the bureaucratic system that he cannot free himself when he must make a massive effort to reshape the governmental environment within which he works? Is he so responsible and so responsive to his own presidential party and to the parties with which it bargains and coalesces that he cannot realign the political forces and hence cannot find the political support and momentum necessary for achieving new goals? Is the steady "presidential" vote over time so turgid and indispensable and so controlling as to inhibit presidential attempts at new voting alignments that might support new goals and new political strategies? In Isaiah Berlin's terms, can the President extricate himself from the centrifugal forces surrounding the fox and pursue, if need be, the coherent and central vision of the hedgehog?

We ask these questions about the President but they are, of course, relevant to leadership in any large organization. For we are not concerned with mere efficiency. In Selznick's terms, we are interested in the Presidency not simply as an organization — as a rational tool engineered to do certain jobs — but as an institution responding to a social environment and trying to reshape that environment in terms of certain values — in this case, democratic values. We are concerned not with management but with leadership. The problem of leadership, Selznick has said, "is always *to choose key values and to create a social structure that embodies them.*" [1]

So I am referring to presidential leadership here as the function of deliberately bringing about a durable change in existing processes and political and other institutions — that is, in means and in instrumental goals — to bring them more in line with a desired pattern of values, through the purposeful deployment of organizational resources. When I speak of presidential leadership I am not primarily concerned with the relation between the one man who is President and his personal staff or his administrative chiefs or congressional lieutenants. This is an important but separate problem. I am dealing with both the President and the other presidential politicians who, by manipulating certain techniques and resources, can durably affect the political context within which they operate. Hence I am more concerned with collective than "one-man" leadership.

I make a distinction here between leadership and management. Every President, every executive, must deal with more or less routine matters that come along in the business of government. These may be knotty and exacting, but essentially they demand no more than the traditionally prized administrative qualities of judgment, common sense, fairness, accommodation, plus a tinge of skepticism and prudence. In short they require *management*. The prompt processing and disposition of these matters is necessary to the functioning of the

[1] Philip Selznick, *Leadership in Administration* (Evanston, Ill.: Row, Peterson and Company, 1957), p. 60.

presidential office and of government generally. Such management is indispensable to stabilizing the political environment, and indeed the character of this management is shaped by the routine problems delivered to the presidential politicians from the particular environment in which they operate.

Leadership, as I will use the term here, is something else. The main organizational objective is to understand, cope with, and ultimately master the changing political environment, and to reshape it more closely toward desired ends. It is to build new institutions that will be capable of shaping political and other human behavior into patterns legitimized by the ideology of the leadership and of the electorate. Though the leaders must forsake both utopianism and opportunism, the emphasis is on goals rather than methods, on change rather than stability, on context rather than process, on innovation rather than routine, on creativity rather than adaptation. Efficiency, keeping the machine running, the handling of routine problems — these are secondary matters.

There is, of course, no sharp line between management and leadership. Any small act of management can have unexpectedly significant effects; the long-run influence of a multitude of specific administrative actions could have a major cumulative influence on broader events. The test is the leader's *purpose*. The question is whether the decision maker is dealing with an issue in order to isolate it and dispose of it, with the least disturbance to the administrative and political environment, or whether he is dealing with it as a means of altering the environment in the light of basic values. It is the difference between the broker who "morselizes" a problem to adjust it in terms of narrow criteria of efficiency and adjustment, and the leader who seeks to deal with, and even exploit, the issue for broader, more substantive goals.

Implicit in my approach to presidential leadership is the assumption of a social, economic, and ideological context of continuous and pervasive change. This assumption might not always be justified. There have been in the United States — and there might come again — calmer periods when the Presidency was concerned less with innovation and creativity than with the maintenance and enforcement of means and instrumental goals appropriate for traditional values. The test is always the realistic organization of such means and goals for the realization of ultimate values, and this process can be put in a static framework as well as a dynamic one. However, I consider my assumption of flux and change to be relevant to conditions in the United States during the late twentieth century.

The Presidency is a seamless web, so that any attempt to isolate certain functions better to examine them is somewhat artificial. However, since the President manages domestic policy on the basis of somewhat different constitutional powers and in response to somewhat different sets of constituencies than those to which he responds in directing foreign policy, it would be useful to examine in turn his actual and potential leadership in each of these broad areas.

The Lineaments of Leadership

What kinds of political leadership may be open to a President?

The most typical and customary type of leadership is the fashioning of innovations following a change of administration. Even if the new President is of the same party as the old, he is expected to do more than simply administer the same programs more efficiently. He is expected at least in a small way to renovate, to innovate, to take new directions. Neither William Howard Taft nor Herbert Hoover was a rabid innovator, but each felt the need to run the Presidency in a different style from that of his predecessor in the same party. Vice-Presidents succeeding in office have wanted sooner or later to put their own stamp on affairs, even though they were elected on the same ticket with the President, and presumably with the same mandate. Theodore Roosevelt, Harry Truman, Lyndon Johnson, and even Calvin Coolidge wanted to be "President in their own right," and largely succeeded.

It is a change in administration combined with a change in party that would seem to set up a firmer basis for presidential leadership. It is assumed that the voters called for a change (even though careful scrutiny of the voting returns later might throw some doubt on this assumption). If new party leadership takes over in Congress too, as in the case of Eisenhower in 1953, the new executive-legislative "team" is supposed to have a clean slate on which to write new laws. The slate may not really be very clean; the continuities and restrictions of the presidential office may gravely limit the new President; but the popular expectations are there and can be exploited. The popular "mandate" may be exceedingly vague, drawn as it is from an ambiguous party platform and fragmentary, episodic, and sometimes contradictory pronouncements by the candidate. But the very ambiguity of the mandate can widen the arc of the new President's discretion.

Wilson's election was the first party overturn in the new century. Even though he was victor in a three-cornered race and had gained neither an electoral nor popular majority, he enjoyed all the psychological and political benefits of the new broom. Wilson united his party behind his program and won a series of notable legislative victories in the long congressional session of 1912–13. Wilson exercised leadership in the simplest, most direct way. He stated his program, presented it to the public, conferred early and often with his congressional lieutenants and advisers, carefully timed the programming of the measures in Congress, maintained pressure on the leaders and rank and file, soothed hurt feelings, and stood firm behind the principles of his bills while allowing some changes in details. Wilson's performance of 1913–14 has become the classic example of presidential marshaling of support behind a predetermined program.

Dwight Eisenhower entered the Presidency in 1953 after a decisive popular victory and with a Republican Congress. He made some innovations in the office of the Presidency, and he won congressional enactment of some of his proposals, such as the St. Lawrence Seaway, a big highway bill, an antisubversive program, and a tax-revision bill. But even with a Republican Congress Eisenhower had many difficulties and frustrations. Not only did he have to deal with a heavily entrenched Republican congressional party and with Senator Joe McCarthy. He lacked the absolute self-confidence and certain conviction that helped make Wilson so effective in exerting leadership over Congress. And the very nature of his program — essentially a consolidation, modification, and in some respects extension of the New Deal–Fair Deal — did not lend itself to building the kind of momentum that helped carry through Wilson's measures. Leadership even of the simplest kind can never be a mere matter of technique. It is inextricably linked with substance — that is, with the goals of the leader.

Another kind of presidential leadership is the establishment of a precedent in such a way that it becomes a permanent fixture of the presidency. I have noted in Chapter II a number of innovations that came to be an enduring part of the Presidency. Woodrow Wilson's appearance before Congress to press for important measures was so striking an act that later Presidents could but follow suit. But here again innovation or precedent must be related to substance. Eisenhower organized an elaborate White House staff system that had some merit for his way of doing things, but in major respects did not survive his administration. Franklin Roosevelt's establishment of the executive office of the President, on the other hand, came just in time for the defense and war emergencies and became an intrinsic part of the presidential establishment. The press conference developed gradually over the years and has become a permanent arrangement. Presidents may run it in different ways. Franklin Roosevelt conducted his conferences like sprightly seminars, with much off-the-record banter; Eisenhower and Kennedy held full-dress affairs, under television lights; Johnson holds off-the-cuff meetings at odd hours, sometimes literally on the run as he leads panting reporters around the White House grounds. But whatever its form, as we have noted, the press conference is as much a White House fixture as the cabinet meeting.

A third type of presidential leadership is the decisive interpretation of events at a time of crisis when traditional doctrine has been shaken and people are willing to turn to new ideas. I distinguish this condition from the normal state of affairs when a President seeks to draw voters behind his program through the regular methods of education and propaganda. In time of crisis and of skepticism about customary ways of doing things, a President's discretion is enormously increased. With some of the old channels and their markers swept away, he can chart a sharply different course if he wishes. The main example of this situation in this century — perhaps the only striking example — was the economic crisis of 1933. Roosevelt did not have a set program when he entered office; he had little more than a bundle of projects and notions and experiments, some of which would be squeezed out of existence in the press of crisis. What he did have was far more important than any possible set "solution" — a willingness to take charge, a faith in the people, and an acceptance of the responsibility of the federal government to act.

While Roosevelt's symbolic leadership was related to definite, concrete acts of government, his interpretation of the situation, in the broadest sense, was more important than any specific program. For he established then and later that the federal government must and could be accountable for the nation's economic well being. The situation had its ironies, for Roosevelt did not re-establish anything approaching full employment during the 1930's. But he acted with such dramatic effect and éclat that people believed that the depression was over, and that the federal government had done the rescue job. Critics of Roosevelt later contended that he could have used the crisis to adopt a far more radical program — for example, nationalization of the banking system — but this view again misses the central point. Roosevelt accomplished a decisive interpretation of events: he dramatized the role of the federal government so that people would see it not as a remote and passive power but as a force that could salvage them and shape the nation's economy. The more enduring legislation of the "second hundred days" — social security, the Wagner Act, holding company legislation, tax reform — could not have passed unless Roosevelt had shifted the voters' expectations of the federal government.

A fourth type of presidential leadership is harder to achieve than any of the foregoing. This kind of leadership is capable of changing basic goals in mid-passage, by reorganizing the coalition supporting the President. Wilson temporarily accomplished this feat in 1916. He had taken office as leader of a patchwork collection of old Cleveland, anti-silver Democrats, city bosses, Bryan Populists, conservative Southerners, and a few urban, middle-class progressives. After accomplishing some legislative goals that represented the lowest common denominator on which these groups could agree, Wilson faced a kind of ideological and policy bankruptcy. Where would the New Freedom Democrats go from there? Not only did the President himself have psychological and ideological need for a new program, but he faced the specter of 1916, when Republicans might reunite around a generally progressive program that would appeal to labor, northern farmers, women, Negroes, and urban progressives. For a time Wilson seemed unsure of his direction. He opposed a rural credits measure for farmers; refused to back a federal child labor law; avoided taking a stand on woman suffrage; opposed the exemption of labor and farm organizations from the Sherman Antitrust Act. He was slow to support a strong federal trade commission; he favored some regulatory legislation but made some conservative appointments; and he made little effort to rid even his own executive agencies of discrimination against Negroes.

But as the election of 1916 approached, Wilson struck out on a new tack. He reversed himself on the rural credits bill; helped push a workmen's compensation and a child labor bill through Congress; persuaded Congress to pass a bill establishing the eight-hour day for railroad workers; and even favored a cooperative effort by government and the export trade to give some protection to American business overseas — a departure from traditional Democratic party policy. As we have noted, Wilson modernized both the appearance and the policy emphasis of the Democratic party as he directed his appeals to urban progressives, professional groups, and intellectuals.[2]

Wilson was not wholly successful in bringing off a lasting change of direction for his party. He barely won the election of 1916, and would not have won at all if he had not retained strong support from the old Democratic party in the South, the Bourbon Democracy in the Midwest, and the western Populists. His capture of the peace issue was probably more decisive than his recent shift to progressivism. America's entrance into the war, the priority of foreign and military policy, Wilson's central postwar concern with a league of nations, and his own illness and disability prevented him from consolidating progressive support even if he had the desire to do so. But Wilson's brief flirtation with urban progressivism had longer-run effects. He made it easier for a later generation of Democrats under Alfred E. Smith and Franklin Roosevelt to steal some of the old Bull Moosers' thunder and to strengthen the urban base of the Democratic party.

A fifth type of presidential leadership is the most exacting of all. This is the effort not only to reshape the alignment of group interests behind one's party and administration, but to reshape the institutional framework within which the political leader seeks to realize his goals. The former may be a simple shuffling or augmentation of coalition support; the latter kind of leadership seeks a structural change that could have a more lasting influence on the realization of political objec-

---

[2] Arthur S. Link, *Woodrow Wilson and the Progressive Era* (New York: Harper & Row, 1954), p. 225.

tives. Hence it is generally the most goal-oriented of all the types of presidential leadership.

Such leadership is difficult because the very institutional arrangements a leader might wish to change, operate against the feasibility of such change. The Democratic party in 1912 was composed of so many factions, and was so handicapped by rural and southern power in Congress, that one critic called it the organized incapacity of the country. Wilson despaired of realizing his program through such an instrument. He considered the possibility of reconstructing his party and drawing to it liberal-minded independents and Republicans. Following his election he promised a New Jersey audience that he would avoid narrow partisanship and would choose "progressives, and only progressives" for his administration. Presumably he could have used such progressive support to dethrone some of the conservative Old Guard in Congress, just as George Norris and his fellow Republican progressives had toppled Speaker Joe Cannon in 1910.

But Wilson was balked by the very citadel of power that he might have been willing to attack. We have noted that when he told his chief patronage dispenser, Postmaster General Burleson, that he was not going to consult "reactionary or standpat Senators or Representatives" in making appointments, Burleson warned him that such a course would ensure the administration's failure. Burleson's reasoning was significant. "These little offices don't amount to anything," he said. "They are inconsequential. It doesn't amount to a damn who is postmaster at Paducah, Kentucky. But these little offices mean a great deal to the Senators and Representatives in Congress. If it goes out that the President has turned down Representative So and So and Senator So and So it means that that member has got bitter trouble at home. . . . I know these Congressmen and Senators. If they are turned down, they will hate you and will not vote for anything you want. It is human nature. . . ." [3]

This was "practical" advice and Wilson followed it. One reason he carried through his initial legislative program was both his willingness to play politics of the most pragmatic sort with the congressional leadership, and his rather surprising skill at the game. But in deciding to operate through the existing political and congressional mechanism Wilson was making another decision, which could also be "practical" in the long run. He was recognizing, perpetuating, and to some extent legitimizing that machinery. He was consolidating the political strength of the men he dealt with, for the more patronage he gave them, the more political resources they gained for building their personal strength within the party and within the district. And the stronger a politician's personal following in the electorate, the more he can bargain with other politicians from a somewhat independent position of power — the more he can bargain with the President himself.

If reshaping the congressional structure was impossible for the President, what about reorganizing the Democratic party at the grass roots? Wilson had some of the materials necessary for such a reorganization, for groups of progressive or independent Democrats had grown up in several states and were seeking presidential recognition. In New York Colonel Edward M. House, Treasury Secretary William G. McAdoo, and young Franklin D. Roosevelt were among those who hoped to reconstruct the state Democratic party, which long had been

---

[3] From interview with Burleson by R. S. Baker, March 17–19, 1927, Baker Collection, cited by Arthur S. Link, *Wilson: The New Freedom* (Princeton: Princeton University Press, 1956), pp. 158–59.

racked by the struggle between Tammany and the reform independents. But as soon as the independent Democrats sought New York patronage for this purpose, the regular Democrats moved to exploit their own power, especially their power on Capitol Hill. They would not have the "regular" party supplanted by an anti-Tammany, presidential organization. Wilson could have forced the issue, but only at the price of alienating men whose votes he needed on Capitol Hill. So the President backed off.

Here again World War I saved Wilson from the political price that his early recognition of the regular Democrats might have exacted. If he had increasingly shifted his political appeal and Administration program during his second term toward urban reformers, independent Democrats, and progressive Republicans, at some point he presumably would have faced entrenched opposition from Southern Democrats in Congress and their allies in the regular party organizations in the North. Wilson did not reach this point, but Franklin Roosevelt did — and paid the price.

Taking office during a crisis, Roosevelt tried to rise above the old party divisions and to build a coalition out of elements from both parties, from third-party forces, and from labor and farm groups. In 1934 and 1936 he even supported Republican and a number of third-party congressional candidates over regular Democrats. He acted like a kind of master broker of group interests. As the presidential election year of 1936 approached, however, the President shifted to the role of party leader and led the Democrats to their biggest victory in history. He did not, however, desert his nonparty allies; progressives such as Mayor Fiorello La Guardia of New York City, Senators Robert La Follette of Wisconsin and George Norris of Nebraska, and union leaders John L. Lewis and Sid-

ney Hillman formed the Progressive National Committee to
work for Roosevelt, and a nonpartisan Good Neighbor
League was established to organize independents, liberal Republicans, civic leaders and churchmen behind Roosevelt.
The President built a Grand Coalition, but it was a coalition
around himself, not a coalition organized within the Democratic party.

Thus, although Roosevelt campaigned as a militantly liberal Democrat in 1936, his victory could be interpreted as essentially a personal one. In his second Inaugural he painted a
picture of one-third of the nation ill-housed, ill-clad, ill-
nourished, and declared that "the Nation, seeing and understanding the injustice in it, proposes to paint it out. . . ."
But then Roosevelt ran into powerful opposition on Capitol
Hill; he failed in his effort to enlarge the Supreme Court, and
his proposals designed to help the one-third floundered in
Congress. He had never solved the problem of unemployment, and with the recession of 1937–38 the number of job-
less soared again. Faced with obstruction in Congress, Roosevelt embarked on his famous effort to "purge" his opponents
in the Democratic state and congressional primaries of 1938,
as we have noted. It was a hastily improvised, widely misunderstood, and badly organized effort, and it largely failed.

On the face of it Roosevelt's purge seemed to be an exercise
of that rare type of presidential leadership that seeks to
change the structure within which the leader acts. If he had
been able to defeat some of his opponents, Roosevelt could
have proceeded with a further realignment of his party and —
more important — with an effort to reform Congress, just as
he had tried to reorganize the Supreme Court, the executive
branch, and even the Democratic party (by getting rid of the
two-thirds rule in the Democratic national convention). But

this must be an extremely tentative judgment, because it never was quite clear as to the kind of leadership, in this sense, that Roosevelt wished to exert.

In 1932 Roosevelt had said to liberal friends like Rexford G. Tugwell: "We'll have eight years in Washington. By that time there may not be a Democratic party, but there will be a Progressive one." [4] Eight years later there was still a Democratic party, but no progressive one — only progressive fragments, as there had been years before. Although Roosevelt in the last year of his life was still talking about coalescing with progressive, internationally minded Republicans, as we have seen, he never seemed to have it clearly in mind whether he wanted simply a liberalized Democratic party — that is, a realigned party base as described in the fourth type of leadership presented above — or whether he wanted to create an essentially new party out of elements of the old, as the Republicans were able to do in the 1850's. Such a new party would have overcome Southern Democratic power in Congress and would have reformed Congress itself. But building such a party would have called for an effort at creative political leadership of the character of Jefferson's and Madison's party-building in the 1790's or of the creation of the Republican party in the 1850's. Roosevelt, a supreme tactician and a brilliant pragmatist, was not the man to undertake such an effort, and he had a number of good reasons — especially the coming of World War II — why he could not try. So in the end he was captive to the old political forces just as Wilson was. The experience of both Presidents underlines the difficulty of achieving this kind of creative political leadership — but also suggests why even such pragmatic Presidents as Franklin

[4] Rexford G. Tugwell, *The Democratic Roosevelt: A Biography of Franklin D. Roosevelt* (New York: Doubleday & Company, 1957), p. 412.

Roosevelt were in the end not wholly content to work within the going system and at least toyed with ways of shaping political environments in which they felt that they could be more effective.

Foreign Policy Leadership

The Framers of the Constitution planned that the President would have broader powers in shaping and executing foreign policy than domestic. Recognizing the special need for speedy and single-minded executive action, they made it possible for the President to be the main spokesman for the nation and the master of the two key agencies of foreign policy, the diplomatic corps and the armed forces. They granted him in effect complete discretion to recognize or not recognize foreign governments. Constitutional usage has sanctioned even stronger presidential power. While the President under the Constitution shares his treaty-making power with the Senate, he can on his sole discretion make executive agreements with foreign nations, and these agreements, unless overturned by Congress, have virtually the same legal validity as treaties in the eyes of the courts. Even at a time when the Supreme Court was circumscribing the President's authority in domestic affairs it was upholding sweeping presidential authority over foreign relations. In 1936 the court recognized the "very delicate, plenary and exclusive power of the President as the sole organ of the federal government in the field of international relations — a power which does not require as a basis for its exercise an act of Congress, but which, of course, like every other governmental power, must be exercised in subordination to the applicable provisions of the Constitution." [5] The President can make, entirely on his own, statements that may rock every chancellery on earth. He can quietly set in motion various approaches and feelers and trial balloons that could have a profound impact on international relationships. He has the power to react to world events in such a way as to prolong and intensify cold war or to plunge the nation and the world into a nuclear hot war. The power of Congress to make a declaration of war has become hardly more than a formality.

Despite all this, Professor Warren concluded after a study of the President's world leadership in this century, "ironically, in a period when the presidency is at the very peak of its influence, probably nowhere in the world is executive leadership more hemmed in, more limited by political considerations, more vulnerable to pressures from within and without than in the United States. For one, Congress by no means has been relegated to a minor position in foreign policy. Farflung commitments involve the Senate in treaty-making functions, and both Houses in appropriating funds for the vast operational programs overseas. . . . Limitations on presidential power come also from the opposing party, from his own party, from the press, and from various organs of public opinion. All of these make his job the most difficult and complicated balancing act on earth while he tries to lead the nation through global agitations that, beyond his capacity to subdue, he can only try to prevent from erupting disastrously." [6]

5 *United States* v. *Curtiss-Wright Export Corporation,* 299 U.S. 304.
6 Sidney Warren, *The President as World Leader* (Philadelphia: J. B. Lippincott Company, 1964), pp. 431–32.

The seeming paradox of the President's sweeping formal powers over foreign policy and the actual restrictions on him can be resolved in part if we distinguish once again between his powers of management and his capacity for innovation and leadership. Much of the President's daily activity is simply a balancing act. The President's latitude is very narrow. As Sorensen has suggested, he must make choices within narrow limits of permissibility, available resources, time, previous commitments, and available information.[7] On the other hand, over the years a kind of policy machine has evolved to handle — to "manage" — foreign problems and even crises.

A disturbance abroad brings into play a vast and interlocked system of interaction and adjustment. Intelligence streams into the White House security room, the State Department, the Pentagon, the Central Intelligence Agency. Quick consultations take place over the telephone; staffs assemble; conferences are set up. Queries and instructions are flashed to men in the field, to our embassies abroad, to foreign embassies in Washington. Our missions at the United Nations and other international agencies, such as NATO, are alerted and consulted. Within the larger departments background material is worked up, precedents examined, specialists called in, various proposals and solutions canvassed. In an acute crisis, the President can communicate directly with heads of foreign powers.

The Cuban missile crisis in 1962 demonstrated how well the system can work under the most intense pressure. Decisions were made not by a "lonely President" somewhere off in an eyrie but were hammered out day after day by fourteen or fifteen men meeting in the White House or the State De-

[7] Theodore Sorensen, *Decision-Making in the White House* (New York: Columbia University Press, 1963), p. 23.

partment, with the Chief Executive not even present most of the time. The group perfectly exemplified the decision-making processes of the modern Presidency; it was composed of old Eisenhower and Stevenson men and new Kennedy men, of presidential Democrats and Republicans, of White House staff members and representatives from CIA and the State and Defense Departments. The group operated in part through committees and subcommittees. It analyzed Khrushchev's possible strategies, a variety of possible responses from Washington, how Moscow would react to those responses, and how the American people and their government might react to those reactions. Options were kept open on each side so that neither would be forced into a corner. Communications were widened to friends, foes, and neutrals. A presidential speech was drafted, circulated, redrafted. The President talked by telephone with former Presidents Hoover, Truman, and Eisenhower. Congressional leaders were informed, though hardly consulted. The group finally had to recommend a choice between limited and unlimited action. Acting by consensus, it recommended the former, and the President agreed.

A key lesson for "crisis management," according to Harlan Cleveland, an experienced State Department official, is to "widen the community of the concerned." He cites the Cuban missile crisis as an example. "In the hours before President Kennedy unveiled the Cuba scenario in his television speech of October 22, dozens of allies were made privy to our plan of action. While the President was speaking, a formal request for an emergency meeting of the Security Council was delivered to its president. The next morning Secretary Rusk presented to the Organization of American States in emergency meeting a proposal for collective action; and that afternoon the Rio Pact nations decided on a quarantine of Cuba and continued aerial surveillance as minimum first steps. The same afternoon, Ambassador Adlai Stevenson opened in the Security Council the case for the United States. And not until that evening, October 23, did President Kennedy, acting under the Rio Pact, proclaim the quarantine." [8] Further negotiations followed in the United Nations.

Whatever exact pattern consultation will follow, it has one vital effect. A wide variety of persons with different views and perspectives become involved. To consult is to ask advice, and to ask advice is to imply at least some need for consent. Even a Washington official's act of merely informing another office in Washington or a ministry abroad provides a kind of access to decision making that the other party may exploit. Thus this system of communication and adjustment incorporates its own checks and balances. At the very least the system produces delays during which tempers may cool and further communication and adjustment may take place.

This system of clearing and adjusting and conciliating is indispensable for a world of sovereign nations. But it is one that binds the President rather severely. At best he can act only as a master broker, trying to find some common denominator among a host of differing ideological camps, national interests, party attitudes, issue-oriented groups, bureaucratic claims, and policy specialists. Often the President may not have any policy goal of his own; his aim is a compromise, a settlement, a reduction of tensions. He may be as impersonal about the substance of the final compromise, within certain limits, as he is about the settlement of a labor conflict that has

---

[8] Harlan Cleveland, "Crisis Diplomacy," *Foreign Affairs,* vol. 41, no. 4 (July 1963), pp. 639, 645–46. On the Cuba crisis see especially Theodore C. Sorensen, *Kennedy* (New York, Harper & Row, 1965).

been projected into the White House by a threatened nation-wide walkout in a critical industry. Adjustment is an object in itself.

Of a very different order is a President's initiative in the face of a far more generalized, remote, and novel situation. Guidelines are lacking; the flow of intelligence is uncertain or even contradictory; presidential estimates must turn on future contingencies and present imponderables. Yet some kind of action, some kind of decision, seems imperative either because of the likely urgency of the future situation or because the President must take action at the time, when options might be open, rather than wait until choices have been greatly narrowed.

President Truman faced such a situation in the spring of 1947. Britain had informed Washington that her straightened financial resources would compel her to withdraw British forces from Greece and that she could not maintain military power in Turkey. The President concluded after consulting his diplomatic and military advisers that the United States must fill the ensuing Middle Eastern vacuum before the Russians could do so. He asked Congress for $400 million for emergency aid to Greece and Turkey. This action marked a sharp turning point for American foreign policy. Franklin Roosevelt had taken leadership on Lend-Lease policy during World War II, but he had been wary of actions that would commit the United States to heavy postwar involvements in Europe or the Near East. And Truman himself had sought to lessen the nation's financial commitments even to Britain during the early days of his Administration. But now, as Professor Warren has said, the nation was undertaking a comprehensive commitment in anticipation of a very general and future danger. "Henceforth, involvement in world crises, however remote, would be a permanent feature of the country's international relations. Truman added a new dimension to the world leadership of the United States. While the Greek-Turkish aid bill was designed to meet an urgent problem in a concrete manner, its implications extended far beyond the immediate purposes of the measure." [9] Those implications were visible later in the Marshall plan, Point Four, and military actions in Berlin, Korea, and Lebanon.

Looking back we may consider Truman's action logical, natural, and sensible. But at the time there were few principles by which people could test its logic or good sense. The policy was new. It was risky. And it was controversial. Some contended that it was a violation of America's long policy of noninterference in Europe during peacetime. Some deplored the fact that we were giving aid to undemocratic governments. Some denounced the action because it was unilateral and seemed to bypass the United Nations. And some said that such assistance would bankrupt the United States and hence weaken our own military security — especially if such aid were extended to other nations. These notions seemed more or less plausible at the time. Some of them seemed about to be vindicated by history. But they were not. For Truman's action in itself, leading to a huge collective effort stretching ultimately over many years, changed the international environment within which the United States was to seek its world objectives for at least another two decades.

Truman's decision to use the atomic bomb against Japan is another example of taking an epochal step in the face of many imponderables. Truman, Secretary of State James F. Byrnes, and Secretary of War Henry Stimson had to calculate the im-

9 Warren, *op. cit.*, p. 312.

mediate military advantages of using atomic warfare against Japan. Among these were the extent of the shock effect on a nation already jolted by severe air attacks; whether the shock effect would harden Japan's will to resist or weaken it; the likely military and civilian casualties resulting from atomic attack as compared to those that would occur after an invasion using conventional weapons; and above all, the saving of American lives as a result of atomic attack. Then there were the possible secondary effects of dropping the bomb: the immediate reaction of national and world opinion; the prospects of defeating Japan before the Russians became heavily involved; the effect on our other wartime allies; the dire need that would arise after the war of restraining the use of atomic power — putting the genii back into the bottle — and the difficulties of achieving this once one nation had used the bomb for immediate military purposes. And then there were the long-term implications of dropping the bomb: the creation of a precedent that could be used some time by another nation; the atomic arms race that might ensue; the spiral of international suspicion that might blight postwar hopes. Scientists who had worked on the bomb, and who by their own mode of thought were deeply concerned with the remote long-term effects of dropping it, had warned that the military advantages of the bomb and the saving of American lives might be outweighed by the resulting loss of world confidence in the United States and by a "wave of horror and repulsion" sweeping over the rest of the world.

Truman made his decision almost exclusively on the basis of the more immediate, military, and calculable criteria. Dropping the two bombs did help bring about an early Japanese offer to lay down arms; the losses in the two bombings, awful though they were, probably were less than an orthodox invasion would have caused; and Japan gave up at a time when the Americans could exploit their military power in Japan proper in dealing with the Russians. But there were also the longer-term consequences. A feeling of revulsion swept the world; Russian and Chinese communists exploited the unilateral American act for propagandistic purposes; an atomic, and later a nuclear, arms race got under way; and it proved difficult if not impossible to put the genii back into the bottle. Such was a passing verdict twenty years after the event; the verdict one hundred years later might be quite different.

The issue here is not the rightness of Truman's act (or of his later decision to begin the manufacture of nuclear weapons). The question that concerns us is the manner in which Truman made his judgment. As a typically pragmatic American politician he dealt with the tangible features of the situation, the immediately probable results. Inevitably his bias was toward the more short-run and controllable elements of the equation. No matter how compelling the longer-term implications of dropping the bomb might have seemed, they posed such huge imponderables and contingencies that they defied easy calculation. The bias was toward immediate results, short-run implications, calculable sequences of action.

Today we can assess some of the longer-run effects of the decision. Surprise use of the bomb did create a precedent that was available indefinitely to any bellicose member of the growing family of nuclear nations. An atomic and nuclear race did ensue (as it probably would have anyway). Not only the Communists but unilateralist and pacifist groups in friendly and neutral nations had a fine propaganda weapon against the United States. And the fear and hysteria aroused by the bomb's effects and sustained by the development of advanced delivery systems hardened peoples' attitudes and immensely complicated international efforts to control the production and deployment of nuclear weapons.

Yet the earlier presidential decision and the resulting tendencies were not irreversible. In 1963 Kennedy conducted his remarkable effort to achieve a limited test ban treaty with the Russians and other powers. Prospects had seemed especially bleak in the wake of the erection of the Berlin wall and of the stiff encounter — and Soviet withdrawal — in the Cuban missile crisis. Kennedy used all the resources of the Presidency in sounding out the Russians, pressing the negotiations, informing and guiding American public opinion, and pushing the treaty through the Senate. The treaty was only a small step, as Kennedy emphasized. But it was part of what he saw as a long-run and purposeful effort at relaxation of dangers and tensions as a prelude to more comprehensive international efforts to improve economic and political relations among nations.

Roosevelt's Lend-Lease program, Truman's decision on the bomb, Truman's military and foreign aid programs, Kennedy's breakthrough on control of nuclear weapons — these and countless other examples of presidential leadership remind us of the inevitable long-run implications of action and inaction. The most prudent and practical short-run step may widen the alternatives of a later President or drastically narrow them. Dwight Eisenhower's refusal to take any significant step in the face of the long-recognized world population explosion may be seen some day as one of the most crucial acts — or non-acts — of his administration. Long-run calculations may produce catastrophes as a result of overcommitment or poor planning; they may also alter the political context so significantly that future Presidents gain an immensely broadened discretion.

These considerations may throw light on the paradox

noted earlier in this chapter — the fact that presidential power in foreign affairs seems so limited even while it is obviously so wide. Each view is correct; everything depends on what the President is trying to do and by what measures his actions are evaluated. In his efforts at day-to-day adjustments he is severely limited by the ineluctable circumstance that he must operate in a world of sovereign nations and through rather old and cumbersome machinery for foreign policy making and action. In this regard, however, he may enjoy considerable latitude, under the Constitution and under custom, from Congress, the opposition party, and the press. In his long-range planning he may find ways of overcoming international restraints if his proposals — like Point Four — are daring, idealistic, and generous. But in such planning he may run into political obstacles at home, especially from congressional and other conservative forces concerned about excessive political and financial commitments abroad. Often his proposals are both short-run and long-run and hence meet a variety of responses in Congress and in foreign capitols.

All things considered, the President has a vast potential for leadership abroad. The huge bureaucratic and other institutional forces that surround and sometimes frustrate him are also powerful instruments for implementing his decisions. The world of divided peoples is also a world yearning for inspired leadership. The events that seem so intractable, like the emplacement of missiles in Cuba or a raging inflation in Latin America, can also be made to open up grand opportunities. Much depends on the energy, tenacity, and resourcefulness of the central decision makers and presidential politicians — on presidential government. And much depends on the availability and accessibility of new ideas and of the men who produce them.

Intellectuals:
The Arc of Innovation

In a static or highly stable society the policy makers can rely on technicians to administer the status quo. The goals of the society are not in doubt, and innovation can be undertaken on the narrow basis of greater efficiency. But a society undergoing change in its basic valuations turns to the intellectuals to redefine the valuations and to reshape the Administration's or party's goals and the means of realizing them. Not only do intellectuals challenge existing assumptions and hence become useful to men in power, or men seeking power, during times of change; intellectuals also articulate that part of a nation's prevailing and rather inchoate ideology that bears on the problem at hand. For without ideological criteria there cannot be a basis of judging the relevance of new policy, and without new policy there cannot be innovation.

The process may not seem orderly on the surface. A sudden crisis or catastrophe will produce the old refrain, "Something must be done." The technicians can only patch up the machinery that had proved unable to prevent crisis or catastrophe; hence the policy makers turn to the innovators of new methods, new institutions, or new means for realizing broader values. There is a little rush toward ideas. Some that have long been shelved by busy administrators are now dusted off, as the policy makers turn to the intellectual community. The pressure to innovate is even stronger in the party out of power, for new ideas can become both a stick to beat the incumbents with, and sources of policy if the opposition takes over the government. Franklin Roosevelt's brain trusters in 1932 served both these purposes.

The type of innovator needed depends, of course, on the extent and nature of the demands on the policy makers. In a more stable situation a government department or a private corporation may require advisers who can base their innovations on rather narrow criteria — for example, more profit making or greater administrative efficiency. The more intense, radical, and wide-ranging the pressures for new policy, the more the policy makers must turn to men who can conceive policy outside the usual criteria and both rearticulate the policy makers' goals and reshape their methods. The broader and fuzzier the ends, the wider latitude for the intellectuals. Roosevelt's brain trusters could come up with an incredible medley of ideas, many of them mutually contradictory, because Roosevelt's standards of judgment were open and complex and shifting. The range of innovation in the early days of the Kennedy and Johnson administrations was much narrower, though no less fruitful potentially.

Intellectual innovators can be found in the governmental service in Washington or in the field, in law firms and big corporations, in state and local government. But the most imaginative, creative and unmanageable intellectuals are found in universities and foundations, which have the obligation to protect and nourish fresh ideas, experimentation, and dissent. The presidential policy makers have little difficulty in tapping these pools of intellectual talent. Intellectuals like others are available from mixed motives of prestige, conviction, patriotism, duty, or they may respond to the call mainly out of curiosity and a wish to deepen their experience, or in the hope of testing their ideas in action. It is a rare person who can resist that call from the White House or even the State Department or the Pentagon. And as Rapoport has said, "After all, in our society the thinker's time comes cheap." [10]

But there are difficulties. The policy makers may have trouble understanding what kind of innovator they need for the problem at hand; they may have trouble even in defining the problem until the adviser is on the premises. They may not know how to exploit — even to communicate with — the innovator who turns up. The classic picture of the literary fellow hired by Hollywood for his talent, sitting around a studio and feeling isolated and useless while the technicians reprocess his script, has many a parallel in government. And the intellectuals have special disabilities. They may be perfectionists or utopians who will not tolerate the compromises required by a nondoctrinaire, disheveled and illogical politics. They may be dogmatists and moralists who cannot work with practical policy makers or even with other intellectuals. They may be orderly thinkers who cannot adjust themselves temperamentally to the sporadic summonses, the wasted motions, the pre-emptory demands, and above all the long periods of inattention and even hostility in the worlds of the policy makers. Or the intellectual, overly sensitive to the caricature of himself in the minds of many administrators, may lean over backward to accommodate. He may concede so much that he loses his value as an outside adviser. He may become a "promoter of technical remedies," as Kissinger has called him, or at worst a person who merely lends his academic or professional credentials to a scheme already drawn up by the practical men. He may veer too far toward the cult of accommodation and success, or too far toward the cult of

[10] Anatol Rapoport, "Various Meanings of 'Theory,'" *The American Political Science Review,* vol. 52, no. 4 (December 1958), p. 988.

alienation and rejection and even cabalism (that is, the feeling that since somehow he cannot seem to get to the chief, certain people are conspiring to keep him out).

Despite this diversity among the innovators and the various and shifting needs for innovation among the policy makers, somewhat patterned relationships may develop between the presidential policy makers and the intellectuals who are advising them. Various members of the White House staff will develop close and fruitful relationships with innovators in academic, bureaucratic, and corporate circles. The innovators will have special points of access to the President through their allies in the White House and agencies. Some intellectuals will act as brokers for others, interpreting presidential policy making needs to the intellectuals and translating the intellectuals' advice for the benefit of the practical men. Panels and committees and task forces may be assembled to establish a "representative" point of view among the outside advisers. Intellectuals taking an active part in the policy-making process may make concessions for the sake of a unanimous report, so that the policy maker can have the ideas neatly packaged and ticketed.

Kissinger and others have noted the dangers of this kind of relation between intellectual and policy maker. The former may become so enmeshed in the policy process that he loses the advantages of an independent perspective. He may be so eager to cooperate, in order not to appear to be a perfectionist or a hairsplitter, that he makes major concessions. He is usually at the mercy of the men of affairs, who can ignore or contort his advice. "The fact that the need for excellence is constantly invoked is no guarantee that its nature will be understood," Kissinger reminds us. "Excellence is more often thought to consist of the ability to perform the familiar as well as possible than of pushing back the frontiers of knowledge or insight. The search for talent more frequently takes the form of seeking personnel for familiar tasks than of an effort to discover individuals capable of new and not yet imagined types of performance." [11] Inescapably the relation between the intellectual and the presidential policy maker is an uneasy one.

Yet the intellectuals have some advantages. The prestige of their name, their command of information, their access to specialists, their standing with other members of the intellectual community, their ability to recruit the services of others, and most important — one hopes — the substantive value of their contributions give them considerable bargaining power with the brokers of ideas in the government. Intellectuals have constituencies too — in the firms or foundations they work with; the people who read their writings; the scholars who share their discipline, monitor their research methods, and stand ready to condemn their recommendations for excessive concessions to compromise and practicality; the ideological or professional groups for whom they may serve as official or unofficial political spokesmen. And whatever the compulsions toward concessions and expediency in a pragmatic polity, forces are working in the other direction toward purity and principle. In a sense every intellectual is somewhat prisoner to the "man on his left." Every intellectual has some feeling of guilt about the concessions required in serving as an adviser, and hence is all the more sensitive to the guardian of his profession or discipline who in the solitude of his study can articulate his doctrine and flay the compromisers. Hence the intellectual community establishes its own kind of checks and balances in its dealings with the men of affairs.

The relations of intellectuals and presidential policy mak-

11 Henry A. Kissinger, *The Necessity for Choice* (New York: Harper & Brothers, 1961), p. 350.

ers has not always assumed this somewhat patterned form. Some Presidents have relied heavily on one adviser to serve as a contact and clearing house with the intellectuals, as Wilson did on Colonel House. Franklin Roosevelt had a brain trust that was far from a trust — his relations with outside advisers were as fluid and helter skelter as with some of his staff and line officials. He was accessible to men whom other advisers considered to be financial cranks. No adviser was ever sure of his standing with Roosevelt, or of the best channel of access to him, or of the President's expectations of him. Sometimes the President preferred to deal with advisers directly, sometimes through intermediaries. Sometimes several advisers might be working on one problem without knowing of one another's activities. Out of this came a good deal of flexibility, experimentation, and creativity; out of it also came hurt feelings, confusion, blind directions, wasted efforts, and lost motion. The difficulties were especially apparent in economic thinking and policy. Roosevelt turned from adviser to adviser and exploited their ideas, many of which turned out to be fruitful. But the "Roosevelt recession" of 1937–38 indicated the instability of economic recovery under the New Deal and the superficial nature of some of the Administration's approaches to recovery. Roosevelt conferred with John Maynard Keynes but the two men did not achieve an engagement of minds. Keynes was disappointed that Roosevelt was not more literate in economics, and the President could not understand the British economist's "rigmarole of figures." It was significant that they could not come to grips with each other.

Today such a President and such an intellectual probably could engage. The creation of the Council of Economic Advisers itself provided the President with an agency that can mediate between him and the intellectuals, that can locate relevant advice and information and establish communication between intellectuals and all the presidential policy makers. Economists in the universities and foundations and corporations have become used to conferring with the Council, the Treasury, the Federal Reserve, and other key agencies. Statistical and research services have been vastly improved. None of this would be important, however, unless the federal government, under both Democratic and Republican presidential policy makers, had become responsible for ensuring prosperity for the nation. It is the importance and urgency of that commitment that guarantees not only a need for innovation in national economic policy but relatively stable mechanisms for insuring that policy maker and outside economic adviser communicate with each other.

Still, the intellectuals pay a price for their heightened presidential influence. Instead of criticizing and proposing from independent positions, they may temper their proposals to meet presidential needs, offer accommodations rather than innovations, present piecemeal remedies rather than grand alternatives — in short, they may simply adjust themselves to the structure of collective leadership. This assimilation is not a new "treason of the intellectuals," but to the same extent that it may strengthen presidential government it may weaken the opposition and blunt the stimulus of new ideas.

Incrementalism or Presidential Leadership?

Viewed in the above terms, presidential leadership must be collective leadership. "Leadership is not an affair of the individual leader," Bentley said. "It is fundamentally an affair of the group. Pomp and circumstance are but details. Leader-

ship by an individual leader is not even the typical form. It is
only a minor form; or, what comes to the same thing, leadership can most often be given an individual statement only
from certain minor and incidental points of view. The great
phenomena of leadership are phenomena of groups differen-
tiated for the purpose of leading other groups. One specialized group leads certain other groups in a special phase of
their activity. Within it are the phenomena of individual
leadership in various grades." [12] One need not accept all the
implications of Bentley's extreme group theory to grasp the
relevance of his remarks for the nature of leadership under a
system of presidential government. To view presidential politicians and their intellectual advisers in either their group or
their institutional contexts, is to be impressed by the central
role of organized leadership and of directed and channeled
innovation as against capricious personal leadership and itin-
erant ideas.

Now we must return to the distinction between the everyday, routine policy making under presidential government
and the undertaking of planned, significant, and long-run
change. For purposes of theoretical analysis we may call the
former "incrementalism" after Dahl and Lindblom — "A
method of social action that takes existing reality as one alternative and compares the probable gains and losses of closely
related alternatives by making relatively small adjustments in
existing reality, or making larger adjustments about whose
consequences approximately as much is known as about the
consequences of existing reality, or both." [13] Since the consequences of the larger affairs of presidential government are

[12] Arthur F. Bentley, *The Process of Government* (Chicago: University of
Chicago Press, 1908), p. 223. See also ch. 14.

[13] Robert A. Dahl and Charles E. Lindblom, *Politics, Economics, and Welfare* (New York: Harper & Brothers, 1953), p. 82.

usually not easily predictable, we are concerned here mainly about the heavy emphasis on day-to-day, short-range, narrowly focused, piecemeal decision making. This is the way of Berlin's fox.

The implicit goal of incrementalism is adjustment, accommodation, balance, harmony. The incrementalists may be central decision makers, exterior decision makers, or bureaucrats. They may be presidential politicians or congressional party leaders. They may be line administrators or (but less often) academic advisers. Their distinguishing characteristic is their — at least to them — hardheaded, workmanlike management of operational problems. Often they *are* hardheaded and workmanlike and bring off impressive feats of managing the most intricate and multi-sided situations.

Incrementalism is necessary but not adequate in a world undergoing continuous and sometimes rapid change. The more that the incrementalists cope successfully with the daily problem and the weekly crisis, the more they may see immediate adjustment and compromise as ends in themselves, even though the world is changing around them. In a revolutionary period, as Kissinger has said, it is precisely the "practical" man who is most likely to become the prisoner of events. "For what seems most natural to him is most in need of being overcome. It is most frequently the administrator who is unable to transcend the routine which has produced an impasse. For bureaucracies are designed to execute, not to conceive — at least not to conceive radical departures. They operate by a standard of average performance. Their effectiveness depends on the existence of some predictable norms. This confers great impetus when the task is technical or when the direction is known. In an age of upheaval, however, the routine which usually confers momentum generates insecurity.

The standard operating procedure will clash with the requirements of creativity." [14] Central decision makers and presidential politicians can bog down in routine just as bureaucrats can.

The vice of incrementalism is its disposition to emphasize means rather than ends, methods rather than goals — indeed, to find its ends *in* its means. It tends to foster adjustment of ends to means instead of reshaping both means and instrumental ends to fundamental goals in a shifting environment. Utopian leadership is guilty of the opposite vice — overemphasis on long-term ends to such a degree that methods are neglected, the needs of accommodation and adjustment are ignored, and immediate problems are allowed to fester and finally to divert leaders from their broader purposes. Creative leadership, on the other hand, while seeing ends and means as a structure of interrelationships, keeps the long-range goals in mind even as it copes with the day-to-day problems.

Administrators and politicians — especially legislative politicians — are usually made the scapegoats for this excessive tendency toward balance, compromise, and accommodation as ends in themselves. American scholars must share some of the blame, however, for many of them have held the major inarticulate premise that a healthy polity is a stable, balanced one, with its many groups in a happy state of mutual interaction. We cannot, of course, dismiss equilibrium and adjustment as important criteria of a healthy polity but the equally significant criteria of instability, imbalance, and movement have been slighted. Twenty years ago Myrdal noted our excessive emphasis on the notion of the "stable equilibrium," which, he said, had been used as a vehicle for introducing

[14] Henry A. Kissinger, *op. cit.*, p. 356.

hidden valuations into research.[15] This emphasis on norms of balance, stability, and equilibrium have stemmed in part from traditional modes of thought in Western society, and in part from some of the biases implicit in leading conceptual approaches to politics, such as group theory, with its concern for mutual interactions within the group and its treatment of outside forces as "disturbances." In particular the study of leadership has suffered from this tendency. The leader has typically been studied as integrator of the group, as at the "juncture of channels of interaction of the group," as the center of transmission belts, an initiator of cues, a focus of responses; as part of a "complex social function in which different types of leadership roles emerge as responses to different types of group needs."[16] The function and possibilities of large-scale leadership in mobilizing latent opinion as well as responding to existing public opinion in a shifting context has been somewhat slighted.

The failure of intellectuals to deal adequately with the concept of creative leadership has an important bearing on the capacity of leaders to deal with problems in the light of long-run goals. A distinguishing feature of the social theorist is not only his ability to articulate the goals. It is also his capacity to see possibilities for heading off problems before they become crises, for dealing with enlarging difficulties that may seem obscure or remote to the practical man, for intervening in the course of social change at some decisive point.

15 Gunnar Myrdal, *An American Dilemma* (New York: Harper & Row, 1962), pp. 1045–57. I have commented on this problem at greater length in "Group Theory and Leadership Theory: A Convergence?"—a paper delivered at the 1963 annual meeting of the American Political Science Association.

16 Alvin W. Gouldner, *Studies in Leadership* (New York: Harper & Brothers, 1950), Part Two; George C. Homans, *The Human Group* (New York: Harcourt, Brace and Co., 1950), *passim*.

The theorist is supposed to have a professional concern with root causes, with factors affecting social change that lie far back in the sequence of political or other action.

The incrementalist, with his bias toward equilibrium, need only analyze the manifest, measurable variables that immediately precede some kind of action. The theorist, with his concern for the pursuit of long-run goals in a changing society, must inquire into original and long-run forces. Thus to him the fact that most Republicans voted for Dwight Eisenhower in 1952 is a significant fact but not a challenging one; he would want also to examine the deeper economic, social, and ideological sources of Republicanism. The fact that Negroes in small towns in the Black Belt of the South are held tightly in a close social embrace of discrimination is an important fact; the historical sources of that rigid social structure challenge the theorist's ability to probe the reasons for social stability or change. His job, in short, is to press back relentlessly for the deep and pervasive forces that produce the more manifest and understandable variables that in turn directly produce various kinds of visible political behavior. If such a theorist wishes to predict he is in somewhat the same difficulty as the weather forecaster. The latter can usually predict the next day's weather with a fair degree of accuracy because the variables he can deal with are limited in number and have a direct and understandable bearing on the weather just ahead. But to make a successful five-day prediction demands an understanding of an infinite number of variables that may undergo an infinite number of shifting interactions during the intervening period.

The theorist must think in terms of a stream of influencing factors that interact over time. He may give priority to economic or ideological or psychological variables, but the modern social scientist would ordinarily grant that these disparate forces interact with one another, sometimes reinforcing one another, sometimes blocking one another. As he moves back from the immediate event that he is interested in (an event that is in itself part of a continuing stream of social action) the theorist looks for major or minor influences that brought about the existing state of affairs.[17]

This is a strategy of *explanation,* but it also can be a strategy of *action* potentially usable by a policy maker. As Myrdal has said, "The relations established in theoretical research are simply *causal.* In practical research the causal relations are transposed into *purposeful* relations. The sequence in theoretical research — from cause to effect — is in social engineering turned into the reverse order of ends and means. In practical research the causal relations established by theoretical research are taken as facts. Theoretical research is primarily concerned with the *present* situation and the *past* development. It attempts to establish, out of systematized experience of the present and the past, a rational knowledge, in as general terms as possible, of the causal relations between elementary forces in the social process. Its final goal is to be able on this basis to forecast the *future* by rational prognoses. . . ."[18] And to forecast the future implications of various present choices is to equip the practical policy maker with a powerful weapon for bringing about social change.

[17] Cf. the discussion of the "funnel of causality" in Angus Campbell, Philip E. Converse, Warren E. Miller, and Donald E. Stokes, *The American Voter* (New York: John Wiley & Sons, Inc., 1960), pp. 24–37. I have used the concept of the "stream" of causality here because I am interested in all the factors that may produce a general political system or state of affairs at a given time, while the "funnel" concept is designed to schematize the steady exclusion of exogenous factors in order to focus on the variables increasingly relevant to a specific behavior, such as the vote decision.

[18] Myrdal, *op. cit.,* p. 1059.

All this is not to say that the theorist can carry off this kind of analysis very effectively. His own understanding, data, and tools are too limited, and the variables are too many and too complex and too indeterminate in social effect to enable the theorist to contribute much to social engineering. Usually he cannot analyze very far "back," or forecast very far "forward," in the stream of events and influences. But there are two circumstances that might enable the theorist to make a reasonably sound estimate of the future impact of a set of social forces.

The first of these is a situation where the planned mobilization of sufficient social forces can be estimated years in advance to bring about a definite and important social change. The protection and improvement of the lot of the Negro in the United States can be cited here. For at least two centuries Negroes and whites have been advancing single proposals toward that end: slavery, colonization (in the United States, in Latin America, or in Africa), emancipation, segregation, "separate but equal treatment" by government, trade union organization of Negroes (along with whites), economic opportunity (Booker T. Washington), political action, direct action, black Chauvinism, and so on. The striking aspect of all these "solutions" is that they were monistic — that is, they would have formed one variable in the stream of causal forces — and that, when tried, they failed to bring about any kind of prompt and comprehensive improvement in the lot of the American Negro. Any theorist could have predicted this failure if he had been armed with an effective theory of the nature and interrelationship of the major forces affecting the Negro's situation and the intense resistance to change built into the social fabric of the South.[19] By the same token, a the-

[19] Myrdal, *op. cit.*, p. 1067, offers a "theory of cumulation" that on first

orist could have predicted that the natural or planned mobilization of a number of forces simultaneously could have brought about a rapid change. Thus he could have estimated that passage of a comprehensive civil rights bill in 1964, combined with direct action by Negroes, political action by civil rights forces, the combined activities of Negro and Northern churches, general prosperity, the force of national public opinion, and the enactment of a strong anti-poverty program, together would have immensely speeded up social change because of the cumulative effect of these influences. He might not have been able to estimate the influence of any single factor; he *could* see that the predominance of the forces inducing change over the forces reinforcing the status quo would have a predictable effect within a roughly measurable period of time.

The second circumstance enabling a theorist to make a reasonably sound estimate of the future impact of social forces is one in which he can see some single force that at a certain point could in itself alter the balance of social or political forces. I am assuming that in the stream of social forces there are times when the boundaries become narrowed and the forces of change and of resistance to change become so balanced that a strategic and well-timed intervention might be-

---

glance might seem to contradict my thesis here. Assuming, for the sake of simplicity, an initially static state of balanced forces, he says, *"any change in any one of these factors, independent of the way in which it is brought about, will, by the aggregate weight of the cumulative effects running back and forth between them all, start the whole system moving* in one direction or the other as the case may be, with a speed depending upon the original push and the functions of causal interrelation within the system." The italics are Myrdal's, and they obscure his point. For the main thrust of the rest of his argument, and of the substantive findings of his study, is that only the cumulative force of a *substantial* number of major and mutually reinforcing forces (especially ideological) can bring about reasonably rapid change in social relationships and behavior.

come decisive for the future shape of things. The Marshall Plan may have been such an intervention. By itself American economic and military aid perhaps could not have countered Soviet expansionism, but combined with other forces at work in western Europe the Marshall Plan may have been the crucial *governmentally planned* effort that bolstered the economic, social, and ideological strength of the West. A more speculative case is that of Franklin Roosevelt and the political situation during his second term. Following the defeat of his court plan and the advent of economic recession in 1937, Roosevelt faced stalemate in Congress over his recovery and reform measures. The question is whether Roosevelt might have overcome this opposition if he had attempted congressional and fundamental party reform in 1937-38 instead of judicial reform. If he had worked with his liberal majorities in House and Senate to reorganize the congressional committee structure and modernize parliamentary procedure, or if he had devoted time to reorganizing the Democratic party at the grass roots into a more effective liberal party instead of trying the hastily improvised, badly conducted, and abortive "purge" of his congressional foes — so goes the reasoning — he might not only have carried through his own economic programs of 1937-39 but made it possible for later Democratic Presidents to effectuate their programs more broadly and quickly. In attacking Senator Walter George and other conservatives in his party Roosevelt, in his usual pragmatic fashion, was dealing with the visible, identifiable manifestations of a long social process; but precisely because the Southern conservatives *did* have roots in that social force — in the political and social structure of the southern Black Belt — they were able to withstand the opportunistic blows of the President. A theorist would have argued that only by overcoming the sources of Southern obstructionism — for example, the political apathy and disorganization of the low-income whites and of Negroes, the courthouse rings that dominated Southern politics, the restricted right to vote, the absence of liberal organizations — could Roosevelt have had any chance at success in strengthening his own political position, or at least that of his successors. And of course, to the pragmatic Roosevelt, such a theorist would have seemed radical, speculative, unrealistic, utopian — as indeed he might have been, for the forces that the theorist wanted to deal with would have been precisely the forces hardest to measure, even though they were the most important and actually offered the greatest opportunity to the President.

The problem of incrementalism versus leadership and theoretical insight especially relates to the President. For the Presidency is the only force in American society that can operate on such a wide scale, with such speed, and with such force and direction, as to have a significant, measurable and predictable effect on the balance of social forces. Only a President can move as swiftly as Truman did in the face of political deterioration in western Europe. Only a President can mobilize public power along a lengthy line of action, as did Kennedy and Johnson in the civil rights struggles of the 1960's. As Dahl and Lindblom have noted, the President is the main instrument of unified action in our political system[20] — and it might be added, the only one. Only the President, in short, can supply the powerful and sustained kind of collective leadership necessary to affect basic social forces.

All these calculations, however, assume one other vital factor: a set of goals toward which the presidential politicians are working. Leadership is impossible unless the leader is con-

[20] Dahl and Lindblom, *op. cit.*, p. 362.

scious of the direction in which he wishes to take the country. Without such a sense of direction leaders run the risk of becoming mere incrementalists trying to maintain a balance of social forces. It is to the relation of national values and presidential government that we must now turn.

PART THREE

THE TESTING OF PRESIDENTIAL GOVERNMENT

VII

The Presidency and the National Purpose

A NATION may be said to exist only when most of its people share some common set of beliefs, expectations, symbols and ultimate values that together make up a national purpose. This purpose may be plain and positive; it may be obscure and unsettled. It may be defined and trumpeted forth from temple of God or government; or it may lie in "the hearts of the people." It may grow out of the conditions of a society; or it may be imported and imposed on it. And it may be badly formulated. "The history of the formulation of the national purpose, in America as elsewhere," Morgenthau says, "is the story of bad theology and absurd metaphysics, of phony theories and fraudulent science, of crude rationalizations and vulgar delusions of grandeur." [1] But it is there.

It is there because people wish to believe that they are engaged in an undertaking that is somewhat broader and more elevating than the advancement of their specific and individual welfares. There must be some transcendental purpose that gives meaning to their everyday activities, and this purpose can be found in religion or in government or — usually — in some combination thereof. The purposes may be manifold and even mutually contradictory. People can compartmentalize their ideological lives just as they do their personal and political. There may be striking differences in the extent

[1] Hans J. Morgenthau, *The Purpose of American Politics* (New York: Vintage Books, 1964), p. 7.

to which the politically informed and active and the politically less involved can think about politics in an ordered and coherent manner.[2] But there is also a strong tendency, depending in part on the balance of other factors tending toward unity or pluralism, toward general support for the wider, somewhat more elevated valuations.

A nation can exist for some time with a loose, disorganized ideology, in a kind of prolonged intellectual fit of absent-mindedness. But eventually it meets some kind of test, in a foreign threat, perhaps, or domestic dispute, which compels it to re-examine its values, sort them out, and establish some rough kind of priority. And once it has done so, and then has dealt with the crisis in the name of these broader valuations, the ideology has become hardened under fire. Now it serves as a more coherent source of direction for national policy.

The national purpose closely affects the process of social change. Changes in a nation with a loose, inchoate ideology, and no pervasive kind of collective control or guidance, tend to take place atomistically and incrementally. They are generated through decentralized processes, through local institutions, such as state or local governments, business corporations, schools, churches, and labor unions. Men make these changes for purposes that may be discrete and pluralistic. But if a society is to realize its *national* purpose, there must also be some institution through which social change can be directed and related to that purpose. In other nations the Church or Crown or some economic estate might serve this purpose; in the United States the national government is the only institution possessing either the power or the mandate to legitimize the national purpose and to attempt to realize it. And consid-

[2] Herbert McClosky, "Consensus and Ideology in American Politics," *The American Political Science Review*, vol. 58, no. 2 (June 1964), pp. 361–82.

ering the pluralistic forces in Congress and working through it and the restricted political role of the judiciary today, the American Presidency has been the institution best equipped to serve as formulator and symbol of the national purpose. How well have the American Presidents performed in fact?

Now that we have considered somewhat systematically the internal operations of the Presidency, the structure of relationships among the presidential politicians, the balance between incrementalism and innovation, we can return to the question posed about the "Hamiltonian formula" in Chapter I. There I suggested that Hamilton framed a set of public policies that lacked precisely the quality we are concerned with here — a sense of overriding national purpose. He had brilliantly related his means — national governmental power and Federalist party dominancy — to the economic policies he sought, and the economic policies were indeed fundamental to the national economic development that Hamilton prized. But something was missing — the ultimate value by which even a prosperous economy would be tested. What was Hamilton's final end — a "freer" society, a more egalitarian one, a more stable or hierarchical or diversified one, a more secure one internationally?

This failure to relate instrumental goals and ultimate ends was not peculiar to Hamilton; later Presidents and other politicians have governed in the Hamiltonian tradition. The main reason has not been an intellectual failure of the politicians but deep fissures and obscurities in the American ideology itself.

Liberty versus Equality

The two great foundations of the American democratic creed are the concepts of liberty and equality. The two ideas make up a tangled skein that runs through the whole course of American history. Visitors from abroad have been struck by their pervasive force; orators have lived off them; politicians have appealed to them as they have to Flag and Country. They have served as unifying symbols for a varied and volatile people.

Yet from the start a vast confusion has surrounded any operational use of these terms. The very words cried for definition and for application to the actual conditions of men. Liberty from what? Liberty to do what? Equality of what sort? In what areas of life? The relation of the two goals to each other was also unclear. Were they both of equal importance? If so, they must be defined to make them mutually compatible. Or must one have priority? If so, just how would a structure or hierarchy of values be established?

The confusion lay deep in Western political thought. It was possible for theologians and philosophers to read a variety of conceptions of liberty and of equality into the sacred writings, including Scripture. The concept of natural equality was especially murky. Man was conceived by some radical thinkers to have an equal right to liberty and happiness, but whether this was a theoretical right that was to be implemented through its own moral power, or an actual right to be protected by the law of Church or State, was left open. And any theoretical right to equality existed as a distant mirage amid the obvious fact of extreme inequality of condition and opportunity.

Argument over such doctrine was not merely the province of philosophers and academicians. The doctrine was important because it affected the settlement of contests over such practical everyday matters as property. The rights of property under the doctrines of liberty and equality were as ambiguous as the doctrines themselves. It was not clear in John Locke's writings, for example, whether property was an end in itself or an instrumental goal in the attainment of some more intrinsic value. Locke was used later both by democrats who preached egalitarianism and by capitalists who considered the protection of private property (even in vast, corporate form) as the main objective of democratic government.

The ambiguity over the meaning and relation of liberty and equality was reflected in the ideology of the American Revolution. The dominant concept in the Declaration of Independence was that of equality; Jefferson stressed equality even more strongly in his original formulation of the first of the "self-evident" truths: "All men are created equal and from that equal creation they derive rights inherent and unalienable, among which are the preservation of life and liberty and the pursuit of happiness." At the same time, the main political thrust of the Declaration and of the Revolution was toward the concept of liberty *from* — liberty from arbitrary overseas rule, and from oppressive institutions and restrictions at home. It was not that the thinkers and polemecists of the time ignored the great questions of ultimate goals and values; they were keenly alive to them and wrote brilliantly about them. But as Robert McCloskey has commented, "early democratic theory in America was never systematically worked out, so that one will search in vain in the

writings of contemporary spokesmen for a consistent statement of the hierarchy of ideals that has been proposed." [3]

The theoretical confusion helps explain much of the difficulty that both Americans and foreign visitors encountered in
understanding American democracy in the nineteenth century. Here was a society that still prated much of equality
and of liberty but tolerated a system of slavery that bluntly
denied the claims of both. Alexis de Tocqueville grasped the
vital place of the concepts of liberty and equality in American
thought, but he defined the concepts so loosely that he reflected the prevailing confusion rather than resolved it. And
much of the special flavor of American politics in the 1830's
and 1840's — the conversion of philosophical and policy issues
into legal and constitutional argumentation, the lively but
often meaningless marchings and countermarchings of the
two parties, the dramatic battles over issues, such as the bank,
that were marginal to the real social and economic problems
of the country — stemmed in large part from the failure to
pose the issues of freedom and equality in ways that made
dialogue coherent and politics more meaningful.

A nation of expanding frontiers and vast social opportunity
can go on for a long time without resolving ideological ambiguities or contradictions, but events ultimately produce
some kind of test. The first great test for America arose out
of moral repugnance for slavery among some Northerners,
and the fervent support of the institution among most Southern whites. The abolitionists, looking on slavery as a direct
challenge to their beliefs in liberty and equality, wanted drastic action not only to close off slavery from the territories but
eventually to annihilate the institution in the South itself.

[3] Robert G. McCloskey, *American Conservatism in the Age of Enterprise*
(Cambridge: Harvard University Press, 1951), p. 4.

But the war was not to be fought on their terms. In the light of the very ambiguity of attitudes toward equality and liberty in the North — especially equality and liberty for the Negro — Lincoln rallied support for containing slavery and for putting down the South on the ideological basis not of equality but of union and of constitutional processes. His statecraft during the war turned on considerations of military victory and ultimate union, as we have noted, not on moral considerations. Politically he was more concerned with winning and retaining the allegiance of white Northern workers, many of whom feared black competition, than with the possible future support of the freedmen.

With his marvelous grasp of ideas Lincoln himself had noted the confusion over the meaning of liberty: "The world has never had a good definition of the word liberty," he said at the Sanitary Fair in Baltimore in 1864, "and the American people, just now, are in want of one. We all declare for liberty; but in using the same word we do not at all mean the same thing. With some the word liberty may mean for each man to do as he pleases with himself, and the product of his labor; while with others the same word may mean for some men to do as they please with other men, and the product of other men's labor. Here are two, not only different, but incompatible things, called by the same name, liberty. And it follows that each of the things is, by the respective parties, called by two different and incompatible names — liberty and tyranny." [4] Lincoln used the homely example of the shepherd who drives the wolf from the sheep's throat, for which the sheep thanks the shepherd as his liberator, while the wolf

[4] Quoted by Franklin D. Roosevelt, October 23, 1940, from Lincoln's speech at the Sanitary Fair; Samuel I. Rosenman (comp.), *The Public Papers and Addresses of Franklin D. Roosevelt* (New York: Random House, 1938), 1940 Volume, p. 484.

denounces him for the same act, as the destroyer of liberty. But if wolf and shepherd could not agree on a definition of liberty, Lincoln concluded, the people were doing so and were repudiating the "wolf's dictionary."

But were they? The Civil War had illustrated once again how the concepts of liberty and equality could be not only confusing but dangerously disruptive depending on how they were defined. Was liberty the right of a slave to be free from his master or the right of the South to be free from oppressive control by the North? Was equality to be seen as equality between sections or as equality among individuals? To be sure, Southern doctrinaries did not find equality to be a concept easily amenable to their goals. It was necessary to shape a complete theory of inequality, as Calhoun did, to counter Northern abolitionist doctrine. But the notable aspect of the Southern theory was that its tenets could be drawn from many of the same founts — natural law, the Bible, revolutionary thought, Jeffersonian ideas and practice (i.e., his ownership of slaves) — that had supplied doctrine to the abolitionists.

So the crucible of civil war, which might have hardened and purified a doctrine of liberty and equality, failed to do so. The old ambiguities remained. Liberty for whom? — Equality with regard to what? And then in the latter part of the century powerful tendencies in American society reinforced an interpretation of liberty that made it incompatible with any meaningful kind of equality.

This new doctrine treated liberty as an essentially negative quality — as the absence of restraint by government over the rights of property and the conduct of economic activity. The state, an unnatural being at best, must not intervene more than is necessary to protect life and property. The less the government interferes, the more freedom is left for individuals. Government or other organized social efforts (except where conducted by private groups such as corporations) automatically cut down on individual freedom. Hence any effort to intervene in the social order to equalize man's working or living conditions meant the suppression of liberty. Defined in these terms, liberty and equality were at opposite poles; they were flatly incompatible.

This doctrine of liberty against the state did not extend over many decades, but it was powerful while it lasted. It had expounders of no small talent in the Englishman Herbert Spencer and the American William Graham Sumner. It found in the United States almost ideal conditions for growth: a loose governmental system that was unable to withstand the force of individualistic doctrine even if it had had the will; great capitalists like Andrew Carnegie who were as articulate in enunciating the doctrine as they were effective in assuming responsibility for economic development; jurists like Stephen J. Field who stood at the vital connecting points between the expressed needs of the new capitalists and the legal permissiveness of government; and an ideology that, as we have noted, was simply too soft and pasty to deal with this radical assertion of the supremacy of a narrow concept of liberty over the old humanitarian canons of equality.

The political leadership of the day responded to the force and relevance of the new doctrine. Congress served as a kind of legislative marketplace where politicians bid for legislative spoils much as capitalists elsewhere traded in the commodity markets. The Supreme Court, after a short period of resistance, became an instrument not only for striking down state and federal laws that restricted economic freedom but for enunciating judicial doctrine that vindicated and even ennobled the activities of industrialists and financiers. The Presidency became the inert instrument described by Wilson in his earlier studies. It was to be expected that good Republicans such as Benjamin Harrison or William McKinley would fit in smoothly with the prevailing doctrine. The real test would come when the leader of the "opposition party" entered the White House. But Cleveland proved himself as solidly against governmental restriction on individual liberty as Garfield and Harrison. When he used troops to break strikes and vetoed an act to provide seed corn for drought-ridden farmers in the Southwest, Cleveland showed the extent to which both parties had elevated laissez-faire to the apex of their hierarchy of political values.

It was not that protest was lacking in the Gilded Age. Labor organized into the nation-wide Knights of Labor and drew up a formidable program of economic reform and governmental intervention. Farmers gathered in a variety of militant protest groups and finally into an organization powerful enough to capture the nomination of one of the two major parties. There was a good deal of tension and unrest among middle-class and professional people. There were eloquent protestants: Henry George with his attack on poverty; Henry Bellamy with his denunciation of cruel and anarchical competition; Washington Gladden with his Social Gospel; Lester Ward with his teachings against the general irrational distrust of government. But nothing seemed to have much effect against the dominant individualistic ethic of the day. The Knights of Labor collapsed and were superseded by a federation of craft unions that shared the supreme economic preconceptions of the time. The price of Populist victory at the Democratic convention in 1896 was a catastrophic defeat at the polls in November. When the Presidency was transferred in March 1897 from the solidly conservative Cleveland to the equally conservative McKinley, one could wonder whether the Presidency more than any other major institution in American politics was reserved for those leaders who saw the American purpose as the apotheosizing of individual liberty almost to the exclusion of the egalitarian principles embodied in the Declaration of Independence.

Freedom Through Equality

Then, in another relatively short span of time, the antithetical doctrines of liberty and equality were reformulated and reconciled by political leaders and converted into a powerful instrument of social reform and of ideological support for the American Presidency today.

The forces producing attitudinal and political change were many and complex: the accelerated growth of capitalism after the Civil War; the growing urbanization of the nation, with all its implications for collective governmental effort in metropolitan areas; the social unrest of the late nineteenth century that finally produced a series of legislative breakthroughs for social welfare policy during the early decades of the twentieth; the huge expansion of the federal government during two world wars; the decline of the vertical and horizontal mobility that had helped make the individualistic ethic operational in American society; the hungering for political leadership, as we noted in Chapter III, after a period of presidential passivity in the face of economic and social problems. But the triggering element in this great process of change was a sheer matter of caprice — the assassination of President McKinley and the elevation to office of a man of furious energy and broadly humanitarian goals.

Theodore Roosevelt entered the Presidency without a system of principled ideas about the role of government in protecting or expanding liberty and equality. As we noted in Chapter II, he was opportunistic in his policy making and often tended toward a lofty moralism that concealed ideas instead of expressing them. But Roosevelt also had certain qualities that made his Presidency a turning point in the growth of democratic ideas and practice. Growing up with some sense of noblesse oblige, he bridled at some of the more atrocious working and living conditions of the day. Equipped with a sensitive feel for the uses of power, he defended the authority of the federal government against the great business combinations of the day, as in his prosecution of the Northern Securities Company and his confrontation of the mine owners in his arbitration of the coal strike. And he had a shrewd insight into capitalism. He saw that business concentration had risen to a great extent out of the radical libertarianism of the day, and could not be overcome by an effort to re-establish the old conditions of individualism. Government must not pulverize the big corporations, he contended, but subordinate them to the public welfare.

Such doctrine was badly needed from someone of Roosevelt's progressive credentials and national standing, for it was precisely on the definition of individual liberty that the progressive intellectuals and politicians of the day were hamstrung. At the turn of the century many reformers and progressives were clinging to the old individualistic ethic that had grown out of the thought and conditions of an earlier America — the Jeffersonian ethic of individual liberty, small-town morality, and governmental decentralization. This ethic had risen as a weapon against the state, but by the turn of the century it was not the state but the big combinations — the combinations of combinations, as Wilson called them — that seemed to be crushing the "little man" and suppressing his individuality. How to deal with the trusts? The answer seemed to lie in an organization and in a power that was at least equal to private combination: government. But believers in individual liberty had been taught to fear public organization. "One of the ironic problems confronting reformers around the turn of the century," Hofstadter has said, "was that the very activities they pursued in attempting to defend or restore the individualistic values they admired brought them closer to the techniques of organization they feared." [5] Roosevelt helped the reformers resolve this dilemma less through his considered beliefs than his style.

Wilson too was caught in the dilemma. His campaign for the New Freedom in 1912 was at heart an effort to mobilize the little man behind some governmental program to restore the old conditions of free enterprise and individual liberty, and to attack private monopoly rooted in high tariffs, banking combinations, and other forms of special privilege. But the role of government was to be quite narrow. It was to hold business in leash, to fragmentize business power, to abolish privilege. Government was not itself to have a decisive role in expanding men's freedoms. For government too was a form of bigness that was to be feared, even though the people might control it through old democratic forms such as elections and new forms such as the initiative, recall and referendum.

[5] Richard Hofstadter, *The Age of Reform* (New York: Alfred A. Knopf, 1955), pp. 6–7.

Yet under the impact of progressive agitation during his first term, and with an eye to picking up vitally needed Progressive votes for his re-election campaign, Wilson gradually shifted toward a position that would permit more positive federal action. The government could intervene to help improve the conditions of some of the less privileged groups in society. Wilson did not swing very far, and he was always caught between the idea of government action to restore traditional individual liberties and the idea of government action to protect and expand individual opportunity. Re-elected on a program that encompassed some of Roosevelt's progressivism of 1912, Wilson could not follow up on his plans before the nation became involved in World War I. But the war itself demanded enormously expanded economic and social action on the part of government and also demonstrated what men could do collectively through government. By 1918 the President was telling a friend that the world was "going to change rapidly, and I am satisfied that governments will have to do many things which are now left to individuals and corporations" — including the take-over of natural resources such as water power, coal mines, and oil fields.[6] This was a far cry from the Wilson of 1912 who had declared to the New York Press Club: "Liberty has never come from the government. Liberty has always come from the subjects of the government. The history of liberty is a history of resistance. The history of liberty is a history of the limitation of governmental power, not the increase of it. . . ."[7]

[6] Quoted in Hofstadter, *The American Political Tradition, op. cit.,* p. 278. See also James Kerney, *The Political Education of Woodrow Wilson* (New York: Century Company, 1926), pp. 437–38.

[7] John Wells Davidson (ed.), *A Crossroads of Freedom* (New Haven: Yale University Press, 1956), p. 130. Davidson contends that such sentences of Wilson's have been exaggerated in their import from having been taken out

Ideological change in a relatively stable society comes about less through the creation of new and different ideas and symbols than through the investing of old and accepted ideas and symbols with new meanings and applications. On the face of it Herbert Hoover would seem to have been a throwback to the radical individualism of the previous century, for he wrote articulately in favor of laissez-faire, individual liberty, and the rest of the old litany. But Hoover was under the same compulsion that Carnegie and others had faced — to justify his views in terms of the widest possible valuations. As an engineer, moreover, Hoover had seen something of the anarchy, waste, and cruelty of individual liberty carried to an extreme. "Our individualism," he wrote in 1922, "differs from all others because it embraces these great ideals: that while we build our society upon the attainment of the individual, we shall safeguard to every individual an equality of opportunity to take that position in the community to which his intelligence, character, ability, and ambition entitle him; that we keep the social solution free from frozen strata of classes; that we shall stimulate effort of each individual to achievement; . . ." [8] Six years later, in his campaign for the Presidency, Hoover stated that "We, through free and universal education provide the training of the runners; we give to them an equal start; we provide in the government the umpire of fairness in the race. . . ." [9]

This would seem to be unexceptional — more of the usual hosannahs to the American Way. But implicit in Hoover's

of context by Roosevelt and others, but a study of the context does not radically alter the meaning as related to the issue of the affirmative possibilities of government.

[8] Herbert Hoover, *American Individualism* (Garden City, N.Y.: Doubleday, Page and Company, 1922), p. 9.

[9] Quoted in Hofstadter, *The American Political Tradition, op. cit.*, p. 298.

definition of equality of opportunity was a radical idea. If the
nation was really interested in safeguarding equality of opportunity and in stimulating individual effort, and if it was
willing to achieve this through public education — the oldest
and biggest socialized enterprise in America — then what was
the logical end of the process? Once one thinks of equality
not in negative Spencerian terms — the victory to the fleetest
and the devil take the hindmost — but in terms of positive
governmental intervention to protect and augment individual opportunity in order really to equalize conditions, then
what was the limit of governmental intervention? On these
grounds government could intervene to control the health,
housing, nutrition, and even the early social and family environment of the individual in order to maximize his chances
for self-realization.

Still, this radical implication of Hoover's doctrine was a
muted sound in a decade given over to business theories that
elevated the narrowest kind of individual (essentially economic) liberty as its highest ideal.[10] It would take a shattering blow to bring down the edifice of radical individualism
that had developed during the late nineteenth century and
had enjoyed an Indian summer during the 1920's. And that
blow came with the depression and with the elevation of
Franklin Roosevelt to the Presidency.

Much has been made of Roosevelt's intellectual eclecticism,
political opportunism, and mixed policies. Like the first
Roosevelt thirty years before, he entered office without a
settled doctrine of political economy and without a principled set of priorities, but with a recognition of the responsibility of government for acting in the face of economic col-

10 James W. Prothro, *Dollar Decade* (Baton Rouge: Louisiana State University Press, 1954), p. 82.

lapse and human suffering. What is more important than Roosevelt's improvisation as we look back today, however, was his gradual shift of direction toward a radical concept of equality and freedom. In his early years in the White House he seemed to conceive of liberty essentially in old Wilsonian terms — as liberty against arbitrary power, whether private or public. American liberties were essentially those embraced by the Bill of Rights. When conservative organizations such as the Liberty League reiterated the old nineteenth century type of liberalism, he answered that the New Deal was trying to protect the liberty of the common man against corporate greed and callousness. Under the pressure of events, and under the influence of that marvelous school that is the White House, Roosevelt immensely broadened his concept of liberty. As early as 1934 he was taking a somewhat cautious step toward such a redefinition. "In our efforts for recovery we have avoided, on the one hand, the theory that business should and must be taken over into an all-embracing Government," he said in a Fireside Chat that year. "We have avoided, on the other hand, the equally untenable theory that it is an interference with liberty to offer reasonable help when private enterprise is in need of help. The course we have followed fits the American practice of Government, a practice of taking action step by step, of regulating only to meet concrete needs, a practice of courageous recognition of change." And he quoted with approval Lincoln's statement that the "legitimate object of Government is to do for a community of people whatever they need to have done but cannot do at all or cannot do so well for themselves in their separate and individual capacities." [11] Roosevelt's militant inaugural address of 1937, in which he promised to deal with the problems of "one-

11 Rosenman, *op. cit.*, vol. 3, pp. 421–22.

third of a nation ill-housed, ill-clad, ill-nourished," was another major step toward a more positive definition of liberty in a democracy.

Despite the egalitarian thrust of the New Deal policies of the 1930's, it was not until the war period that Roosevelt completed a reformulation of the concept of liberty — now a concept of *freedom* — in a way that would require heavy and comprehensive intervention of government in order to maximize equality of opportunity and positive liberty. By now he was fashioning his final credo of the Four Freedoms, in part as a foil against Adolf Hitler's effort to redefine the concept of freedom to fit his own purposes.[12] And he was projecting this concept on a world-wide basis. The four freedoms, he said in 1942, "are the rights of men of every creed and every race, wherever they live. This is their heritage, long withheld. We of the United Nations have the power and the men and the will at last to assure man's heritage." [13]

Everything depended on giving substance to these generalities and this Roosevelt proceeded to do in his State of the Union message to Congress in January 1944:

> This Republic had its beginning, and grew to its present strength, under the protection of certain inalienable political rights — among them the right of free speech, free press, free worship, trial by jury, freedom from unreasonable searches and seizures. They were our rights to life and liberty.
>
> As our Nation has grown in size and stature, however — as our industrial economy expanded — these political rights proved inadequate to assure us equality in the pursuit of happiness.

[12] James M. Burns, "Roosevelt, Hitler and the Battle of Symbols," *The Antioch Review*, vol. 2, no. 1 (Spring 1942), pp. 407–21.
[13] Rosenman, *op. cit.*, 1942 Volume, pp. 287–88.

We have come to a clear realization of the fact that true individual freedom cannot exist without economic security and independence. "Necessitous men are not free men." People who are hungry and out of a job are the stuff of which dictatorships are made.

In our day these economic truths have become accepted as self-evident. We have accepted, so to speak, a second Bill of Rights under which a new basis of security and prosperity can be established for all — regardless of station, race, or creed.

Among these are:

The right to a useful and remunerative job in the industries or shops or farms or mines of the Nation;

The right to earn enough to provide adequate food and clothing and recreation;

The right of every farmer to raise and sell his products at a return which will give him and his family a decent living;

The right of every businessman, large or small, to trade in an atmosphere of freedom from unfair competition and domination by monopolies at home or abroad;

The right of every family to a decent home;

The right to adequate medical care and the opportunity to achieve and enjoy good health;

The right to adequate protection from the economic fears of old age, sickness, accident, and unemployment;

The right to a good education.[14]

The vital concept here was the indispensable linkage of economic security and equality to individual freedom, under a second Bill of Rights. From Cleveland's definition of liberty as the individual's liberty against the state to Theodore Roosevelt's opportunistic use of government to thwart evil, to Wilson's development of a more positive concept of free-

[14] Rosenman, *op. cit.*, 1944–1945 Volume, pp. 40–41.

dom, to Hoover's redefinition of the conditions of equality, to Roosevelt's reconciliation of liberty and equality — the course had been erratic and the ideas somewhat improvised. But the consequence was definite and of crucial importance to the modern Presidency. The deadly dichotomy between liberty and equality, as defined, had been broken. A concept of American democracy had developed under which the two ideas were not only compatible but mutually fortifying. While the new definition of liberty did not (and probably never could) settle certain questions of priority in the relation with equality, each concept now could make the other more fruitful in practice. This is not a very novel notion today, but it had taken a long time to hammer out its foundations and to make this invigorated and broadened concept of democracy politically acceptable.

But the implication was more than political. It was also philosophical, in that now Americans had the intellectual underpinnings for a straightforward and unassailable rationale for the extension of governmental power and program. Now Americans could regard the relation of freedom and institutional arrangements with a knowing eye. No longer need they swallow the old doctrine that the more government — or for that matter, the more big business or big labor — the less liberty. Everything depended on the extent to which institutional arrangements promoted relationships among persons and groups that maximized meaningful choice, with as little coercion as possible over spontaneity and creativity. Hobhouse had long insisted that collective action need produce neither the enlargement nor the narrowing of restraint, but the reorganization of restraints. Restraining and liberating forces are found in all areas of life, not just in government — found in parents, supervisors, teachers, union leaders, college deans, corporation chiefs, and in personal relationships. A person can be held captive by a possessive parent, by a faithless lover, by a dictatorial boss, as well as by the chief of police or by the local draft board. Government of course could not break down all such restraints — especially the self-imposed ones. But government could regulate unfair restraints by one man or group over another and, more important, by its own actions could enormously expand equality of opportunity and hence collective freedom by egalitarian policies in education, health, fair employment, social welfare, and many other sectors.

And this is precisely what the American government — and especially the American President — has been doing in the years since World War II. It is not necessary to go into detail. We need only remember the Employment Act of 1946 that formally committed the federal government to the economic goals developed during the New Deal; or Harry Truman's success in running on the New Deal issues of positive liberty and equality of opportunity; or the extent to which the presidential Republican party had to accept this doctrine before it could hope to win the Presidency; or the effort of the Eisenhower Administration to continue and expand Fair Deal social welfare programs; or the strong social welfare emphasis of the Kennedy-Johnson administration; or Barry Goldwater's attack on the new concept of liberty and his thorough repudiation in the election of 1964. All this was related to the slow philosophical shift from negative liberty to positive freedom and to the policies and programs of the Roosevelt administration, with one exception domestically. Roosevelt had not been wholly explicit about the postwar role of government in broadening the liberty and equality of the most neglected group of Americans, the Negroes, and this was to be the contribution of later Presidents, notably Harry Truman. The passage of the Civil Rights Act in 1964 was the culmination of a political and philosophical excursion that had stretched over a century of intellectual travail and political lost directions, and then had rediscovered the purpose of American democracy.

The American Purpose Abroad

I have been contending that Presidents in this century have reformulated American values of liberty and equality, long confused in their relation and often considered dichotomous; that these values have converged in the supreme value of freedom *through* equality; and that this convergence has vital implications for the relation today of the American President and the national purpose. Now I shall suggest that a similar convergence has taken place in the relations of ends and means in American foreign policy, with equally important meaning for the Presidency.

If the establishment of a rational relation among assumptions, objectives, and methods has seemed difficult in domestic policy, it has seemed virtually impossible in the conduct of our policies abroad, where we are so subject to the wills of foreign peoples and leaders and the caprices of history. Yet even here men inevitably try to work out priorities of ends and means, however crude and untidy. Van Vorys has formulated a model set of ends-means relationships: (1) ultimate end-interests postulated with a high degree of regularity (utopian images of the international order); (2) proximate end-interests postulated with a high degree of regularity (self-preservation, territorial integrity, military security, subsistence); (3) means-interests regularly pursued (security techniques, economic measures, anti-subversive techniques, etc.); (4) means-interests irregularly pursued (all typical state goals, such as the renunciation of war.)[15] No state could even approximate such a model in establishing priorities, but as Lerche has said, "we would not expect a national policy-maker to endanger an end-interest in order to advance a means-interest." [16] Policy divorced from some overriding purpose becomes empty and meaningless in the long run, just as the pursuit of ends divorced from available means becomes utopian and self-defeating.

To look back on the long history of American foreign policy making is to marvel at the shifting assumptions on which it has been based, the variety of basic goals toward which it was directed, and the wavering and inconsistent doctrines in the name of which it has been executed.

The early period of the Republic is regarded by some historians as a time of high realism in American foreign policy making, as a time when Presidents and Secretaries of State pursued sober, hardheaded policies based on prudent calculations of national interest and relative national power. Hamilton defended this policy with his usual brilliance, and he epitomizes it today. Faith and justice were necessary between nations, he said, but not generosity or benevolence. Between individuals, yes; between nations, no. "Instances of

15 Karl Von Vorys, "The Concept of National Interest," in Vernon Van Dyke (ed.), *Some Approaches and Concepts Used in the Teaching of International Politics* (Iowa City: State University of Iowa, 1957), pp. 49–54, cited in Charles O. Lerche, Jr., *Foreign Policy of the American People* (Englewood Cliffs, N.J.: Prentice-Hall, Inc., 1958), p. 15.
16 *Ibid.*

conferring benefits from kind and benevolent dispositions or feelings toward the person benefited, without any other interest on the part of the person who renders the service, than the pleasure of doing a good action, occur every day among individuals. But among nations they perhaps never occur. It may be affirmed as a general principle, that the predominant motive of good offices from one nation to another, is the interest or advantage of the nation which performs them." [17]

This concept of international relations underlay much of the foreign policy of the young Republic. But there were numerous difficulties. It was a foreign policy better adapted to a struggling young nation intent on following a narrow definition of its own security than for a world power, such as the United States was destined to become. A "realistic" conception of national self-interest was nebulous enough to permit a wide variety of different policies to be followed in its name. Thus realism dictated a balance of power policy in regard to European nations, while the United States flatly contradicted this policy in the War of 1812. But the main weakness of Hamiltonian realism was precisely the crucial failing of the Hamiltonian model: its failure to gear instrumental policies, such as balance of power methods, to ultimate ends. In the long run Americans would demand something more than realism. They looked for a *purpose* that gave meaning to the competition of nations, the striving, the loss of blood and treasure. Hamilton had worked out everything except what ultimately a nation — even an economically well developed nation — was *for*.

Still, the foreign-policy demands of continental expansion

---

[17] "Pacificus," Essay No. IV, July 10, 1793, Henry Cabot Lodge (ed.), *The Works of Alexander Hamilton* (New York: Knickerbocker Press, 1885), vol. IV, p. 464.

gave some immediate meaning and purpose to American foreign policy during the early decades. It was the formation of broader concepts for hemispheric policy that tested the longer-term purpose of the nation. And here again our policies betrayed confusion and discontinuity of policy. The Monroe Doctrine, seemingly so clear and limited a policy, and in some respects the most consistently supported policy, turned out on application to have a dozen meanings. And it rested on an assumption of American national power, whereas in fact it was supported by the British who for their own reasons were eager to keep the European states out of Latin America. The greatest consistency of American foreign policy for decades stemmed, without much acknowledgment, from British strategy and the Royal Navy.

Perhaps it would have been impossible for the new nation to gear its means and instrumental goals to a great national purpose, considering the changing world environment during its first century, the limited scope of action possible for a relatively small power, and the kind of obscurities in the national ideology that we noted earlier in this chapter. But the purpose of American foreign policy seemed even more ambiguous following the first century, and at a time when the international balance of power was relatively stable.

Most peculiar, for a nation that had preached continentalism and anti-imperialism, was our spree of expansionism at the turn of the century. "Before the war," Professor Bemis has noted, "there had not been the slightest demand for the acquisition of the Philippine Islands. The average American could not have told you whether Filipinos were Far Eastern aborigines or a species of tropical nuts. The American people had no more interest in the islands than they have today in Madagascar. At the time of Dewey's victory, President Mc-

Kinley himself had to look them up on the globe; he could not have told their locality, he said, within two thousand miles. But the expansionists of 1898, the new imperialists, the Roosevelts, the Lodges, the Mahans, the exponents of a 'large' policy, knew where the Philippines were, and they soon wanted them for the United States, wanted them as a valorous young swain yearns for the immediate object of his feelings, knowing only the passion of the present and seeing only the more appealing allurements of the hour." [18] And Mc-Kinley later told visiting clergymen puzzled over the disposition of the Philippines, that he walked the floor of the White House night after night "and I am not ashamed to tell you, gentlemen, that I went down on my knees and prayed Almighty God for light and guidance more than one night" [19] — and the Almighty seemed to propose accession of the whole archipelago.

If the expansion of 1898 was a "great aberration," as Bemis suggests, the background of the Open Door policy suggests even more sharply the absence of planning in terms of principle and long-term purpose during these years. The Open Door — the concept of the territorial and administrative integrity of China, with equal access and equal rights for all nations bent on commerce — was long glorified as a master stroke of diplomacy that arose directly from the American tradition of benevolence, fair play, and practical idealism. Actually, as George Kennan has shown, the Open Door had been conceived by the British, was not very relevant to the Chinese situation, and had little practical importance in the end. Nor was it any kind of logically planned effort to express the American purpose abroad. Its origins lay more in chance

---

[18] Samuel Flagg Bemis, *A Diplomatic History of the United States* (New York: Henry Holt and Company, 1950), p. 469.

[19] Quoted in Bemis, *op. cit.*, p. 472.

developments: a fleeting (and for some time unsuccessful) British effort to interest the United States in adhering to the policy; the elevation to Secretary of State of John Hay, who had become interested in the problem probably because of his recent ambassadorial service in London; the happenstance that an Englishman who was second in command of the Chinese Customs Service was concerned that German, Russian, and especially British interests, might take certain steps that would threaten the Service and the financial strength of the Chinese government and that he had an old friend who was close to Secretary Hay. There is no evidence, according to Kennan, that the formula in the note that was dispatched "was given any serious critical study in the United States government or that any effort was made to assess the practical significance it would have when measured against events in China." [20] And Hay himself, only a few months after calling for the upholding of the territorial and administrative integrity of China, tried secretly to acquire a naval coaling station in the Chinese province of Fukien.

Hans Morgenthau has said that there were three choices implicit in the American purpose from the beginning and in the reality of American power as it developed during the first century: acceptance of our continental limits on the basis of an abstentionist and restrictive conception of the American future; territorial expansion beyond our continental limits; a utopian effort to liberate other nations and help them improve their economies and acquire or strengthen democratic forms of government through the use of American influence beyond the continental limits.[21] Within a twenty-year period after the turn of the century the United States repudiated its

20 George F. Kennan, *American Diplomacy 1900–1950* (Chicago: University of Chicago Press, 1951), p. 31.

21 *Op. cit.*, p. 102.

isolationist or insular beginnings, later dallied with the second, expansionism and imperialism, and then plunged into the "Great Crusade" under Wilson. "Our object now, as then," Wilson proclaimed in his war message of April 2, 1917, "is to vindicate the principles of peace and justice in the life of the world as against selfish and autocratic power and to set up amongst the really free and self-governed peoples of the world such a concert of purpose and of action as will henceforth insure the observance of those principles. . . . The world must be made safe for democracy." And Wilson won a martyr's mantle in staking his prestige and political power on a dramatic effort to line up the people of the nation behind his crusade for the League.

The incredible thing about the Great Crusade was not its occurrence but its brevity. By 1920 Harding was taking a mushy stand on the League — or *a* League — and he interpreted his huge majority as a mandate against internationalism. For fifteen years the nation sought to withdraw from the world, except for millenarian gestures such as the Kellogg-Briand Pact. Economic isolationism buttressed the political. Franklin Roosevelt, once a Wilsonian and a firm advocate of the League of Nations during his campaign for the Vice-Presidency in 1920, retreated before the force of the feeling that America had had enough of foreign involvement and of attempts at moral leadership of the world. In the face of aggression in Europe and Asia during the mid-thirties, Congress tried to legislate neutrality, and Roosevelt somewhat reluctantly went along with the effort to institutionalize isolationism.

Once again, under the press of cataclysmic events, the pendulum abruptly swung back. By 1941 the United States was committed to throw its material weight into the defense against the Axis, and once again we were off on a crusade.

Roosevelt tried to evade some of the loftier phrases and promises of Wilson, but he saw the war as far more than a mere effort to protect the national interest narrowly defined. "We are fighting today for security, for progress, and for peace," he said a month after Pearl Harbor, "not only for ourselves but for all men, not only for one generation but for all generations. We are fighting to cleanse the world of ancient evils, ancient ills. Our enemies are guided by brutal cynicism, by unholy contempt for the human race. We are inspired by a faith that goes back through all the years to the first chapter of the Book of Genesis: 'God created man in His own image.' We on our side are striving to be true to that divine heritage. We are fighting, as our fathers have fought, to uphold the doctrine that all men are equal in the sight of God. . . ." [22] And Secretary of State Cordell Hull, a stalwart Wilsonian, went even farther, promising a postwar world based not on power politics but on free trade and economic cooperation. As the Russians counterattacked the Germans and drove westward, Hull spurned a proposal from London that Russia be given a controlling interest in Roumania and Britain in Greece. The creation of zones of influence, Hull said, would sow the seeds of future conflict and impair the authority of the planned international security organization. And on returning from Yalta Roosevelt proclaimed that the Crimean conference spelled "the end of the system of unilateral action, the exclusive alliances, the spheres of influence, the balances of power, and all the other expedients that have been tried for centuries — and have always failed. We propose to substitute for all these, a universal organization in which all peace-loving Nations will finally have a chance to join." [23]

[22] Rosenman, *op. cit.*, 1942 Volume, pp. 41–42.
[23] Rosenman, *Public Papers*, 1944–45 Volume, p. 586.

With the abrupt termination of Lend-Lease and the demo-
bilization of our armed forces following World War II, it
seemed that the United States might be headed toward another of its historic reversals in foreign policy. Soviet expansion in eastern Europe, the rise of a second Communist power
in China, the hysterical reaction of many Americans, ranging
from extreme interventionism to extreme isolationism, the
enthusiastic intercession in Korea followed by popular disil-
lusionment and impatience, the coming to power in 1952 of a
Republican administration that talked grandly of liberation
of captured peoples — all this seemed to constitute a new period of turmoil in which foreign policy would continue to
zigzag indefinitely in response to emotional popular attitudes,
party politics, and economic and ideological pressures, all in
an unstable world setting. Yet something quite different was
happening.

What actually happened amid the hysteria and floundering
was the reaffirmation of a bipartisan policy that slowly took
on an almost unprecedented purposefulness, consistency, and
steadiness.

The hallmark of this policy is an extraordinary flexibility
of means in the pursuit of a relatively well ordered set of national goals. During most of their history the American people and their leaders have tended to substitute means for ends
in conducting their foreign policy. Neutrality, isolationism,
interventionism, internationalism, opposition to spheres of
influence, military build-up on the one hand or disarmament
on the other, hemispheric or regional solidarity, and other
policies for conducting foreign policy have become cardinal
issues over which parties have divided and elections have in
part been fought. The implication of the debate was often
that America must choose cleanly and permanently between

such competing concepts or policies, and that to try to employ seemingly different or antithetical policies at the same time in different parts of the globe revealed a foreign policy of inconsistency and indecision. Foreign policy pundits have often sounded like generals and admirals of yesteryear contending that ground power or sea power was the sole decisive weapon and must be employed at all the crucial points.

Today we employ simultaneously a battery of concepts and policies that would baffle the ideologue of the 1930's or the 1940's. The United States has built up a formidable military establishment, including nuclear weapons, and has made efforts to disarm; has fostered spheres of influence, cordons sanitaires, and buffer zones in some areas while working for regional and hemispheric action on a collective basis elsewhere; has intervened with military power in Korea and Cuba but not in Hungary or the Suez; has acted multilaterally in a host of dangerous international situations and unilaterally in others; has supported free trade in some areas and restrictive policies in others; has given economic and military aid to some nations and not to others; has been neutral in some situations and not in others; has retaliated against provocative incidents in some instances and not in others; has given warm support to the United Nations without being unduly restricted when it wished to act on its own.

Such flexibility of policy making has come to turn, I think, on a far more stable and sophisticated set of assumptions than those that shaped our actions abroad only a couple of decades ago. We have overcome a series of myths: the myth of American omnipotence and the myth first of Soviet incompetence and then of Soviet invincibility; the myth that utopian gestures of ours such as unilateral disarmament will be followed by equally benevolent actions on the part of other powers;

the myth that economic aid and democratic indoctrination automatically influence developing nations toward democratic ways and the myth that they never can; the myth that some one instrument of national policy, such as nuclear weapons or free trade or humanitarianism or ideological warfare or pacifism or international organization or brinksmanship or neutrality or balance of power, will, if pursued long and hard enough, bring about a resolution of our difficulties abroad. We realize that all of these instruments must be used at given times and in given situations, but not one of them is a safe foundation for foreign policy in a complex and changing environment. "We must be willing to face the paradox," Henry Kissinger wrote in 1960, "that we must be dedicated both to military strength and to arms control, to security as well as to negotiation, to assisting the new nations towards freedom and self-respect without accepting their interpretation of all issues." [24] These paradoxes — and many others — are precisely the paradoxes of policy and assumption that we have learned to live with in the 1960's.

This foreign policy of eclectic means and relatively principled ends owes part of its steadiness and consistency to the institutional arrangements that support it: the bipartisan foreign policy procedures of consultation and consensus building that helped both to provide support in Congress for policies backed by the Presidential parties and also to ensure considerable continuity between the Truman and Eisenhower administrations and between the Eisenhower and Kennedy-Johnson administrations; the relatively stable alliances in the Atlantic and the South Pacific that provide an elastic but durable structure of international policy making and action; a

[24] Henry A. Kissinger, *The Necessity for Choice* (New York: Harper & Brothers, 1960), p. 9.

large, professional foreign service that has now had a half century of experience in the management of multi-national programs and projects and in dealing with an enormous variety of foreign problems and crises; and a rise in the maturity, stability, and homogeneity of popular attitudes and moods sustaining bipartisan foreign policies. On this last point Almond has commented, after citing polling data, "Thus it appears that there has been a real stabilization in foreign policy awareness and attention, a broad plateau of appreciation of the continued gravity and salience of international and security problems." [25] The American people have begun to learn how to live patiently and yet purposefully in a world of complexity, a world of grays and shadows rather than black and white.

Both a source of this more purposeful foreign policy, and a reflection of it, is the Presidency itself. The enormous range of the President's responsibilities, representation, and powers abroad; the growth within his Executive Office of foreign policy making machinery; his almost exclusive responsibility for the disposition and employment of nuclear power; his capacity to be prudent (in Berlin, after the erection of the Wall) and his capacity to be bold (as in the missile crisis in Cuba); and his pivotal role in alliance-building — all these have contributed to the stability and continuity of American foreign policy in recent years, just as that stability and continuity in turn have contributed to sustained presidential influence. During recent years the Presidency has proved its absolute indispensability in the long and complex pursuit of peace, just as it has always been indispensable in the successful conduct of war. ". . . Where there is zeal in the search

[25] Gabriel A. Almond, *The American People and Foreign Policy* (New York: Frederick A. Praeger, 1960), p. xxii.

for agreement, refusal to accept initial disappointment as final, a cool and balanced assessment of the risks of agreement against the risks of unlimited competition, and a firm use of the powers of the office," McGeorge Bundy has said, "the Presidency can become . . . an instrument of hope for all men everywhere. . . . [But] There is more in the Presidency than the special powers of the Commander-in-Chief or the special responsibility for pressing the hard cause of disarmament. There is more, too, than a need for understanding of Soviet realities. The Presidency is a powerful element in the strength or weakness of the United Nations, as every Secretary-General has known. The Presidency remains the headquarters of the Great Alliance, as even the most separated of national leaders has recognized. The Presidency is an indispensable stimulus to Progress in the Americas. The Presidency must make the hard choices of commitment that have brought both honor and difficulty, as in Korea in 1950, or in South Viet Nam in 1954. The White House visit and the White House photograph are elements of democratic electioneering not just in the United States, but wherever the name of the American President can bring a cheer. The death of a President men loved has shown how wide this larger constituency is. Allies, neutrals, and even adversaries attend to the Presidency. When the American President shows that he can understand and respect the opinions and hopes of distant nations, when he proves able to represent the interests of his own people without neglecting the interests of others, when in his own person he represents decency, hope, and freedom — then he is strengthened in his duty to be the leader of man's quest for peace in the age of nuclear weapons. . . ." [26]

[26] McGeorge Bundy, "The Presidency and the Peace," *Foreign Affairs*, vol. 42, no. 3 (April 1964), pp. 363–64.

The Convergence of Purpose

What, then, are the goals — what is the national purpose — in pursuit of which these various policies are being so flexibly administered? Here we find a convergence of purpose between our domestic and foreign policies.

In a pluralistic world of separate sovereignties our essential goal continues, of course, to be the national interest. It is in our definition of the necessary conditions of the national interest that our domestic and foreign purposes have converged. Just as we redefined and united the twin values of freedom and equality at home, so we have done abroad. Our concept of a world in which our national interest can most effectively be protected is a world of free nations characterized by a growing equality of condition both within nations and between nations. This is not a goal we are prepared to fight and die for, but a goal to which our diplomatic, military and foreign policies are directed. We are willing to help nations improve and equalize the living conditions of their people and to develop more democratic or at least representative institutions. We are willing to help protect such nations from aggression from outside. And we are willing to share on a massive basis the material abundance and industrial technique and equipment of our own nation.

I do not contend that these are tightly ordered objectives and rigidly adhered to; or that the best means are always adopted to reach them; or that we do not make serious blunders of the order of the U–2 incident or the Bay of Pigs. Nor do I argue that this national policy of protecting national security by fostering equality and freedom abroad is a good policy for all time. I do suggest that foreign and domestic policy have converged between these twin and now inseparable goals.

The reasons for the convergence are several-fold. During World War II — the great dividing line of foreign policy in this century — the very nature of the Nazi enemy compelled the United States to proclaim objectives of freedom and equality abroad as well as at home. Since in the long run the conduct of foreign and domestic policy is inseparable, the Democratic party could hardly deny the assumptions and goals in its foreign policy that it was stressing in its policies at home. The much touted "revolution of rising expectations" in the developing nations has demanded a humanitarian emphasis in American social and economic policy abroad. And there has been a significant change in the electoral and attitudinal bases of internationalist and interventionist foreign policies. For decades the South was a bastion of internationalism, sending to Washington representatives such as Cordell Hull. In recent years, while old isolationist sections of the Midwest seem to have become more internationalist, the South has been moving toward economic isolationism. Lerche has found a shift toward unilateralism in foreign policy on the part of Southern congressmen, especially during the 1950's. While opposite tendencies are also at work, he expects that the South's effect on congressional action in foreign policy matters will "continue on balance to be a disruptive one, at least for the next several national administrations. Unilateralism, tending steadily toward ideological militancy, will speak for a major sector of Southern opinion and will for much of the time succeed in throwing Southern multilaterialism on the defensive." [27]

[27] Charles O. Lerche, Jr., *The Uncertain South* (Chicago: Quadrangle Books, 1964), p. 290.

Thus, partly as a result of the hardened conservative attitudes arising from the struggle over race relations, there has occurred in the South a convergence of sentiment opposed to the social welfare state at home and to redistributionist economic policies abroad. This "convergence of conservatism" in the South has in turn helped polarize the tendencies toward a convergence of liberal ideas of freedom and equality in most other parts of the country.

This trend in the South also helped precipitate the most dramatic challenge so far in this century to the growing national consensus over the meaning of freedom and equality.

VIII

The Embattled Presidency

THE NOMINATION of Barry Goldwater for President in 1964 was a clear challenge to the deepening national purpose expressed in our bipartisan foreign policies and in our domestic policies of freedom through equality. As a strategist the Arizona Senator saw the relation of means and end. He not only attacked the general direction and specific policies of the Roosevelt-Truman-Eisenhower-Kennedy-Johnson Presidencies. He also attacked the mechanisms — the big federal executive department headed by a powerful President — through which the national purpose was largely being achieved. As Louis Koenig has said, Goldwater in a real sense was running against the Presidency rather than for it.

The Republican nominee chastised believers in a strong Presidency for holding a "totalitarian philosophy that the end justifies the means." He espoused pure Madisonianism. "What, then, is the best distribution of power for our society?" the Senator demanded. "Our answer to this question has traditionally been a *balance* of power among the various parts of the society. . . . I submit that this balance is being upset today by the trend toward increasing concentration of power in the Presidency. . . . *The more complete and concentrated executive power becomes, the greater will be the temptation to employ it to wipe out all opposing power. . . .*" [1]

[1] Barry Goldwater, "Powers of the Presidency," *Yale Political*, vol. 3, no. 1 (Fall 1964), p. 18.

Goldwater's defeat was a historic validation both of the interlaced purpose of American domestic and foreign policy and of the role of the Presidency in achieving that purpose. But that defeat did not of course end the 175-year-old debate about the powers of the office. The Presidency never has been a neutral office and never can be, for the hopes and interests of multitudes have been too much part of it. Huge constituencies at home and abroad achieve representation through it, while other interests find it less responsive to their appeals and proddings. Individual Presidents have tried sometimes to lift themselves and their office out of the ruck of routine politics and individual or group concern. They have failed because the office is political in every sense of the word, and being political must affect men's interests.

It is not only the "strong" Presidency that is biased against some interests and in favor of others. A weak Presidency can decisively affect the answer to the famous question of who gets what, when and how in American — and now in world — politics. It was the weakness of the Presidency, not its strength, that helped put us into our most unsuccessful military effort, the War of 1812. It was not Buchanan's grasping for power but his effort to evade responsibility that had a critical effect on the nation's wavering course toward civil war. It was Hoover's failure to comprehend the power and responsibilities of the Presidency that hardened the grip of the depression on the nation and shaped the direction of national politics for at least a generation. It was Eisenhower's failure to exploit his opportunities as party chief that may well have given John Kennedy and Lyndon Johnson their narrow margin of victory in 1960, and that same failure was a partial cause of Goldwater's capture of the Republican nomination in 1964 and the crushing Republican defeat later that year.

Nor is the bias of the Presidency corrected by the tendencies toward institutionalization and collective decision making that we have noted in the last three chapters. The forces that influence the President as an individual — his electoral sensitivity to urban, national origin, labor, low-income Americans, his exposure to leaders and interests outside the nation, and his special concern for his place in history combined with his knowledge of the basis of historians' judgments — all these factors pervade his administration as a whole. Exterior decision makers and other officials may operate independently of the President, and even act contrary to his views, but the general direction of presidential government is the direction of the President.

From Jefferson's misgivings on hearing of the proposed new office, to the Republicans' attacks on the monarchical Washington, to Clay's protests against Jackson, to the Democratic censure of Lincoln, to the denunciations of the strong Presidents in this century, to Barry Goldwater's admonitions on the Presidency in 1964 — the long cry of outrage over executive power runs through our whole history. "The President carries on the government," one critic thundered in the Senate, "all the rest are but subcontractors. Sir, whatever *name* we give him we have but one executive officer. A Briareus sits in the center of our system, and with his hundred hands, touches everything, moves everything, controls everything. I ask, Sir, is this republicanism? Is this legal responsibility?" [2] This question happened to be asked by Daniel Webster; it was asked before and has been repeated since; and as long as such questions are asked, the Presidency as an institution will be in a state of battle.

[2] Quoted in Wilfred E. Binkley, *President and Congress* (New York: Alfred A. Knopf, 1947), p. 81.

Many of the attacks against the Presidency have grown out of interests and attitudes that have been neglected or rejected by the President in the ordinary course of affairs. These do not need detain us here. But three charges against the Presidency have deep roots in American traditions and ideas:

1. Executive power in general, and the Presidency in particular, are a threat to individual liberty.

2. The Presidency as an institution misrepresents the American electorate.

3. An unworthy man — a demagogue or an incompetent — may be elected to the Presidency, with incalculable dangers to the nation and the world because of the huge enhancement of presidential power.

The President and Individual Liberty

Deep in the tradition of Western man is a tendency to equate the loss of individual liberty with the expansion of government, and to equate the threatening forces of government with the executive. Centuries of suppression of liberties by absolute and not-so-absolute monarchs and princes have left a heavy imprint on the modern mind. "The history of tyranny," Professor Patterson wrote in 1947, "is primarily a record of executive despotism which has generally taken place at the expense of legislative and judicial agencies either by their coercion or by their abolition. The history of liberty therefore, is essentially an account of man's struggles against executive tyranny. . . . Liberty and democracy are the products of legislative assemblies. It is no accident that liberty and democracy were born on British soil where legislative control of the executive was first established. . . . Executive authority by virtue of its inherent centralized and absolute character is incompatible with democracy. . . ." [3]

Politicians have been even more agitated than academics. "The 'executive establishment,'" according to Senator Gordon Allott of Colorado, "is not just the President, but a monstrosity that has grown, theoretically under his direction. It is as arrogant as it is power hungry. It is as self confident as it is contemptuous of the good sense of the American people. Its goal is to force a retreat from liberty by creating an atmosphere of impatience. In such an atmosphere, progress often is mere velocity. And action, not wisdom, becomes a status symbol. . . ." [4]

The Framers of the Constitution knew better than this; harsh experience and long reflection and study had taught them that suppression of liberties could come from any branch of the government, including the judicial and legislative, and hence they devised a constitution with devices for holding all three branches in check. But the Framers too had a special fear of the executive. One of them noted in the convention that executive power had a tendency to increase, and another feared that the proposed President was headed toward monarchy, and an especially dangerous form of monarchy — an elective one. The more republican-minded took the strongest stand, outside the convention as well as within. Jefferson feared the potential power of the new President, especially in the absence of a bill of rights. He wanted the new charter to provide clearly, "and without the aid of soph-

[3] C. Perry Patterson, *Presidential Government in the United States* (Chapel Hill: University of North Carolina Press, 1947), p. 39.
[4] New York *Herald Tribune*, March 7, 1964.

ism, for freedom of religion, freedom of the press, protection
against standing armies, restriction of monopolies, the eter-
nal and unremitting force of the habeas corpus laws, and
trials by jury in all matters of fact triable by the laws of the
land and not by the laws of nations." [5] It is precisely Jefferson's definition of the problem that interests us here: a strong
Presidential office hostile to individual liberty (defined as the
civil and political liberties now set forth mainly in our Bill of
Rights).

What has happened is precisely the opposite of what Jefferson and his fellow Republicans feared. The powerful modern Presidency has in fact become the most effective single
protector of individual liberty in our governmental system.
To heighten the paradox, recent Presidents who had the very
means of oppression that the republicans feared — a huge centralized military establishment and a far-flung federal law enforcement agency — have protected civil liberty far more
than they have restricted it. And the very libertarians who
feared a strong President in the 1780's — Jefferson and Adams
— actually did override political liberties as Presidents.
Adams, always sensitive to criticism, denounced demagogues
who fomented political animosity. He helped arouse the
public feeling that produced the adoption of the Alien and
Sedition Acts, which authorized the President to deport undesirable aliens and made it a crime to criticize the government
or its officials. Under these measures about twenty-five persons were arrested and ten jailed or fined for criticizing President Adams.

The fact that Jefferson, the libertarian, won the Presidency
in 1800 partly because of the reaction to the Federalists' Alien

[5] Jefferson to Madison, Dec. 20, 1787, in *Library of the World's Best Literature* (New York: R. S. Peale and J. A. Hill, 1897), vol. XIV, p. 8253.

and Sedition laws makes Jefferson's behavior in office even more mystifying today. As President he spoke eloquently of the liberties of the people, just as he had in earlier days. Thus in his second Inaugural he declared: "If there be any among us who would wish to dissolve this Union or to change its republican form, let them stand undisturbed as monuments of the safety with which error of opinion may be tolerated where reason is left free to combat it." But in fact he failed to back up this noble concept. He opposed federal interference with the right of a free press, but he easily tolerated — indeed encouraged — state interference. In enforcing the embargo, he violated such specific and ancient a right as that against the quartering of troops in the people's homes. Upset by the excesses of the "tory press," he wrote the governor of Pennsylvania that he had long thought "that a few prosecutions of the most prominent offenders would have a wholesome effect in restoring the integrity of the presses." [6] According to Leonard Levy, who has studied this "darker" side of Jefferson, these inconsistencies reflected "the fact he had no systematic and consistent philosophy of freedom. . . . He had not . . . thought through the tough and perplexing problems posed by liberty: the conditions for its survival and promotion; the types of liberty and conflicts between them; the validity of various legal tests for measuring the scope of liberty or its permissible area of operation; and the competing claims of other values." [7]

The irony deepens with Lincoln. Brought up in the Whig tradition, he had inveighed against executive power while a member of Congress. But no President overrode constitu-

---

[6] Jefferson to McKean, Feb. 19, 1803, in Ford, *op. cit.*, vol. VIII, pp. 218–19.
[7] Leonard W. Levy, *Jefferson & Civil Liberties* (Cambridge: Belknap Press, 1963), pp. 170–71.

tional liberties as sweepingly as the Civil War President. The ancient right of habeas corpus was suspended wholesale. All persons "discouraging enlistments, resisting militia drafts, or persons discouraging military drafts or guilty of any disloyal practice affording aid and comfort to the rebels" were subject to martial law and liable to trial and punishment by court martial or military tribunal.[8] He allowed his subordinates to indulge in sporadic efforts to censor the mails and even arrest and detain editors. There were thousands of arbitrary arrests, many followed by long drawn out trials. Lincoln had the excuse that the North was fighting for its existence. "I felt . . ." he said, "that measures otherwise unconstitutional might become lawful by becoming indispensable to the preservation of the Constitution through the preservation of the nation."[9] Yet he established precedents that could be exploited in less critical times.

Most of the late nineteenth century Presidents had the virtue of their defects: just as they generally opposed governmental interference in economic affairs they also generally shunned interference with mens' political rights, except perhaps when it came to anarchists, radicals, and fomentors of labor strikes. The real test would come when the nation was again plunged into war.

Wilson is another anomaly. He had been raised in an intellectual tradition of political liberty even stronger than Lincoln's: in the nineteenth century liberal heritage of free speech, press, and religion, due process, and protection against arbitrary action by government. Yet he seemed little disposed to fight for this tradition, at least during wartime.

8 James D. Richardson, *Messages and Papers of the Presidents, 1789–1897* (Washington, D.C.: Bureau of National Literature, 1897), vol. VI, pp. 98, 99.
9 Nicolay and Hay, *Complete Works of Abraham Lincoln* (Lincoln Memorial University, 1894), vol. X, p. 66.

Oddly, he seemed to have a fatalistic view of the plight of liberty once hostilities were under way. A week before the United States entered World War I he told Frank Cobb of the *New York World:* "Once lead this people into war, and they'll forget there ever was such a thing as tolerance. To fight you must be brutal and ruthless and the spirit of ruthless brutality will enter into the very fibre of our national life, infecting Congress, the courts, the policeman on the beat, the man in the street." Wilson thought, according to Cobb, that the Constitution would not survive the war; that free speech and the right of assembly would go; that a nation could not put its strength into a war and keep its head level — it had never been done.[10]

Was this a self-fulfilling prophecy? During the war the federal government indicted almost two thousand persons under the extraordinary Espionage Act of 1917, almost half of whom were convicted. The Justice Department officially sponsored the American Protective League, which had enrolled a quarter million members by the end of the war. The League, according to Roche, "was nothing less than a government-sponsored lynch mob which proudly took the law into its own hands in summary and brutal fashion. Its specialty was not arrest and trial in courts duly appointed for that purpose; it specialized in direct prophylaxis: tar and feathers, beatings, and flag-kissing." [11] Concerned over the mob-rule tendencies of the League, Wilson asked his Attorney General, A. Mitchell Palmer, if it should not be curbed, but Palmer stood his ground and Wilson did not pursue the matter.

Contrast with this Roosevelt's concern for civil liberties during War II. Things could have been much the same, for

[10] Quoted in Horace C. Peterson and Gilbert C. Fite, *Opponents of War, 1917–1918* (Madison: University of Wisconsin Press, 1957), p. 11.

[11] John P. Roche, *The Quest for the Dream* (New York: Macmillan Company, 1963), pp. 43–44.

national origin and racial feeling in the country were still sharp, and once again we faced German aggression, this time under a savage regime. But there were relatively few criminal prosecutions compared to the first war; only one periodical (Father Coughlin's *Social Justice*) was suppressed; and Roosevelt and his Attorney General, Francis Biddle, would not tolerate any executive campaign for ideological conformity. There was one gaping exception — the forced evacuation of over 100,000 Japanese-Americans from their West Coast homes, on the grounds of military necessity. Otherwise the Roosevelt administration not only refused to go in for organized suppression of liberty, but took the initiative, through the Office of War Information and other agencies, to combat racial, ethnic, and religious prejudice, and to vivify the "First Freedom" — freedom of speech.

Why this difference between World War I and II? Certainly not because of divergences in Wilson's and Roosevelt's ideological backgrounds; they both shared nineteenth century beliefs in political liberty. The difference, I think, was more institutional than personal. By the 1930's and 1940's the Presidency had become sensitive to the political power of groups that had been socially and economically disadvantaged, and to liberal intellectuals who took a militant stand on civil liberties. Presidential policymakers during World War II could not forget the fact that an earlier administration had a blemished record in history because of its passivity during the war in protecting civil liberties, and because of its excesses during the Palmer raids after the war. The very nature of the enemy in World War II — especially his vaunted suppression of individual liberties and minority rights — made it both possible and necessary to defend civil liberty in this country.

That presidential protection of civil liberties had become

essentially institutional rather than personal was further indicated by Harry Truman's administration. There was very little in Truman's background, as compared with Wilson's and
Roosevelt's, to suggest that he would become a champion of
individual rights. And he too presided over a war — a small
and intense hot war in Korea and a long cold war — that
might have inflamed vigilante groups to crack down on unpopular minorities. Yet Truman vetoed the Internal Security Act of 1950 as a "mockery of the Bill of Rights and of our
claims to stand for freedom in the world." He established a
loyalty program for federal personnel but he required the
government to establish reasonable grounds for belief in a
person's disloyalty. Privately in the White House, and publicly before such skeptical groups as the American Legion, he
contended that "real Americanism" meant that freedom of
speech and religion must be protected, that "a man who is
accused of a crime shall be considered innocent until he has
been proved guilty" and that "people are not to be penalized
and prosecuted for exercising their Constitutional liberties." [12]

Above all it was Truman's understanding of the potential
role of the *President* that helped establish the responsibility
of presidential government for the protection of civil liberty.
Referring to the irrational anti-Communist fears that dominated American politics during his years in office, Truman
said later: ". . . The office of the presidency is the one office
to which all the people turn when they are beset by fears like
these. It is to the President that they look to say a firm 'No' to
those who wish to destroy others through fear and innu-
endo." [13]

[12] Speech dedicating the headquarters of the American Legion, Washington,
D.C., *New York Times,* August 15, 1951, p. 12.
[13] *New York Times,* May 9, 1954, p. 54.

Roosevelt, Truman, and the later Presidents established presidential responsibility not only for restraining the federal government from unduly curbing civil liberty, but also for reaching outside the government and taking a positive approach to the strengthening of civil liberties in other public and in private sectors. The President can no longer profess neutrality when state governments or powerful private groups threaten the Bill of Rights. He does not dare to be silent. Even Eisenhower, usually restrained in his statements, denounced the "book burners" directly and Senator Joe Mc-Carthy by indirection. Institutionally also the Presidency has the power to broaden or narrow liberty, through the Justice Department, the Post Office, and the State Department (as in the issuance of passports). The character of his appointments — a Biddle rather than a Palmer — can be decisive. The kind of private citizen he honors, the kind of committee he sets up, the kind of staff man he appoints, the kind of telephone call he puts in at a critical moment, the kind of speech he delivers in a crucial hour — all these reflect the power of the Presidency in affirming the guarantees of the Bill of Rights. "Where once presidential involvement with constitutional rights was brief and intermittent," Longaker says, "it is now direct, inevitable, and enduring." [14] It will, I think, survive any incumbent who might show less concern. The Presidency has come to be a major institutional protection of the civil liberties of Americans.

The contrast with Congress is significant. Individual Senators such as the two Robert La Follettes, father and son, and Robert A. Taft were valiant supporters of civil liberties. But institutionally Congress has become a source of threats to individual liberty. It is not accidental that the Senate should

[14] Richard P. Longaker, *The Presidency and Individual Liberties* (Ithaca: Cornell University Press, 1961), p. 3.

have become the permissive arena for Joe McCarthy's assaults on innocent Americans (until near the end, when the Senate censured him on non–civil liberties grounds), or that the House of Representatives should have made its committee on un-American activities a permanent committee consistently reflecting the attitudes of Martin Dies, J. Parnell Thomas, and their ilk. One does not need to undertake statistical comparison or elaborate research to see the institutional forces in Congress — the power of the demagogue and his immunity from public feeling, the privileged position of investigating committees, the small-town ethic that once idealized but now seems to have turned against the idea of liberty "for the thought we hate," the coalitions between congressional Democrats and congressional Republicans that have supported the forays against the Bill of Rights.

The fact is that in this nation the historic relation of legislature and executive to individual liberty has simply been reversed. "Although there is abundant evidence in recent years of the misuse of executive power," Longaker concluded after a careful study, "the essential genius of the American Presidency has made it a liberating rather than constricting force in the American scheme of constitutionalism." [15] A committee of Congress, appointed in 1789 to consider the proper formal title for the President, recommended that he be addressed as "His Highness, the President of the United States of America, and Protector of Their Liberties." This long and somewhat royal title was not very popular, but recent Presidents, through the "essential genius of the Presidency," have given that title to themselves and to their office.

[15] Longaker, *op. cit.*, p. 232.

Is Presidential Government Representative?

An assumption on which the Framers established our constitutional system was that Congress, and especially the House of Representatives, would act as the great representative institution, and that the President and the courts served somewhat different, though not necessarily less important, purposes. "What is the principle of representation?" asked William Paterson in the Convention of 1787. "It is an expedient by which an assembly of certain individuals chosen by the people is substituted in place of the inconvenient meeting of the people themselves." [16] The President, who was to be indirectly elected, was not set up to be "representative" in this sense. But as the President came to be party leader and popular spokesman, and as the presidential electoral system was changed, the President came to take on a highly representative function. In this century it has become customary to refer to the Presidency as the "people's office." Yet just who the "people" are is left undefined. And the question as to "representative of *what*" is also left unanswered.

Those who consider Congress "representative" and the President "unrepresentative" often share the old concept of Paterson and others — the concept that a multitude of representatives elected from small districts can express the peoples' wishes and meet their needs more effectively than one elected representative in the Presidency. But to hold this view is to

[16] Quoted in Max Farrand (ed.), *Records of the Federal Convention of 1787* (New Haven: Yale University Press, 1937), vol. I, p. 561.

share the prevailing confusion over the meanings of representation.

There is the false view, to begin with, that an effective representative system can produce in government a mirrorlike reflection of the great varieties of interests in the constituencies — that the elected legislator can literally re-present the voters, and that the legislators collectively simply substitute for the people. This is impossible. To begin with, the voter cannot accurately compute his own interests and communicate them to the representative. The voter has too many interests, marginal and secondary as well as primary and vital, to present to the legislator for the re-presenting. Even if the legislator by some miracle — or through some computer — were able to reflect the myriad interests within each of his constituents and hence the stupendous aggregation of interests throughout his whole constituency, he would not know what to do. He is but one of hundreds of legislators in his state capitol or in Congress. He could not by any political or mechanical device "plug in" the myriad interests of his constituency into the even vaster array of interests reflected throughout the whole assembly, in such a way as to obtain exact representation in the actions of the whole legislature.

Even if all this were possible, the legislator would still be stymied. Even if somehow he could recognize all the interests, he could not respond to them impartially. He speaks for a political party, for various interests, for a majority or a minority, perhaps for past and future interests as well as present. He must calculate not only his constituency's interests but his own. Of course he does the best he can, in a rough sort of way. Certain of the interests in his district will be more visible and influential, and he can combine with other legislators representing somewhat similar interests back home. But even so there will be enormous distortion of the real interests of the voters. The mirror is at best a badly cracked one.

All this is to presuppose, moreover, that careful identification and slavish reflection of the constituents' interests is the representative's objective. But he may not be operating on any such theory of direct democracy. Many congressmen claim that they base their voting decisions on their independent judgment rather than on party loyalty, constituents' views, or other considerations.[17] They do not want to act as the carefully circumscribed agent who tries to read his constituency's mind and then express it. They want to express their own minds, as informed men who are far closer to the nation's problems. The best way that they can truly represent their constituents, in short, is *not* to sacrifice to them their unbiased opinions, mature judgment, and enlightened conscience, as Edmund Burke pleaded in his famous address to the electors of Bristol.

It is clear that "mirror" representation is impossible and may well be undesirable. Whom, then, *should* the representative represent? And how should he represent them? To these questions political science gives no final answer, because the modes of representation turn on questions of goals and values.[18] Direct representation, indirection representation, "virtual" representation, functional representation, majority rule, minority rights, "direct democracy" through the initiative, referendum, and recall — these and many other theories, procedures, and institutions have been tried (none of them, it might be added, with any magical results). There are theories, too, of *non*-representation — for example, the theory that

17 L. E. Gleeck, "96 Congressmen Make Up Their Minds," *Public Opinion Quarterly*, vol. XXI (February 1945), pp. 105–14.
18 Charles E. Gilbert, "Operative Doctrines of Representation," *The American Political Science Review*, vol. LVII, no. 3 (Sept. 1963), pp. 604–18.

the political leader must represent the past and the future, as well as the present, that ultimately he is responsible to history — which leaves the representative a large discretion indeed.

If the theory of representation is shot through with obscurities and contradictions, and with the most challenging questions as to the relation of individual interests and the political process,[19] the *practice* of representation in a democracy is not so difficult. In practice we have worked out a relatively simple system: the representative is elected as a result of winning a majority or plurality of the votes in his district, whether local, state, or national. To win office he obviously had to be acceptable to that plurality or majority, but in office he has a relatively free hand until the next election, when he again presents himself to the people. The constituents exert control over their representative not by directly participating in the governmental decision-making process but by delegating that function to him (except in a number of states where voters can act directly through the initiative and referendum). He has discretion to cater to them or to ignore them, but he must face them in another election if he wishes to stay in office — a motive that is evident in most politicians.

Viewed in these terms, congressional representation takes on no special legitimacy as compared with presidential. Each officeholder must simply work out his own mixture of responsiveness or nonresponsiveness to varying interests in his constituency. There is no structural or institutional or theoretical reason why the representation of a "single" broader constituency by the President is necessarily better or worse than the representation of many "separate" constituencies by

[19] See, for example, Anthony Downs, *An Economic Theory of Democracy* (New York: Harper & Brothers, 1957), and James M. Buchanan and Gordon Tullock, *The Calculus of Consent* (Ann Arbor: University of Michigan Press, 1962).

several hundred legislators. Some distortion is inevitable in either arrangement, and the question of the good or evil of either form of distortion simply leads one back to varying value judgments.

Still, critics of presidential government as unrepresentative advance two special arguments: first, that the President, in trying to respond to some kind of totality or collectivity, cannot give individual voters the special attention and help and recognition that they want; second, that the electoral college badly distorts presidential representation.

The special role of the congressman in catering to his constituents' special needs has long been a byword in American government. Anyone who has seen a congressional office in action will recognize this role. But the argument as to the contrast with the President should not be pressed too far. The presidential office also receives countless letters from individuals; also replies, sometimes under the President's name; and through the bureaucracy takes care of literally millions of special requests. Often the congressional office expedites the process for a particular constituent, but it is the executive office and bureaucracy that actually handles the requests for passports, social security adjustments, home leaves, rural mail service, and the like. In this sense the federal bureaucracy is probably the most elaborately and sensitively representative institution that we have.

As for the electoral college, this is an old object of disapproval. The argument is that the big states, under the winner-take-all arrangement, force the presidential candidates to cater to the big organized minorities — the labor, ethnic, racial, and religious groups — that politicians feel hold the balance of power in those states. Practically this means, according to the argument, that both presidential candidates make unwarranted pledges to labor and other liberal organizations, and that both presidential parties make sweeping and unjustified promises on social welfare and regulatory policy — in short, they both become too liberal.

This argument might have been important in earlier times when there was some polarization between a small number of big industrial states and the more rural states. But the spread of urbanization and suburbanization throughout large sectors of the nation has partly solved this problem. The main reason that presidential candidates cater to the "urban masses" or to the "organized big-city groups" is simply that these masses or groups have such heavy voting power in so many of the states. Presidential candidates would cater to these elements whether the electoral college existed or not. To be sure, there may be some residue of distortion, but this is relatively small compared with the bias of congressional districts in a rural and conservative direction as a result of deliberate or natural gerrymandering. Actually, with the urbanization of the country, and with the eventual effects of the Supreme Court's decisions on apportionment, there will probably be a long-run tendency toward a diminution of both these counterbalancing distortions and toward a greater coincidence of the presidential and congressional constituencies.

To answer the critics who consider the presidency unrepresentative is not necessarily to defend the representativeness of that office. My effort here has been only to rebut those who contend that by its *very nature* a single executive form of representation is necessarily inferior to the kind of representation achieved through several hundred legislators. The case for presidential representation cannot be presented except on the basis of the values one seeks to serve. Nor can the question of presidential representation be separated from other qualities — responsibility, effectiveness, leadership, and the like — that may also represent instrumental goals for the polity. All these goals — and the processes and institutions to serve them — will be considered together in the last chapter of this book.

Why Great Men Are Chosen President

Bryce wrote his famous essay on the Presidency at the nadir of presidential quality and impact — before the century of the two Roosevelts, Wilson, and other "great" Presidents. He wrote long enough after the times of Jefferson, Jackson, and even Lincoln for those figures to have receded into history and to seem exceptional. As we look at Presidents in this century we might ask whether it is time for another essay, "Why Great Men *Are* Chosen President," or perhaps better, why the presidential election process and the Presidency itself bring out the potentially great in men.

Only one President in this century bears out Lord Bryce's fears, Warren G. Harding, and perhaps one of these days some iconoclastic young historian or political scientist will reassess Harding and astonish the world by promoting him a few notches in the historians' pantheon of Presidents. Some of the other so-called "weak" Presidents in this century had considerable strength and tenacity and purposefulness. William Howard Taft was a man of huge abilities whose place in history has been clouded by the somewhat fortuitous events of 1912. Coolidge and Hoover also suffered from the hindsight of historians, but Coolidge had real political abilities and

Hoover striking intellectual and executive ones. I am not trying to restore these figures, but certainly they are far removed from the Harding type.

Even more important is the evident impact of the Presidency on the incumbent. Four Vice-Presidents in this century have gone on to the Presidency: Theodore Roosevelt, Calvin Coolidge, Harry Truman, and Lyndon Johnson. All four passed the acid test of winning a term on their own. At least two of them rank as among the great or near-great Presidents. I do not propose to resurrect the "Gabriel over the White House" theory of the Presidency, or contend that the White House exercises a kind of magic over the incumbent or invests him with divine power. But we do have ample indication by now that the Presidency, with its built-in educational processes, its spacious view of the world, its command of talent, and above all its self-conscious historic role, does work its way on the man in the Oval Office.

Is it a string of good luck that has elevated potentially great men to the Presidency? Or does our selection process have something to do with the generally impressive results? That process — from presidential primaries and state conventions to the national conventions to the fall campaign — has come in for a great deal of criticism. The empty slogans and tired war cries of the spring presidential primaries; the preposterous claims before each primary election and the elaborate rationalizations afterwards; the frenzied attention to local problems in New Hampshire or Wisconsin or California at the expense of fresh and creative proposals on national problems — this and the rest of the confused and sometimes zany process has often bored and depressed us. Above all, the scramble by celebrated men such as Adlai Stevenson or Nelson Rockefeller to grab a few hands in a drugstore or address a dozen people in a café has affronted our idea of how we should choose a man fit for the power and majesty of the White House. The conventions have come in for criticism too; they have seemed rigged by back-room politicians and swayed by phony demonstrations. And the fall presidential campaigns have been criticized as too long, too expensive, and too subject to the distortions and caprices of the electoral college. Is all this really the way to choose great men for the Presidency?

Our system for choosing Presidents is almost ideal, it seems to me, and certainly preferable to the major alternatives that have been proposed, such as a single nation-wide presidential primary.

The seeming disorder of the present presidential primary system reflects a great virtue — its openness. Presidential aspirants who otherwise might be closed out by party leaders can use the primaries as a way to demonstrate their popular appeal. In 1960 John Kennedy was cut off from two key centers of Democratic party power: the old presidential Democratic party leadership headed by Truman, and the Senate Democratic leadership under Lyndon B. Johnson. Kennedy outflanked these power centers by invading the primaries. Estes Kefauver also used this access route; such tactics may not always bring victory in the end, but at least the candidates have a chance to show their mettle.

Another virtue of the presidential primaries is that they favor the more broadly representative candidates. The aspirant must test his standing with a variety of interests, sections, and ideologies. He can demonstrate his strength in urban and suburban areas such as New Jersey, big states such as California and Illinois, eastern seaboard states like New Hampshire, western states like Oregon, farm states like Nebraska and South Dakota. The states with presidential primaries are, mainly by coincidence, a fairly good cross section of the whole country, aside from the Mountain area.

The seeming confusion of the many different types of primaries is actually a virtue. The different types of primaries subject the candidates to varying kinds of election machinery, shifting sets of competitors, diverse ranges of popular attitudes and voter participation. Some primaries are in effect "sudden death" contests between two men, as was that between Kennedy and Hubert Humphrey in West Virginia in 1960; others are less conclusive. Some primaries allow only party regulars to vote; others permit independents to take part, and even members of the opposition party. In 1964, for example, the New Hampshire primary was a wide open popularity contest that enabled voters to write in the name of Henry Cabot Lodge, who was 10,000 miles away. The Wisconsin primary required aspiring delegates to indicate their presidential preferences; Illinois delegates were not able to offer their preferences on the ballot; the Oregon ballot listed the name of every widely recognized presidential possibility, whether he liked it or not. Other primaries provided other permutations and combinations.

The main argument for the presidential selection process is that it tests men for the very qualities they must display in the White House. No selection machinery is guaranteed to produce great Presidents, but the system should measure a man against the specific demands of the job he seeks. The American Presidency is widely recognized as "the toughest job on earth." The selection process is exacting and it should be. If the primaries and the conventions and the fall campaigns are exhausting and nerve-wracking, so is the crisis-ridden Presidency.

Stripped to its essentials, the Presidency requires two cardinal political skills: the ability to appeal directly to mass publics, at home or abroad, and the ability to negotiate with rival leaders holding independent bases of power. A President must be both preacher and politician. Obviously he must know how to reach and inform and arouse popular feeling in his own country; magnetic and articulate Presidents like Wilson, the two Roosevelts, and Kennedy have known also how to stir tremendous responses abroad.

The presidential primaries test a candidate's ability to enter a political situation a long way from his home base, to sense the voters' needs and attitudes, and to win support even against local favorite sons. Kennedy did all this in 1960 when he overcame a formidable local vote-getter in Oregon, Senator Wayne Morse. Candidates must give a convincing demonstration of their popular appeal if they wish to make any inroads in the primaries. Less obvious — because it is a much less visible part of the nomination process — is the way in which our presidential selection process measures the second great talent that a politician must display — negotiating with rival leaders. Only a third of the states hold presidential primaries for the selecting and directing of their delegates. Most of the states choose convention delegates in party conventions and committees, often with little attempt to discern the preferences of the party rank and file. The delegation is often dominated by leading officeholders, such as the Governor or a Senator, or by a coalition of leaders.

The candidate must employ all the arts of persuasion, conciliation, gentle threat, and virtuous temptation in dealing with these men. For the state leaders hold most of the political cards. They can court other candidates; make promises that may or may not be kept; indulge in the fine art of political bluff; yield on some matters (e.g., delegates) and not on others; maneuver and compromise — just as foreign leaders do. The presidential aspirant indulges in all these arts too. The result is often a political trade in the form of implicit understandings and expectations. Thus in 1932 James A. Farley made with John N. Garner of Texas a classic deal — actually an implicit understanding — that later helped put Roosevelt across at a critical point in the Democratic convention.

This is not a closed-off game wholly controlled by the political leaders and insiders. It all takes place in a political context of ultimate popular control. Even a state party leader who runs his delegation "lock, stock and barrel" knows that some day he and his fellow leaders must face the voters in some election, and hence he cannot cavalierly reject a popular national candidate. Nor are the states with presidential primaries free of influence from party leaders. In some primary states these leaders control the outcome of the presidential primaries far in advance by arranging one "official" slate that often meets no opposition in the primary. Typically a state offers a complex combination of leadership control and rank-and-file expression.

And such a mixed situation supplies the acid test of a candidate's presidential quality. For here he confronts a political situation that will face him time and again in the White House, whether he is dealing with a Senator, House committee chairman, Southern governor, or foreign leader. The President must analyze, calculate, bargain, and negotiate, always with the ultimate possibility — at least outside the Communist countries — of some kind of direct popular appeal. The President must face the toughest questions: How much power does the rival leader have? What kind of opposition does the rival face in his own bailiwick? Can he come through on either his threats or his promises? How much is bluff? Can his local leaders be defected?

The presidential candidate, in short, must deal not merely with one political leader or with the rank and file; he must deal with the whole structure of leadership and followership in a state, just as a President must do in dealing with a foreign nation. This superb training system for statesmen comes to a grand climax at the presidential nominating convention, when the candidate calls in all his political credits under the rapt gaze of the nation. Much has been made of boss-controlled conventions, but actually the candidate must deal not only with heads of state "machines" but with subleaders, factions, and scores of individual delegates — just as he would have to deal as President with a highly pluralistic nation and a fragmented world.

The presidential campaign is a training ground not only for a future President but for his entourage. Under the intense pressures of the campaign the candidate builds close relations of loyalty and understanding with his staff. Together they establish the state foundations for the President's personal organization across the nation. Indeed, the institutionalization of the President's staff actually begins during the campaign period. The communications lines, points of access, and debts and obligations that are built up or channeled through the campaign staff are reflected later in the organization and political operations of the presidential office. The presidential campaign forces the staff to deal with an enormous variety of politicians, journalists, policy advisers, interest group leaders, party fat cats, and political camp followers, free lancers, and prima donnas; all these experiences and contacts are indispensable later on. Education in a campaign may be nasty, brutish, and short; it is no less valuable for a staff that must deal with the political world in which a President operates.

Kennedy's tremendous effort of 1957–1960 may come to stand as the prototype of the presidential nomination campaign of the future, at least in the out-of-power party. Kennedy made his decision early; planned his tactics carefully; negotiated with party leaders at the same time that he cultivated his personal popularity with the voters; built a brilliant campaign staff with such men as Theodore Sorensen, Stephen Smith, Kenneth O'Donnell, and his own brothers; raised a big campaign chest; and fashioned so complex and versatile a personal organization that he could operate on many fronts at the same time. He carried every primary he chose to contest, and won support in every leader-dominated delegation where he chose to fight — a virtuoso performance that foretold much of Kennedy's capacity as President and one that presidential aspirants will be restudying with awe for some time to come.

The crowning glory of the whole system is the fall campaign. Walt Whitman said that he knew "nothing grander, better exercise, better digestion, more positive proof of the past, the triumphant result of faith in human kind, than a well contested American election," and the system has probably improved in time. In the short span of ten or twelve weeks, under the closest scrutiny of the press, the candidates must mount a vast political enterprise, pose and reinterpret their party platforms, link their campaign tightly or loosely with those of hundreds of other candidates, and try to bring the whole effort to a grand climax just before election day. The candidate must aim appeals at special interests without alienating more general ones; hew to the party line without seeming to be overly partisan; appear forthright but not extremist, specific but not tedious, explicit but not overly committed; he must engage his opponent without being overly dominated by him.

A national election is the supreme expression of democracy, a time of direct, deep, and uninhibited sharing by the people in the nation's decision making, a time when we tolerate the confusion and the clowning and the vulgarity because the people's voice in the end rises above all this and registers their collective wisdom and aspirations. Our presidential elections have met the harshest tests of history, operating triumphantly amid depressions, hot wars and cold, domestic strife. They ruthlessly cast aside the aspirants who cannot organize a large campaign organization, who cannot bargain with other leaders, who cannot appeal to the mass of voters, who cannot spell out their programs, who cannot hold their tempers and keep their sense of humor. The whole presidential selection system is almost ideally suited for the selection of men who *can* become great in the White House.

The Alleged Perils
of the Presidency

Not long ago I received a letter from a Chicagoan who had seen me defend President Kennedy in a television discussion. He wrote:

It is a great tragedy that our young people in seeking higher learning should be taught by men of your caliber.

You took the position that president of the U.S. should dictate to Congress. You took the position before a national audience that the president was the dominant factor in our form

of government and that congress should be subservient to
him.

Every school child knows that the president is the chief administrator of the federal system — that he can propose laws
but that congress alone can pass them. . . . He is an executive, not a legislator.

You showed an appalling bias in favor of the powers of the
president knowing full well that you lied in what you said.

A professor in a college should stick to facts and not what
he thinks. It is obvious that you believe the constitution of
this nation is outmoded. Either that or you are being well
paid to promote the Kennedy image of greatness before he
was great or became great. . . . In any case you are totally
unfit to be a professor of history in any college. . . .

I would suggest that your college get a better professor of
history. This unless a Kennedy endowment makes this impossible. . . ."

To my mind this was a wrong-minded but reassuring letter.
My friend in Chicago misinterpreted my real position, as I
have long favored an active partnership between President
and Congress rather than presidential supremacy, but it was
reassuring because this correspondent is one of thousands of
Americans who in effect stand guard behind the Constitution.
These people often see the relation between their own interest or ideology and the Constitution, and only a nation with
such people in it can make a Constitution work and endure.

In effect I have tried in this chapter, and indeed in much of
the rest of the book, to set to rest some of the fears of people
like our Chicago friend who worry about the perils of the
Presidency. But there are two particular fears that demand
separate attention. They both turn on questions of chance.
One is that we might somehow elect an authoritarian type of

person to the Presidency. The other is that some President might, because of personality defects, crumble under pressure and perpetrate a terrible act of violence such as a nuclear attack.

The first fear finds no support in history. The Aaron Burrs, William Randolph Hearsts, Huey Longs, and Joe McCarthys have never come close to the Presidency (Burr was regarded as a vice-presidential candidate); they have not even come close to winning a major-party nomination. The party and electoral systems have their own checks and balances that operate to exclude adventurers from high office. Some conservatives argue that this misses the point, that some of the men actually elected — notably Jackson, Lincoln, the two Roosevelts — upset the traditional balance of power and hence threatened our liberties. But the notable thing that divides such men from the Huey Long type is that none of these so-called strong Presidents has threatened the two solid and indispensable underpinnings of a democratic polity — open, competitive elections and the essential civil liberties that make such elections meaningful. It is significant that we have gone ahead with presidential elections during civil war and world war. Many factors tend to make the President sensitive to democratic processes — the fact that he has been conditioned by these very processes in his long journey to the White House; the checks and balances operating within the executive branch, as discussed in Chapter IV; and above all the robustness and pervasiveness of the nation's civil liberties — liberties that are too powerfully entrenched for any President to ignore.

The other alleged peril of the Presidency is more substantial. The argument is that we have made the Presidency so powerful, we have allowed it to become so pressed by crisis, that we run the enormous risk that some incumbent will crumble under the pressure and even take some erratic or desperate action. This problem is the theme of a recent study of the life and death of James Forrestal, the first Secretary of Defense.[20] On May 22, 1949, Forrestal plunged to his death from the sixteenth floor of the Bethesda Naval Hospital, where he was undergoing psychiatric treatment. Earlier he had exhibited the classic signs of paranoia — he had complained that the Communists or the Jews were out to "get him." Rogow says:

"Since 1900 two American Presidents (excluding McKinley) have died in office, one was incapacitated before the expiration of his term, and one was forced to curtail seriously his activities as a result of heart illness. There is a body of opinion which holds that illness and exhaustion affected decisions made by Presidents Woodrow Wilson and Franklin D. Roosevelt during their last years in the White House. More recently ulcers, hypertension, coronary diseases, and 'exhaustion' have affected or terminated the political careers of Generals George C. Marshall and Walter Bedell Smith, former Secretaries of State Hull, Stettinius, Byrnes, and Acheson, Under-Secretary of State Sumner Welles and Deputy Secretary of Defense Robert A. Lovett." After citing some British and Russian examples of the same problem, Rogow wonders: "Is the fate of the world — *our* fate — in the hands of sick men?"[21]

All this, it seems to me, constitutes a serious, even frightening problem. But it is not a problem that can be met by tightening the old constitutional restraints on the Presidency.

[20] Arnold A. Rogow, *James Forrestal* (New York: Macmillan Company, 1963).
[21] *Ibid.*, p. xi.

The only people who could actually restrain the President from erratic, irrational, or psychotic action are those close to him — and not Senators or congressmen or judges. The checks and balances were never designed to cope with the problem posed by the "red telephone" that the President may turn to in a moment of desperation or even hysteria. Thus, here I reassert the argument of Chapters IV and V — that decision making has become such a collective process that a solitary act of lunacy would be virtually impossible. The White House has its own "fail-safe."

The whole situation, however, is quite ironic. Political scientists talk about — we practically live off — the existence of checks and balances against presidential and other forms of power. These checks do not operate in the making of war or even in the making of foreign policies that could precipitate war — for example, Franklin Roosevelt's instructions to the Navy Department in the months before Pearl Harbor. Yet these are almost irreversible decisions; if the President makes a colossal mistake, there is no institutional safeguard against its consequences. The President is actually checked by Congress only in making those decisions that could indeed be reversed if they turned out badly — for example, in social or economic policy. Thus the President might make a decision on taxes as irresponsible or daft as a decision for a showdown with a foreign power — but on the former matter there would always be a majority of the voters at the next election to repudiate his action. A presidential course set for war cannot be reversed. A nuclear holocaust would wipe out all the checks and balances — including the voters. In short, the whole concept of restraints in this area is topsy-turvy — a fact I sometimes reflect on dourly as I sit each fall teaching freshmen about the traditional checks and balances.

Still, the power of the President to make a catastrophic blunder while fatigued or under great stress is not the price we pay for the Presidency. It is the price we pay for living in the kind of world that we do. The only protection possible is the one the White House already affords: a group of men closely related to the President who can restrain him if need be. If power and decision making in the White House are collective, prudence is collective too.

IX

The Crucible of Leadership

ONE DAY during the early years of the Wilson Administration Franklin D. Roosevelt and his wife were lunching with worldly old Henry Adams who listened to the young Assistant Secretary describe a governmental problem that was worrying him. Adams broke in sharply: "Young man, I have lived in this house many years and seen the occupants of that White House across the square come and go, and nothing that you minor officials or the occupants of that house can do will affect the history of the world for long." [1] That Adams, a connoisseur of power, could make this statement hardly more than fifty years ago suggests the tempo of the rise in the power and scope of the modern Presidency. The enormously heightened expectations of the President on the part of both leaders and general public; the institutionalization of the office; the growth of a secure political base in the presidential parties; and the converging ideas of freedom and equality which have given direction and purpose to the Presidency and which Presidents in turn have strengthened and vivified — all these forces have transformed the office in the short span of time since the beginning of the century.

The events of 1964 brought to a climax this sixty years growth of presidential government. For 1964 brought not just another campaign, not just another conservative defeat.

[1] Eleanor Roosevelt, *This Is My Story* (New York: Harper & Brothers, 1937), p. 237.

Not only was Goldwater's candidacy a dramatically unsuccessful attack on both the national purpose of freedom through equality and on the major instrument — the Presidency — through which to achieve that purpose; but the effect of that candidacy was to compress into a few months a fundamental shift that had been under way for some years. Many liberals and some conservatives had been calling for a realignment of parties that would enable presidential and other candidates to confront the electorate with sharper choices between liberal and conservative doctrines. Changes had come slowly because of the tenacity of a four-party system that was anchored in a firm set of attitudes, institutions, and customs and that produced shifting coalitions among all four parties rather than a firm and clear-cut division over doctrine. Then in 1964 the Goldwater forces in a series of dramatic challenges catalyzed the four-party forces, drove liberal and moderate Republicans into the Johnson camp, won in return some Democratic party leaders in the South and a host of conservative Democrats, and cleared the way for an altered set of party relationships.

The Goldwater defeat in the election indicated that not only Presidents and presidential party politicians supported the broad liberal doctrine of freedom through equality, but that vast numbers of voters did too. Conservatism as a doctrine seemed to have received a clear rebuff. There had already been considerable evidence in election returns, polls, and other data that Americans were coming to endorse strongly the welfare state, federal regulation, and other redistributionist policies. McClosky, using 1958 polling data, had found "reason to believe that ideological sophistication and the general acceptance of liberal democratic values are increasing rather than declining in the United States. . . .

Democratic ideology in the United States, linked as it is with the articulate classes, gives promise of growing as the articulate class grows. Many developments in recent American life point to an increase in 'articulateness': the extraordinary spread of education, rapid social mobility, urbanization, the proliferation of mass media that disseminate public information, the expansion of the middle class, the decline in the size and number of isolated rural groups, the reduction in the proportion of people with submarginal living standards, the incorporation of ethnic minority groups into the culture and their increasing entrance into the professions, and so on." [2]

Success feeds on success: Johnson's sweeping victory suggested a more pronounced liberal tendency in the electorate than may in fact exist. The mass of people have somewhat fuzzy attitudes toward questions of social and economic equality, McClosky finds. And they also have ambivalent attitudes toward presidential power, as we have noted earlier. But the effect of Goldwater's repudiation was to strengthen the impression of powerful popular support both for the welfare state and for the modern Presidency. Thus it would be a courageous man indeed who would run on a Goldwater platform again. And the 1964 results will long be interpreted as a vindication of the Roosevelt-Truman-Kennedy-Johnson Presidencies even though many ambivalent attitudes will be concealed in the neat columns of election figures.

This confirming of the national purpose has vital implications for the Presidency. It represents a convergence of institution and ideology. We noted, in exploring the Hamiltonian model of the Presidency, that opportunistic chief executives shaped powerful means and instrumental goals even

2 Herbert McClosky, "Consensus and Ideology in American Politics," *The American Political Science Review*, vol. 58, no. 2 (June 1964), p. 379.

when their ultimate values were not clear. We noted in considering the Jeffersonian model that effective long-run political strategies turned on the existence of doctrine — such as his Republican doctrine of the early years — that could establish an intellectual context and policy program to which the strategies were instrumental. What we have achieved in the modern era is a combination of presidential opportunism and strong national purpose — a new combination of the Hamiltonian means and the Jeffersonian ends that historians have long juxtaposed. These factors both strengthen and limit presidential leadership today.

The Triumph of Presidential Government

The power and paradox of the Presidency have reached a new peak in the administration of Lyndon B. Johnson.

The intellectuals have been put on panels and assigned tasks; their ideas have been welcomed, channeled, and morselized. The President has virtually monopolized the output of the presidential press by making news, by being news, and by insisting that the best stories be released through the White House. Specific military and diplomatic issues from far-off theatres are routed to Johnson for decision, even more than they were to Kennedy. The Vice-President, by express prior agreement, acts as a political and executive assistant to the President. Departmental lobbying strategy on Capitol Hill, clearance of speeches by agency heads, line appointments in the agencies — all have been lodged more tightly in the White House. Legislation is drafted in the White House and openly submitted to Congress just as the President would like to have it pass, instead of being introduced independently by a friendly legislator. The vast new federal programs established in the mid-1960's have made the Chief Executive more than ever the President of the Cities. Independent power centers hardly exist — certainly not in the State Department or Congress, least of all in the Republican national headquarters.

More than ever the White House is a command post for economic, political, diplomatic, and military combat. But what is the nature of the long-term struggle?

The Presidency today is at the peak of its prestige. Journalists describe it as the toughest job on earth, the presiding office of the free world, the linchpin of Western alliance, America's greatest contribution to the art of self-government. Foreigners are fascinated by the Presidency, just as they are appalled by Congress and perplexed by party and election shenanigans. Scholars describe it as the most popular and democratic — and withal the most elevated and even most elitist — part of American government. They lovingly dissect the Presidency, slicing up its essentially indivisible power into that of Chief Executive, Chief of State, Chief Legislator, and so on. And they worry about its infirmities even as they marvel at its strength.

Even so, we may have underestimated the long-term impact of presidential government on the whole structure of American government. Past trends and current tendencies may permit some guarded speculations as to the future.

Conservatives have long held that the Presidency, as idealized and operated by liberals and internationalists, was imperialistic and exploitative and hence that it would eventually overpower the other branches of government. They are

substantially right. For almost a century now, the Presidency
has been warding off forays against its own constitutional do-
main and drawing other governmental and political institutions into the orbit of its influence. At least since the days of
President Grant the defense and expansion of the office have
been conducted not only by the strong Presidents but by
"weak" ones; hence we can say that the growth of the Presidency has been in part an institutional tendency and not one
turning merely on the accident of crisis and personality.

As we have noted earlier, Hayes successfully withstood a
vigorous effort by the Senate to dominate his major appointments and thus to exercise direct influence over the executive
establishment. Cleveland refused to give in to Senate demands that he submit to that body executive papers relating
to the nomination of federal officials. The Tenure of Office
Act, "designed to transfer control of the public service from
the President to the Senate, and thus to strike a vital blow
both to executive power and to the capacity of a President to
maintain a coordinate position with the legislative branch," [3]
was hamstrung under Grant and Hayes and repealed under
Cleveland. Hayes overcame an attack on the President's legislative power when he vetoed an appropriation bill to which
House Democrats had attached a rider relating to reconstruction policy in the South.

All this was good defense; and it confirmed the President's
formal control of the executive department. As we noted in
Chapter IV, the President in recent decades has seemed to
bring the Cabinet more certainly under his personal influence than was often the case in the nineteenth century. Lincoln's famous episode of "seven noes, one aye — the ayes have
it" would be impossible today; cabinet members would not

[3] Leonard D. White, *The Republican Era: 1869–1901* (New York: Macmillan Company, 1958), p. 28.

dare risk such a posture of opposition to the chief. The Vice-Presidency also has been tucked securely into the executive establishment. Some agencies, such as the Federal Bureau of Investigation, remain classic examples of the limitations of the President's control, but this independence is in part a product of unique personality and will probably diminish in time.

Presidential aggrandizement has been even more marked in the sphere of party politics. There was a time when conventions refused to renominate incumbent Presidents, when the national chairman was independent of presidential control, when the national party apparatus was dominated by competing leaders or factions. Things are very different now. The most important change affecting the nominating process since 1896 in the party in power, according to David, Goldman, and Bain, "has been the rising position of the Presidency and the increased recognition accorded the President as party leader. Other circles of influence continue to exist; but the group consisting of the President and his immediate associates has become the innermost inner circle; the others can now be regarded as a loose constellation of groups surrounding the White House as the center of power." [4] Recently the national party chairman has been simply one more political lieutenant of the President's and one who often had less power than political aides in the White House. The President's party influence does not run much beyond the scope of the presidential party, as noted in Chapter V; but the scope of the presidential party may be expanding too, depending in part on the President's influence over other sectors of the whole government.

Perhaps the most extraordinary but least remarked expan-

[4] Paul T. David, Ralph M. Goldman, Richard C. Bain, *The Politics of National Party Conventions* (The Brookings Institution, 1960), p. 72.

sion of presidential government lies in the extension of its influence to the Supreme Court. Prior to the modern presidential epoch, successive Presidents held sharply different doctrines and hence put men of varying viewpoints on the bench. Judicial appointees of a Theodore Roosevelt versus a Taft, of a Wilson versus a Harding, of a Hoover versus a Franklin Roosevelt, could hardly be expected to agree in their socioeconomic doctrine, and generally their decisions reflected their differences. This does not mean that Presidents always appointed men who slavishly expressed the presidential line. Indeed, they sometimes chose men who in time diverged widely from the President's basic doctrine, as in the case of Wilson's appointment of James C. McReynolds. But inescapably the type of appointment, and the appointee's social and economic doctrine on the bench, were affected by the general set of ideas, as well as by the political interrelationships,[5] of a presidential administration. Thus it was not surprising that the Supreme Court of 1933–37, composed mainly of appointees of Republican Presidents, rejected major New Deal legislation. Since 1937, however, the Supreme Court has not invalidated a major piece of national social legislation. The Court is composed of men who respond to the same general ideas of freedom and equality as have recent Presidents. Eisenhower's appointees are almost indistinguishable on social and economic legislation from Roosevelt's and Kennedy's; indeed, Eisenhower's major appointee, Earl Warren, has led the court in some of its historic egalitarian decisions, notably the *Brown* school desegregation case. The election of Barry Goldwater, and the kind of judicial appointments he

[5] For a striking example of a Supreme Court appointment of this type, see David J. Danelski, *A Supreme Court Justice Is Appointed* (New York: Random House, 1964).

would have made, would of course have disrupted the harmony between the two branches, at least if Goldwater could have put enough of his own men on the bench, but Goldwater's rejection diminishes the likelihood of a sharp presidential-judicial break in the foreseeable future. As long as we elect liberal Presidents from either of the presidential parties we can anticipate a generally liberal court.

Federalism has also felt the impact of presidential government. Modern Presidents have overturned old doctrines and practices of states' rights by extending their policy-making power into the urban areas of the nation. Historically the growth of cities has brought more need for public regulation and control and hence the growth of government. This tendency has been evident in public health, public transportation, social welfare services, traffic and crime control, and many other sectors. These developments in turn have produced financial crises in many cities; as the burden on city government has increased, its fiscal resources have proved inadequate. City officials have had to go cup in hand to state legislatures. But the states too have been struggling with financial limitations, and rurally dominated state legislatures have not been eager to hand out money to their city brethren. So the cities have turned to Washington. But here too they often have met frustration, for Congress too is heavily influenced by the rurally based congressional party coalition, especially in the appropriations committees. So the mayors head for the White House.

And the President is there to welcome them. Whatever his political party, the modern President must be sensitive to the needs of the cities. The alliance between the President and the cities is one of the oldest facts of American politics. As far back as 1800 a presidential candidate foresaw that his success might turn on the vote in New York City. In that year Jefferson wrote to Madison: "If the city election of New York is in favor of the Republican ticket, the issue will be Republican; if the federal ticket for the city of New York prevails, the probabilities will be in favor of a federal issue because it would then require a Republican vote both from New Jersey and Pennsylvania to preponderate against New York, on which we could not count with any confidence." [6] The spread of urbanization and the electoral college "gerrymander" have made New York and the other big urban states "preponderate" in most recent presidential elections.

Thus the man in the White House has become the President of the Cities; he has become the Chief Executive of Metropolis. He has provided the main motive power for shaping legislation needed by the cities; he pushes through the federal money bills with their provision for matching grants; he commands the executive departments — Labor, Justice, Health, Education and Welfare — that work closely with metropolitan governments; he appoints the heads of promotional and regulatory agencies for housing, urban renewal, transportation, communication, that affect the city. The President of course extends aid to the cities with strings attached — strings in the form of presidentially approved standards, procedures, safeguards, and the like. But the community of doctrine and interest between presidential government and big-city government is so close that major conflicts of politics and policy do not arise. More often the President and the mayors are allied against hostile or indifferent officials in other parts of the "marble cake" of federalism — against state legislators, county officials, congressional appropriations committees and subcommittees, even Governors.

6 Ford, *Works*, vol. VII, p. 434.

It is dangerous to generalize about such a complex set of governmental interrelationships as these. But the population explosion in metropolitan areas, the President's sensitivity to urban needs, the proliferation of urban and suburban areas cutting across county and state lines, the fiscal parsimony of municipalities, counties, and state legislatures, and the modern liberal assumption that government is an effective tool for realizing freedom and equality — all these forces are powerful ones that will operate for years to come. As a vital force behind the President's political and legislative leadership, the cities constitute a lasting foundation of presidential government. Inevitably, as presidential government cuts across and deranges the old formal division between local, state, and national authority, it will dominate policy making in and around metropolis.

Thus the Presidency has absorbed the Cabinet, the executive departments, the Vice-Presidency. It has taken over the national party apparatus. Through consistently liberal appointments over the years it has a powerful influence on the doctrine of the Supreme Court. It has transformed the federal system. What about its impact on Congress, historically and constitutionally the great counterforce to the presidential office?

Here the change may be the most profound of all, at least in the long run. Our speculations need not be overly influenced by short-run developments, such as President Johnson's great success with Congress in his first two years in office. This success, coming on the heels of the congressional deadlock over many of Kennedy's major proposals, was largely due to some special circumstances: Johnson's standing on Capitol Hill, his particular legislative experience, the consolidation of presidential support after the rout of the Goldwater forces, and a congressional and popular urge to honor the late President's memory by supporting some of his major proposals. We must consider more basic and continuing forces that shape the relations of Congress and President as institutions.

One such force is reapportionment. The granting of greater representation in the House (and in state legislatures) to urban and suburban areas will bring the presidential and congressional constituencies into closer approximation and hence diminish some of the structural forces making for divergent policy. This shift may take longer than some expect, because it is the one-party district rather than the malapportioned district that lies at the heart of congressional party power on Capitol Hill.[7] But in the long run reapportionment, along with the spread of heterogeneous urban and suburban population into presently rural districts, will diversify one-party areas and stimulate competitive two-party politics.

Another tendency that may bring Congress more into the presidential orbit is continuing congressional reform. Some of this might consist of formal change in organization and procedures, such as the strengthening of the Speaker early in 1965. Other changes will be less obvious, embracing the distribution of prestige and informal influence in the structure of both houses. The elected party leadership in Congress tends to support a President of the same party, as in the case of Senator Robert Taft lining up behind Eisenhower (just as the elected congressional leadership tends to diverge from the presidential party when the Presidency is in opposition hands). As the elected leadership continues to gain strength

[7] See James MacGregor Burns, *The Deadlock of Democracy: Four-Party Politics in America* (New York: Prentice-Hall, 1963), especially ch. 10, "The Structure of Coalition Politics."

in Congress as compared to the committee chairmen — as in the long run I believe it will — the President will gain added influence over the legislature.

The most powerful force for unifying President and Congress will be the continuing and probably increasing consensus over freedom and equality. As long as the nation was deeply and closely divided over these goals, Congress with its bias toward conservatism was bound to be at odds with a President biased toward liberalism, except in times of crisis. Without a broad consensus it was impossible to mobilize steady congressional majorities behind presidential proposals for social welfare and other egalitarian measures. Congress has been slow to act when only a bare popular majority seemed to support Fair Deal or New Frontier programs, as suggested by the fate of major presidential proposals in Congress following the close popular majorities won by Truman in 1948 and Kennedy in 1960. Kennedy liked to quote Jefferson's remark that "great innovations should not be forced on slender majorities." They have not been, in Congress. Often a three-fifths or two-thirds majority of the electorate supporting liberal programs has been necessary to produce a dependable straight majority behind those programs in Congress, because of the distortions in congressional representation. But judging from polls, election data, and other indices, about three-fifths or two-thirds of the American voters have come to uphold in a general way federal welfare and regulatory measures at home and policies designed to support freedom and equality abroad. This consensus is bound to show in Congress.

This is not to predict joyous harmony between President and Congress. Relations will continue to be marked by misunderstanding, jealousies over status and protocol, and differences over policy. Oscillations between presidential and congressional power will continue, though probably with the balance of power continuing to shift toward the executive over the long run. Conflict will probably be especially acute in the fiscal sector, for the conservative grip on the spending and taxing committees and machinery of Congress will not soon be relaxed. But it is precisely in the fiscal sector of policy that the President will be under the greatest pressure to meet the claims of freedom and equality. The question will be whether the President has enough power to channel funds into federal programs for health, education, urban development, housing, and the like; whether he has the funds to staff effectively promotional, regulatory, and control agencies in civil rights and related fields. If congressional conservatives could not thwart passage of social legislation, they still might try to starve or cripple its implementation.

But even here the big guns seem to be on the President's side. The same consensus over freedom and equality that now pervades Congress as a whole should affect its fiscal policy making too in the long run. If in the short run fiscal conservatives in Congress are able to stymie presidential programs, the White House can retaliate by mobilizing interests that favor spending, dramatizing the social and economic ills that need to be attacked, returning to Congress for deficiency and emergency appropriations, using discretionary funds of the President, and other devices. The President has already been granted significant latitude in the use of funds to influence policy; the most notable example is the Civil Rights Act of 1964, which granted him power to withhold federal funds from any program or activity receiving direct or indirect federal assistance, in which racial discrimination was found to exist. President Kennedy asked Congress for presidential authority to change tax ratios within certain limits, in order to strengthen the arsenal of anti-recession weapons; Congress balked at granting this power, but may well change its mind in the future, especially in the face of a deepening economic recession. The actual coming of a recession would precipitate an even speedier and more drastic shift of fiscal authority to the White House, for no President today can afford to bear the political burden of a slump. In March 1933 Roosevelt warned that unless Congress acted in the economic emergency, "I shall ask the Congress for the one remaining instrument to meet the crisis — broad Executive power to wage a war against the emergency, as great as the power that would be given to me if we were in fact invaded by a foreign foe." No President could ask for less than this in a future crisis; he probably would ask for more. And no modern Congress could resist him, for part of the nation's consensus over freedom and equality is a commitment to federal action against depression and poverty. And because that commitment first and foremost binds the President and will do so indefinitely, it is part of the edifice of presidential government.

The Corruption of Consensus

"I am the President of the United States, the only President you will have, God willing, until January of next year," Lyndon Johnson said a few months after his election, before a group of newspaper editors assembled in the flower garden. "One of the hardest tasks that a President faces is to keep the time scale of his decisions always in mind and to try to be the

President of all the people. He is not simply responsible to an immediate electorate, either. He knows over the long stretch of time how great can be the repercussions of all that he does or that he fails to do, and over that span of time the President always has to think of America as a continuing community.

"He has to try to see how his decisions will affect not only today's citizens, but their children and their children's children unto the third and fourth generation. He has to try to peer into the future, and he has to prepare for that future.

". . . Irresistible forces of change have been unleashed by modern science and technology, and the very facts dissolve and regroup as we look into them. To make no predictions is to be sure to be wrong. . . .

"The President of this country, more than any other single man in the world, must grapple with the course of events and the directions of history. What he must try to do, try to do always, is to build for tomorrow in the immediacy of today, for if we can, the President, and the Congress, and you leaders of the communities throughout the Nation, will have made their mark in history. Somehow we must ignite a fire in the breast of this land, a flaming spirit of adventure that soars beyond the ordinary and the contented, and really demands greatness from our society, and demands achievement in our Government. . . ." [8]

No presidential speech could have caught more aptly the paradox of the modern Presidency. To serve the needs of the present and the future, to satisfy current electorates and future ones, to conceive of America as a present community and a continuing one, to anticipate the future by preparing for it now, to make long-run predictions in the face of opaque facts,

[8] Remarks of President Johnson to American Society of Newspaper Editors, Office of the White House Press Secretary, April 17, 1964.

to "build for tomorrow in the immediacy of today," to foster greatness in the midst of so much that is mediocre and complacent — all these alternatives pose dilemmas for the President who aspires to his own greatness in history but must work in a tangle of day-to-day problems.

The crowning paradox is an old one for the American President — the need to be both the "President of all the people" and yet to respond to the interests and expectations of the majority that elected him. Since the beginning the President has had to serve both as the ceremonial and symbolic head of the whole nation and also as the head politician. He has had to be Chief of State at the same time that he has served as legislative and party chief. He has had to combine roles that are neatly divided in parliamentary countries between a king and a prime minister, or between a largely ceremonial president and a *premier*. He has had to be both a unifier and a divider of the people.

Filling these two roles has been awkward but not impossible. The President has had almost literally to don and doff his partisan or ceremonial costume for differing occasions. The shift from a "President of all the people" stance to a "politician looking for votes" stance is marked rather cleanly during election years by the day that the President formally begins his campaign for re-election and no longer can command television and radio channels free. The shifting back and forth between the roles has led to humorous byplays, as when reporters used to question Franklin Roosevelt as to whether his campaign-year inspection trips were part of his presidential or his electioneering responsibilities. The inconsistency and tension between the two roles, indeed, served a useful purpose in reminding people — including the President himself — that as leader of the whole nation he was always subject to the claims of the people who voted for him, and that as party chief he had obligations to the whole nation. The President could never be seen simply as a hero, for he had crass political obligations, but neither could he be perceived as a mere politician. The two roles both complemented each other and held each other in check. Their very inconsistency was a sign of health.

Note the striking contrast with today. As the modern Presidency has become increasingly the expression of a consensus over political goals — the goals of freedom through equality — the holder of the office has come increasingly to represent the same kind of national unity and harmony in his political role as in his symbolic and ceremonial. The old tension — and hence the balance and safeguards — between the two roles is disappearing. Columnists have poked fun at Lyndon Johnson because he clothed the most obviously political ideas and goals in the most bland and magisterial phrases. But this is not simply Lyndon Johnson's doing. The fact is that any President articulating the modern values of freedom and equality *seems* to be speaking for the great bulk of the nation for the simple reason that he *is* so speaking.

The implications of this development for the future can be grasped if we consider what has also been happening to the President's role as ceremonial and symbolic and even heroic leader. That role is of course an old one — even older than the Presidency itself, having begun when George Washington, in resplendent array, stepped out on the balcony overlooking Wall Street and took his solemn oath. By the end of the nineteenth century Henry Jones Ford was noting that in the Presidency America had revived the oldest political institution of the race, the elective kingship — precisely what Patrick Henry had feared. The sheer magnitude of the President's ceremonial duties today is staggering. "He lights the national Christmas tree on the White House lawn in the season of good will to men," Herman Finer has summed it up; "he issues the Thanksgiving Day message in the season of thankfulness and bicarbonated repletion; his office sends greetings to societies and persons on their birthdays, offering national recognition and a reason for gratitude; he throws out the first baseball of the season and attends the army-navy football game in a spirit of good-fellowship and as a votary of the sport; he is host at brilliant banquets for kings and queens and potentates, representing America in its dignity in the comity of nations; he sponsors movements for health and wealth and happiness; gigantic dams and electric works pound into operation as his finger touches the proper button, enhancing America's pride; and he is in mourning on Memorial Day, his hat over his heart, one with the heroes of the past, one with those who mourn the men who died so that the nation might live; at military parades on the Fourth of July he embodies the vigor of American independence; and he is at home, for hand-shaking, to scores of thousands of worthy and ordinary citizens throughout the year. And with him is the First Lady of the land, presiding, the smartly dressed descendant of Dolly Madison and the rest, over the social life of the capital, the epitome of grace for the women of the nation." [9] The facilities of the White House have been augmented to permit the President's home to be almost continuously on show, both to the hordes of tourists and the stream of dignitaries. The ceremonial and symbolic life of the Presidency has become almost as formal and stylized as that of the court of Versailles. The White House has even had court

[9] Herman Finer, *The Presidency: Crisis and Regeneration* (Chicago: University of Chicago Press, 1960), pp. 111–12.

jesters about, and the Gridiron Club, now in its seventh decade of existence, serves as the occasion when men can try to
make fools of Presidents and get away with it.

All this is familiar; what we must gauge is the longtime
effect of this kind of symbolism on attitudes toward the Presidency. Consider the attitudes that children develop toward
the office during their most formative years. Since the beginning of the Republic, no doubt, little boys have wanted to be
President, but recent investigations of children's perceptions
of the President make one pause. In a study of the grade-
school student's image of political authority, Hess and Easton
discovered that two figures appear first on the horizon of the
child's political awareness — the local policeman and the President of the United States. The children's attitudes toward
the President were highly idealized. They saw him as much
more hardworking than most men, more honest, having more
liking for people, knowing much more. As a person he was
"best in the world" to 61 percent of the second-graders, and
either best in the world or "good" to all but a very small minority of the children. They saw him also as a potent figure,
having the main part in making the laws, with congressmen as
helpers and governors and mayors as subordinates. The children have ideas about the office, not just the man; there was,
report the authors, "a base line of expectations about the conduct and qualifications of the man who occupies or seeks to
occupy it." [10] While the perception of the President in positive terms decreases a bit with age, it stays high, and it did not
seem to be dependent on social status or partisanship (of the
child's parents). In commenting on this and other studies,
Roberta Sigel has suggested that the school is probably one of

[10] Robert D. Hess and David Easton, "The Child's Changing Image of the
President," *Public Opinion Quarterly*, vol. 24, no. 4 (Winter 1960), pp. 632-44.

the important sources of the child's image of political authority and that most children's books "are designed to increase pride in our Presidents and our history." And she notes that the "President being far away enjoys an added advantage over local authority figures: the child has no opportunity to check against reality the idealized image taught him by the adult world." [11] From her own set of findings about children's reactions to President Kennedy's assassination she concluded that the image of the Presidency remained highly positive despite a slight decrease in the power image and that the children could in a rudimentary way distinguish between the person of the President and the institution of the government. "Their sense of political security seems to be a function of their faith in the institution of government as well as of their faith in individual Presidents." [12] These early attitudes inevitably shape people's views of the Presidency in their adult years.

The increasing dominance of the Presidency over the rest of the government, its embodiment of the national purpose, its symbolic expression of the nation's glory and solidarity, its tremendous impact on Americans during their most formative years — what does all this imply for the future of the nation and of the Presidency?

The old and accepted fears of presidential power, I have contended in the last chapter, do not seem justified on the basis of actual experience. Increased authority and scope have not made the Presidency a tyrannical institution; on the contrary, the office has become the main governmental bastion for the protection of individual liberty and the expansion of civil rights. The office "represents" the electorate at

11 Roberta S. Sigel, "Death of a President and School Children's Reaction To It — An Exploration Into Political Socialization," Wayne State University, 1964.
12 *Ibid.*

least as effectively and democratically as does Congress, though in a different way. The office has attracted neither power-mad politicians nor bland incompetents but the ablest political leaders in the land, and these leaders in turn have brought the highest talent to the White House. We must, under modern conditions, reassess the old idea that the *main* governmental protection of civil liberty, social and economic rights, and due process of law lies in the legislature or the courts or state and local government. The main protection lies today in the national executive branch. As a general proposition the Presidency has become the chief protector of our procedural and substantive liberties; as a general proposition, the stronger we make the Presidency, the more we strengthen democratic procedures and can hope to realize modern liberal democratic goals.

The danger of presidential dominance lies in a different and more subtle tendency. It lies not in presidential failure but in presidential success. It lies not in the failure to achieve our essential contemporary goals of freedom and equality but in their substantial realization and in the incapacity of presidential government to turn to new human purposes.

The prospects seem good that presidential government will continue to help broaden equality of opportunity at the same time that it protects our basic freedoms. All the Presidencies since that of Hoover have made some kind of commitment to this goal; they have aroused strong expectations; they have perfected the governmental machinery necessary to realize the goals; and we can expect that the contest between the presidential parties on domestic issues will turn mainly on the incumbent Administration's successes and failures in combating poverty, expanding opportunity, and enlarging civil rights, especially for Negroes. In foreign policy the election tests will be the efficient management of crisis plus the long-run effectiveness of military and economic programs abroad designed to strengthen the foundations of freedom and equality in other nations. Given the harmony between ends and means — between the ends of freedom and equality and the means of presidential government — we can expect that well before the end of this century, and perhaps much sooner, we will have achieved substantial equality of opportunity in this nation. We need not expect equality of *condition,* nor full equality of opportunity, for gray areas of deprivation and discrimination will remain. Some of the old tension between equality and freedom will always be found in a diverse and changing society. But to the extent that public and private measures can realize freedom and equality, the goals will be substantially achieved.

And precisely here lies the problem. As freedom and equality are achieved presidential government will exhaust the purpose for which it has been such an eminently suited means. The great machinery of government that has been shaped to distribute welfare and overcome poverty and broaden opportunity and protect liberty will become devoted to increasingly automatic tasks. The passion will long since have disappeared, and increasingly the compulsion of purpose will be dissipated. Purpose will no longer be toughened in conflict; creativity will no longer rise from challenge and crisis. As the ends of government become increasingly agreed upon among the people, between the parties, between President and Congress, between national and state and local governments, issues will resolve mainly around questions of technique. And the more humdrum these matters become, the more the President will turn to his ceremonial and symbolic role to provide circuses to the people — the bread already being in abundance.

According to Morgenthau, we are already facing this problem, even with the goals of freedom and equality not yet achieved. In this nation there have been purposes, he reminds us, to which we could pledge our lives, our fortunes, and our sacred honor. "There is no such issue today. None of the contemporary issues of domestic politics of which the public at large is aware commands for its alternative solutions those loyalties out of which great political conflicts are made. There are divergent opinions and interests, to be sure; but there is no great issue that men deem worthy of sacrifice and risk. In consequence, the integrating principle of American society has lost both its dynamic and its substantive qualities. . . . The American consensus, which in the past was monistic in form and pluralistic in substance, has become monistic in both respects. In consequence, conformism now extends to the substance of policies and constitutional arrangements. Since no issue is any longer worth fighting over, a position must be 'moderate,' and what was once a compromise between seemingly irreconcilable positions now transforms itself into the adjustment of positions differing only in degree. Since the purpose of America seems to have been achieved — the need for improvement notwithstanding — the *status quo* tends to become as sacred as the purpose itself, and an attack upon the *status quo* almost as unpalatable as dissent from the purpose. Since there is nothing left to fight for, there is nothing to fight against. . . ." [13] Morgenthau was writing during the Eisenhower Administration, and he did not anticipate the force of Kennedy's challenge to Republicanism and of the Negroes' revolt against the status quo in the early 1960's. But he was right in a broader sense, for it was precisely Eisenhower's acceptance of the purposes of the New

[13] Hans J. Morgenthau, *The Purpose of American Politics* (New York: Vintage Books, 1964), pp. 213–14.

Deal and the Fair Deal, and his blandness in his methods of realizing them, that made his administration an ominous indication of the likely nature of late twentieth century politics in America.

Many would reject any call today for high purposes and fighting issues. They prefer a polity that is not rent by great issues, scarred by savage conflict, absorbed in passionate controversy, or even distracted by political problems. Considering the nature of the early and middle epochs of the twentieth century, they would cherish a period of calm in which people could indeed, in John Adams' words, turn to painting, poetry, music, architecture, statuary, tapestry and porcelain. The very realization of the grand aims of freedom and equality, they believe, would create a basis on which people could turn to the enduring problems of the richness and quality of life, and could forsake some of the old ideological quarrels.

Those who spurn ideology will contend, moreover, that progress emerges not from the pursuit of central, synoptic visions or plans or purposes, but from the pursuit of a wide range of alternative policies, from flexible methods, from refusal to make an ultimate commitment to any means or any end, from incremental and adjustive tactics that permit day-to-day reconciliation of differences. Such an approach, they hold, produces innovation, creativity, and excitement. It rejects the grand formulations of interrelated ends and means in favor of special angles of vision, sharpened individual or group motivation, the social dynamics of a loosely articulated, highly accessible, and open-ended polity. The incrementalists would proceed step by step, renouncing passion and commitment in favor of prudence and calculation.

Yet many who have lived through the decades of traumatic and even bloody political conflict, at home or abroad, will wonder about a nation in which the great issues have dwindled to matters of technique. They will worry first about a people so bored by the relatively trivial political issues of the day that they have become largely absorbed in the minutiae of their private lives. They will doubt whether in the long run even architecture and poetry can be kept out of politics. They will worry that people might fall into adjustment, conformity, undiscriminating tolerance, and aimless, time-filling activities, and that this will lead to the acceptance of mediocrity and a compulsive togetherness rather than the pursuit of excellence and individuality.

They will be concerned about the governors as well as the governed. For a government agreed on the larger issues and proceeding by calculation and adjustment is likely to attract to its service the little foxes who know many little things — the operators, the careerists, the opportunists, the technicians, the fixers, the managers. Some of these men may be resourceful, zealous, dedicated, flexible, and adjustable. But they will be so absorbed in technique that it will be difficult for them to separate issues of policy from questions of their own immediate self-enhancement. Certainly there would be little room for the Churchills who give up office in the pursuit of broader principles, or even for the administrative innovators who wish to create something more exalted than a better administrative mousetrap. Thus the governors too would lose their way, become lost in technique, would become absorbed in private motives, would substitute means for ends.

For this is the corruption of consensus — the attempt to find universal agreement on so many issues that great public purposes are eroded by a torrent of tiny problems solved by adjustment and adaptation. Ways and means are more and more rationally elaborated by increasing numbers of technicians for a society having less and less human purpose. In government this would mean Hamiltonianism gone wild; in the Presidency it would mean the submergence of the nation's supreme political decision-maker in an ever widening tide of incremental adjustments. The President might still be a hero to most of his people, but his policy and program would not be heroic, only his image. He would still seem a potent figure to children — and grownups — but his actual influence over events would be dwindling. He would still be visible as he mediated among the technicians and occasionally coped with crises; but it would be the visibility of the tightrope walker whom the great public watches with emotional involvement but without actual participation. The defeat of presidential government would be inherent in its very success. Having taken over the Cabinet and the rest of the government, presidential government would finally have taken over the President.

Creative Presidency,
Shadow Presidency

People were freely predicting at the time of Lyndon Johnson's inaugural in January 1965 that the nation was headed for a modern era of good feelings. The President himself had said after his election that the country had reached a new "consensus on national purpose and policy." He was quite right — the nation had indeed reached a consensus over the goals of freedom and equality. But these are not the only problems that occupy men, and history warned that eras of apparent good feelings could conceal heats and ferments that would erupt in turbulence and strife years later.

And an unblinking look at the world and the nation in the

mid-sixties disclosed a profusion of interlaced problems, any one cluster of which could occupy a people's energies: at home the problems of rapidly changing group and class and generational relationships, education, urban disorder, mounting crime rates, social anomie and alienation, automation, political apathy, along with the more old-fashioned issues such as transportation, farm subsidies, labor-management relations, tax reform, monopoly and administered prices, medical care; and abroad, nuclear proliferation, the continuing and in many areas deepening poverty of tens of millions, the population explosion, the disruption of old rural cultures and the flood of people into the restless cities, the fragmentization of Africa, the social unrest of Latin America, communist expansion in Asia, along with the week-to-week "little" crises, any one of which could explode into a major one.

It was impossible in the mid-sixties to predict in what forms these problems would emerge with the passage of time. One might speculate, though, that many of the most crucial domestic problems might revolve around certain old but still compelling value-questions. Given the trends in the nation that one could predict with the greatest certainty — huge population increases in the urban and suburban areas, accelerated social mobility, a constantly enlarging and increasingly homogenized middle-class population, a decline in ethnic solidarity and variety — one might guess that once the old problems of equality and freedom had been subdued, sharper questions might emerge over the possibilities of individuality and privacy in a mass culture. If the past century has seen the early tension and later partial reconciliation of values of liberty and equality, we might be at the threshold of an age increasingly preoccupied with the relation of liberty and fraternity, of privacy and community, of the individual and the group. If in past years we have been concerned with mainly quantitative problems — the amount of goods and services produced and how they were distributed — we might be more occupied in the future with the quality of American life in a great, affluent, complacent, and perhaps mediocre society.

The quality of American life — this is not a new phrase nor a new political issue. It is older than Jefferson's dreams and as young as the Great Society. No one has defined the hope and the promise better than President Johnson. "The great society," he proclaimed at the University of Michigan in May 1964, "is a place where every child can find knowledge to enrich his mind and enlarge his talents. It is a place where leisure is a welcome chance to build and reflect, not a feared cause of boredom and restlessness. It is a place where the city of man serves not only the needs of the body and the demands of commerce, but the desire for beauty and the hunger for community.

"It is a place where man can renew contact with nature. It is a place which honors creation for its own sake and for what it adds to the understanding of the race. It is a place where men are more concerned with the quality of their goals than the quantity of their goods. But most of all, the Great Society is not a safe harbor, a resting place, a final objective, a finished work. It is a challenge constantly renewed, beckoning us toward a destiny where the meaning of our lives matches the marvellous products of our labor."

The crux of the problem is whether a system of presidential government so perfectly adapted to, and so largely facilitative of, quantitative liberalism — that is, of the augmentation and fairer distribution of goods — can redefine its purpose and shift its strategy in order to embrace new values with their implications for changes in means and instrumental goals.

Such a shift calls for much more than making the White House into a showplace of the arts, or awarding medals to heroes of culture, or bestowing presidential recognition on private cultural enterprises. It means a concerted and sustained and expensive effort to impart values like those of Johnson to the barren lives of millions of Americans, middle class as well as deprived. It means diverting the kind of resources into cultural, recreational, and educational activities that we have in the past poured into economic recovery, or even into national defense. And such an effort might be controversial and even unpopular. Many Americans would oppose it and deride it; by its very nature such an effort would bring foolish blunders and mishaps that could be easily caricatured; and certain ventures — perhaps an effort to improve the quality of commercial radio and television — could precipitate clashes with powerful interests.

Above all, the shift from the pursuit of quantitative to qualitative goals would call for comprehensive, sustained, and broadly unified policies — in short, for planning. Effective planning is impossible except in the context of at least a rough ordering of values, instrumental goals, and means. It will be as important to have clearly thought out, long-range priorities in this respect as it would be in planning increased productivity. Winston Churchill once said that "those who are possessed of a definite body of doctrine and of deeply rooted convictions upon it will be in a much better position to deal with the shifts and surprises of daily affairs than those who are merely taking short views, and indulging their natural impulses as they are evoked by what they read from day to day." [14] Considering the intractable nature of the many hu-

---

[14] Quoted by W. W. Rostow, "The Planning of Foreign Policy," School of Advanced International Studies, The Johns Hopkins University.

man problems implicit in the quest for a qualitatively grea⋅ society, Churchill's remarks are as relevant to a cultural strat⋅ egy as to a foreign or economic.

Presidential government is a superb planning institution. The President has the attention of the country, the administrative tools, the command of information, and the fiscal resources that are necessary for intelligent planning, and he is gaining the institutional power that will make such planning operational. Better than any other human instrumentality he can order the relations of his ends and means, alter existing institutions and procedures or create new ones, calculate the consequences of different policies, experiment with various methods, control the timing of action, anticipate the reactions of affected interests, and conciliate them or at least mediate among them.[15] If as Hubert Humphrey has said, we need not a planned society but a continuously planning society, the Presidency provides strong and versatile tools for that purpose.

Still, we must acknowledge that the Presidency has become an effective planning agency for reasons of chance as well as volition. In this century the Presidency has been the center of the conflict between labor and capital and later between segregationists and civil rights forces; it has steeled its will and its ideology in the struggles against Nazi tyranny and communist expansion. After a century of planless growth the Presidency found its place as a key part of the American system of ends and means. The question is whether presidential government can detach itself enough from set ideas and existing institutions and old ways in order to embrace new goals. With leadership, to quote Selznick further, "the problem is

15 Cf. David Braybrooke and Charles E. Lindblom, *A Strategy of Decision* (New York: Free Press of Glencoe, 1963).

always *to choose key values and to create a social structure that embodies them.* The task of building values into social structure is not necessarily consistent, especially in early stages, with rules of administration based on economic premises. Only after key choices have been made and related policies firmly established can criteria of efficient administration play a significant role. Even then, the smooth-running machine must accept disturbance when critical problems of adaptation and change arise." [16]

To define new goals, to fashion new institutions to realize those goals, to avoid both utopianism and opportunism, to build popular support without improper manipulation, to allow for flexibility of means and redefinition of ends, and always to elevate purpose over technique — all this is the test of creative leadership. It will be the test of presidential government in the years ahead. To define leadership in this way is to see the importance of a number of proposals that have been made to strengthen the Presidency and hence to enable the President to reshape institutions and processes: four-year terms for Representatives (to bring presidential and congressional constituencies into closer correspondence); the granting of full power to the President to control executive department organization; finding means of attracting the highest talent to the executive department, especially to its major staff positions; efforts to bring into the policy-making process intellectuals with creative and innovative gifts; providing the President with greater discretionary power over fiscal policy, including the item veto and the granting of authority to change tax rates within certain limits; and above all, the further strengthening of the elected leadership of Congress so

[16] Philip Selznick, *Leadership in Administration* (Evanston: Row, Peterson and Company, 1957), p. 60.

that it can act more quickly and comprehensively in harmony with the President. But the greatest need of presidential government does not lie in this kind of reform. We can expect many of these changes to take place in any event as the Presidency becomes increasingly institutionalized. Indeed, some are already taking place, in substance if not in form. Some of them at best will simply speed up transitions that already are under way — for example, greater presidential control of fiscal policy.

The greatest need of the Presidency in the years ahead will not lie in internal changes, important though these are, or even in its relations with Congress. The greatest need will be an opposition that challenges presidential values, presidential methods, presidential institutions, that is eager to take power and to present its own definition of the national purpose.

Of all the vital elements of American democratic government the national opposition is the most disorganized, fragmented, and ineffective. As a responsible opposition to the President, Congress is an almost total failure. Hostile Senators and Representatives bombard the White House from all directions. Typically they fail to advance alternative proposals and hence they do not provide the voters with an idea as to how the opposition would govern if it got the chance. The congressmen usually prefer to play the game of bargain and even various forms of genteel blackmail with the President rather than to criticize forthrightly and dramatically. No wonder that Presidents in recent years have been far more sensitive to criticism in the press than on Capitol Hill.

There are good reasons for the debility of the opposition. In part it is a simple reflection of the power of presidential government. "The aggrandizement of the President, especially by the electronic media," as Key has said, "has made the dispersed minority leadership one of low public visibility." [17] The main difficulty is the bifurcation of the opposition into the presidential and congressional parties. Once the presidential candidate — the presidential party's leader — has made his strenuous campaign and lost, he then becomes "titular" leader of the whole party. This is a polite term for shelved or even repudiated. For once the campaign is lost, the congressional party leaders try to assume the opposition role. They hold formal and visible positions from which to conduct the attack, while the titular leader usually has no formal position to fall back on, as in the cases of Stevenson in 1956, Nixon in 1960, and Goldwater in 1964. But the congressional party cannot carry the burden of militant leadership, because of its own internal divisions, its separation between the House and the Senate, and its lack of institutional structure (as compared with the Shadow Cabinet in Great Britain). If the opposition party has lost the Presidency but still controls one or both branches of Congress, as in the case of the Democrats after 1956, it lacks the advantage of being completely in the opposition; it suffers from having a modicum of power and responsibility. If the opposition party lacks control of Congress as well as of the White House, it has a poor forum from which to appeal to the public and virtually no machinery to support a focused and sustained attack on the government.

The impotence of the opposition becomes more serious as presidential government becomes more powerful. No matter how benign a government may be, it will be tempted to manipulate public opinion, to try to dominate the flow of opinion, to cover up mistakes, and to cast doubt on the patriotism

17 V. O. Key, Jr., *Public Opinion and American Democracy* (New York: Alfred A. Knopf, 1961), p. 457.

or at least the honesty of outside critics. The more that government represents a consensus, or claims to, the more tempted it may be to succumb to some of these tendencies. Above all a consensus government may become flabby and complacent and lose the cutting edge of energy, initiative, and innovation. The very tendencies toward excessive concern with technique that we noted above can cause a government to lose direction and momentum unless the opposition holds it to its promises and threatens to oust it from power.

The problem is especially acute in the United States because of the lack of well organized and programmatic parties. This is less of a problem for the President because, as we have seen, he has built up his own presidential party to provide him with an electoral footing and other political resources. The opposition presidential party, lacking a President and having to make do with a titular leader, is not anchored in an organized mass following and a militant cadre. It must improvise — and that in turn encourages a similar opportunism and absence of direction in the presidential establishment.

The greatest need of the American Presidency is a potent and competitive Shadow Presidency. At the very least the opposition party should establish some kind of collective leadership modeled perhaps after the Democratic Advisory Council of the 1950's, to give the presidential party a strong voice. More than this, it should experiment with an annual or biennial convention or conference both to choose a top leader and to renovate its program. The failure of the opposition to take this primitive step is not due to any innate difficulty but mainly to the divergent constituencies and institutional jealousies of the congressional party, which wants to dominate the opposition role even though it fills that role so feebly. Ideally there would be an annual convention, a dependable system for collecting adequate funds, a large national staff with regional and state units under it, an effective propaganda apparatus, and talented, articulate, and highly visible leadership. Whatever the exact form, it is clear that the opposition party today has a rare opportunity to exercise Jeffersonian leadership — that is, to build a new political institution.

Even more important, the opposition party must display creative leadership in defining its own version of the national purpose. It is not for outsiders to lecture the opposition party as to the goals it might propose, but one must note the great opportunity that may lie before it. If presidential government as shaped by liberals for egalitarian purposes cannot shift its own strategy toward qualitative goals, if presidential government under Democratic party leadership may be hobbled by its own successes, then the opposition could seize the initiative. American conservatives have long been interested in the now intensifying problems of individuality and community, identity and alienation, liberty and fraternity, innovation and tradition, equality and hierarchy. As Clinton Rossiter has argued, they have not blinked at the hard questions about man in society. And it was under Abraham Lincoln and Theodore Roosevelt, both Republicans, that the nation first addressed itself most directly to problems of the quality of American life. In executing one of the oldest of political and military strategies — shifting the very grounds of the combat — modern conservatives can come to grips with liberal Democracy and its presidential establishment.

Perhaps all this is unnecessary — perhaps we can give in to the acknowledged rewards and virtues of presidential government, without worrying much about competition, criticism, alternatives, and the tasks of an opposition. But a great people will not be content long to float in such a slack tide. At the conclusion of his study of a group of working men in an eastern city — a group that was not technically a cross section of a larger population but may be highly indicative of social trends — Robert Lane wrote: "The man of Eastport has no cathedral building in his air space to raise his sense of importance and mission; he is not engaged anywhere in a struggle against want or fear or squalor in such a way as to engage his mind and take him out of himself; he is not, like the Italian Fascists who were his uncles, rebuilding a glorious Roman history; manifest destiny, the conquering of a continent, are parts of a history not quite his own, and anyway they refer to completed tasks. What shall he do that will call out the greatness in him? Against the background of a great purpose, he might measure the political system and say whether or not it is just. But he has no way to conjure up such a vision, and hence no way to take the measure of his society." [18]

The Epoch of Executive Government?

There remains only to summarize the thesis of this book and to inquire whether other great nations may also have entered their own eras of presidential or executive government.

The Hamiltonian President — the resourceful, heroic, opportunistic leader — was from the outset an alternative to the weak Madisonian executive and to the Jeffersonian model of the party chief who both acted for, and was constrained by,

18 Robert E. Lane, *Political Ideology* (New York: Free Press of Glencoe, 1962), p. 475.

the popular majority that he led. The Hamiltonian President aroused ambivalent attitudes among Americans — including many intellectuals — who wanted strong leadership
and honored it in past Presidents but who feared that a current or future strong man in the White House might threaten
American democracy. The expansion of the President's political, military, diplomatic, and economic power, combined
with the huge enlargement of the executive department,
posed the threat that an independent leader, manipulating
various constituencies, freely wielding his broad executive
and emergency authority, and drawing party, Cabinet, Congress, and even the courts into his political orbit, would start
the nation on the road to tyranny. But this threat never
materialized. On the contrary, the executive and political institutionalization of the Presidency generated internal checks
and balances and stable bases of support in the presidential
parties in such a way as to channel and stabilize presidential
power. And the convergence of the long ambivalent American ideology in the modern doctrines of freedom and equality has both empowered the President to act for quantitative
liberalism and set broad limits for his actions.

Hence presidential government, far from being a threat to
American democracy, has become the major single institution
sustaining it — a bulwark of individual liberty, an agency of
popular representation, and a magnet for political talent and
leadership. But the situation has its drawbacks and dangers.
Presidential government has become such a fitting means of
realizing agreed-on ends of freedom and equality that it runs
the risk of losing sight of its purpose in its preoccupation with
technique and of becoming irrelevant to new ends. As the
President comes increasingly to speak for the whole nation in
his political and policy and planning role, just as he has al-

ways done in his ceremonial role; as he comes to act for the people in general rather than for his party or for Congress or for some particular constituency; as he cultivates a consensus that may become flabby and complacent — presidential government may lose its potency for anticipating new problems and realizing new values. The politics of adjustment and adaptation threatens to take the place of a politics of principle and passion. Political affairs tend to fall into the hands of the little foxes — the tacticians, technicians, and fixers concerned chiefly with the allocation of quantitative values in an already affluent society. Thus presidential government faces the question as to whether it is merely a vehicle of the current status quo or an instrument of creative planning in the pursuit of news ways of realizing human and qualitative values in our public affairs. The future of presidential government turns less on constitutional and other reforms, useful though these would be, than on the access of intellectuals and innovators to the White House and on the creation of a vigorous, coherent, creative opposition — on a Shadow Presidency that could provide a continuing challenge and stimulus to the presidential establishment.

To what degree are similar trends toward executive government discernible in other populous nations? If the sixteenth and seventeenth centuries were characterized in the Western world by the rule of strong monarchs with centralized power, and if the eighteenth century was the great epoch of popular assemblies and legislatures, and if the nineteenth and early twentieth centuries were an era of party-building, is it possible that we are entering a world-wide epoch of executive government?

Britain has so long been noted for her system of strong party government that the tendency toward executive power has been somewhat obscured. And indeed the parties do remain powerful instruments for consolidating the leaders' support in Parliament and country. But for some time the relative power of the Prime Minister seems to have been increasing. Today he is in much the same position as the President — he controls the party organization, broadly sets party policy, forms and re-forms his Cabinet almost at will, treats his Ministers as his personal administrative assistants, makes policy less with the Cabinet than with shifting *ad hoc* groups of Ministers, personal advisers, and civil servants. The Prime Minister enjoys greater power than the President over the substance, timing, and passage of legislation. He also controls a larger supply of patronage — not only ordinary political and executive posts but highly prized Honors.

Like Presidents, prime ministers dominate the election campaign. For good or ill British politicians have studied American campaign techniques and have borrowed some of them — especially the mobilizing of television and radio attention to the head of the ticket, to his "image," personality, family, hobbies, and pets. The voters respond to the commanding role of the leader of the party and recognize that the man who wins will tower over the rest of the administration. Even the British Foreign Secretary, holder of a proud and ancient post, tends today to be a quiet and rather colorless technician — a tendency visible in American Secretaries of State and in the foreign ministers of other nations. Whatever their borrowings from American practice, however, the British have created one great democratic institution that has so far eluded the Americans — a responsible opposition party operating through a visible and articulate Shadow Cabinet.

France has exhibited the most dramatic shift to executive government. Behind the weak, multi-party coalitions of legislative blocs there has always been a powerful administrative organization and executive impetus in the French state. These are now expressed in a President that dominates party, Cabinet, Premier, and Parliament. He dictates foreign and military policy and holds wide authority over domestic affairs through his control of administrative rule making and his restricted power to govern through executive ordinance. In time of actual or asserted crisis the President can assume almost unlimited emergency power.

Some fear, or hope, that presidential government in France will not outlive its modern exemplifier, General de Gaulle. But the old executive urge in French government, combined with the need today of strong and stable executive leadership, doubtless will continue to find expression in some form of presidential government. And De Gaulle has made some effort to institutionalize the system, especially in constitutional provisions subordinating the Premier to the President and in the provision of direct election of the President.

Soviet tendencies are more enigmatic. Both Stalin's and Khrushchev's rule indicated that single leaders controlling large staffs and military, police, and party power could operate a system of executive government. Such a system responded not only to the party but to huge bureaucratic pressure groups, such as the military, heavy industry, trade unions, agriculture, education and the scientific institutes. Stalin's manipulation and suppression of leaders and power groups within the Communist Party may be a precedent for any party leader who, as Prime Minister, turns to bureaucracies outside the party in coping with rivalry and rebellion inside it. In the wake of Khrushchev's ouster his successors reestablished collegial party rule, but the party Presidium was still dominated by bureaucratic czars who were far more responsive to claims of administrative pressure groups than to party ideology. Whether some kind of opposition element could become institutionalized would depend on incalculable long-run forces operating in the interstices of the system. Press, literary, scientific, technical and academic groups might become sources of questioning and innovating and even of a semi-legitimate opposition.

India has a remarkable combination of executive and parliamentary government. A Prime Minister governs through a cabinet in the tradition of Western parliamentary systems, but at the top of the governmental pyramid sits a President with far more power than the ceremonial Presidents in Europe. The President of India has a set of limited legislative and executive powers and wide emergency authority in the event of external or internal threat, financial instability, or the breakdown of constitutional machinery in a state. The last power has been exercised in the imposition of President's rule in the Communist-dominated state of Kerala. The Prime Minister will doubtless remain the chief policy maker in normal times, but in the event of economic crisis, external attack, or regional fragmentization (as in the language problem), the President could establish a form of executive government. Much would depend on the personalities and political resources of President and Prime Minister. They could become rivals, or they could pool their constitutional authority and operate a system of executive government somewhat independently of Parliament and party.

Tendencies toward executive government can be found in other nations, such as Germany. Whether the executive impetus in the great nations in time will produce systems of executive government — of executive leaders taking their mandates directly from the people, dominating party and parliament, manipulating constituencies and pressure groups directing huge public agencies and holding at least a veto power over big private bureaucracies — cannot yet be discerned. But to the extent that nations deliberately adopt systems of executive government the American experience may be instructive.

For in presidential government Americans have established one of the most powerful political institutions in the free world. They have fashioned, sometimes unwittingly, a weapon that has served them well in the long struggle for freedom and equality at home and in the search for stable and democratic politics abroad. They have grasped the uses of this power, and as Harold Laski said, great power makes great leadership possible. Yet power alone is inadequate. It must be linked with purpose. Ultimately it must embody a Jeffersonian thrust toward the most elevated goals of man; it must express the single central vision of the hedgehog. But purpose in turn is steeled not amid agreement, adjustment, conformity, but in crisis and conflict; it was out of crisis and conflict that Roosevelt, Nehru, Lenin, Churchill, and the other great leaders of this century emerged.

A great society needs not consensus but creative leadership and creative opposition — hence it needs the sting of challenge in a society rich in diversity and in a politics rich with dissent.

ACKNOWLEDGMENTS

I WISH to thank Professor MacAlister Brown of the Political Science Department at Williams for reviewing the entire manuscript and for making suggestions on the basis of his own close study of national institutions. Kurt Tauber and other colleagues in the Political Science Department have reviewed parts of the manuscript. I am grateful to Miss Paula Levine for assistance on footnotes and bibliography; to Mrs. Mary Rita Healey for her cheerful typing against deadlines; to Margaret D. Thompson for untiring proofreading; and to my wife, Janet Thompson Burns, for reviewing the galleys.

The Roper Public Opinion Research Center at Williams provided me with public opinion data relating to the Presidency, and the personnel of the Williams College Library made it, as usual, a pleasant and efficient place to work.

Portions of Chapters VI, VIII, and IX have appeared previously in a paper, "Group Theory and Leadership Theory: A Convergence?", presented by the author to a panel of the American Political Science Association, September 1963; in *The New York Times Sunday Magazine;* in *The Nation;* and in the James Lecture, University of Illinois, February 1964.

J. M. B.

INDEX

(continued on next page)

42. More in Sorrow *by Wolcott Gibbs*
43. The Coming of the New Deal
   by Arthur M. Schlesinger, Jr.
44. The Big Sky *by A. B. Guthrie, Jr.*
45. The Dartmouth Bible *edited by Roy B. Chamberlin and*
   Herman Feldman
46. The Far Side of Paradise *by Arthur Mizener*
47. The Politics of Upheaval *by Arthur M. Schlesinger, Jr.*
48. Jefferson and Hamilton *by Claude G. Bowers*
49. The Price of Union *by Herbert Agar*
50. Mark Twain's America *and* Mark Twain at Work
   by Bernard DeVoto
51. Jefferson in Power *by Claude G. Bowers*
52. Fifty Best American Short Stories 1915–1965
   edited by Martha Foley
53. Names on the Land *by George R. Stewart*
54. Two Kinds of Time *by Graham Peck*
55. The Young Jefferson 1743–1789 *by Claude G. Bowers*
56. The Promised Land *by Mary Antin*
57. Personal History *by Vincent Sheean*
58. The New Industrial State *by John Kenneth Galbraith*
59. The Battle of Gettysburg *by Frank A. Haskell,*
   edited by Bruce Catton
60. On Becoming a Person *by Carl R. Rogers*
61. A History of Mexico *by Henry Bamford Parkes*
62. Flaubert and Madame Bovary *by Francis Steegmuller*
63. Paths of American Thought
edited by Arthur M. Schlesinger, Jr., and Morton White
64. The South Since the War *by Sidney Andrews*
65. The Elizabethan World *by Lacey Baldwin Smith*
66. Literature and the Sixth Sense *by Philip Rahv*
67. Turbulent Years *by Irving Bernstein*
68. Renaissance Diplomacy *by Garrett Mattingly*
69. The Death of the Past *by J. H. Plumb*
70. The Affluent Society *by John Kenneth Galbraith*
71. The Way We Go to War *by Merlo J. Pusey*
72. Roosevelt and Morgenthau *by John Morton Blum*
73. The Lean Years *by Irving Bernstein*
74. Henry VIII *by Lacey Baldwin Smith*
75. Presidential Government *by James MacGregor Burns*
76. Silent Spring *by Rachel Carson*
77. The Book of Family Therapy *by Andrew Ferber,*
   Marilyn Mendelsohn, and Augustus Napier
78. The Beginnings of Modern American Psychiatry
   by Patrick Mullahy
79. A World Restored *by Henry A. Kissinger*